D1713837

Verschollen

Verschollen

WORLD WAR I
U-Boat Losses

Dwight R. Messimer

Naval Institute Press

Annapolis, Maryland

Naval Institute Press
291 Wood Road
Annapolis, MD 21402

Distributed internationally by Chatham Publishing, 99 High Street, Roches-
ter, Kent ME1 1LX United Kingdom

Library of Congress Cataloging-in-Publication Data
Messimer, Dwight R., 1937–
Verschollen : World War I U-boat losses / Dwight R. Messimer.
    p. cm.
Includes bibliographical references and index.
  ISBN 1-55750-475-X (alk. paper)
  1. World War, 1914–1918–Naval operations–Submarine. 2. World War,
1914–1918–Naval operations, German. 3. World War, 1914–1918–Personal
narratives, German. 4. Submarines (Ships)–Germany–History. 5. Germany.
Kriegsmarine–Lists of vessels. I. Title.
D591 .M47 2002
940.4'512–dc21

                                                          2002004313

Printed in the United States of America on acid-free paper ⊚
09 08 07 06 05 04 03 02   9 8 7 6 5 4 3 2
First printing

To Charles Burdick, Ph.D.,
A good friend who I miss very much

Contents

Preface

My goal in writing this book was to provide readers with a comprehensive, easily used, and readable source of information on how Germany's U-boats were lost during World War I. Wherever possible, I have provided the firsthand accounts of men who survived the sinkings. And I have provided the official and unofficial opinions about what happened to the U-boats in each case where the cause of the boat's loss is uncertain. I have, based on my own research, rebutted those opinions that I think are wrong. The translations from the original German documents are my own as are the drawings and the maps. The maps are accurate, but do not use them for navigation. I assure the traditionalists among the readers that I do know that ships are referred to as "she" and "her." I too am a traditionalist. But in this book the publisher prefers to use the gender-neutral pronoun "it" instead. If you have comments or questions, you may e-mail me at drmessimer@aol.com.

Verschollen

Introduction

When Germany went to war with Great Britain on 4 August 1914, the German navy had no plans for using its U-boats in an anti-shipping role. Instead, the Germans deployed their U-boats as pickets in the North Sea with the mission to intercept the Grand Fleet as it steamed toward Helgoland.[1] The Germans were slow to launch even a tactical anti-shipping campaign intended to interdict military supply lines across the English Channel, and it was not until February 1915 that the Germans launched an anti-shipping campaign aimed at Great Britain's commercial seaborne traffic.

In 1915 an insufficient number of U-boats for the job, and concerns about political repercussions, prevented the Germans from achieving the strategic potential of an unrestricted U-boat war against commercial shipping. The legal obstacle to an unrestricted U-boat war on shipping was the 1909 Declaration of London, the terms of which were embodied in the Prize Regulations.

Under the Prize Regulations, warships-including U-boats—were allowed to stop any merchant vessel, board it, and inspect it for contraband. If no contraband was found, the warship had to release the merchant ship. That happened occasionally, but not often when compared with the number of seizures that the British made. If contraband was found, the warship could put a prize crew aboard and send the merchant ship into either an allied or a neutral port where the cargo was condemned. If the tactical situation demanded it, the warship could sink the merchant vessel after first seeing to the safety of the crew. Obviously, torpedoing a merchant ship without warning was a violation of the Prize Regulations. By January 1917 the increasingly effective British blockade and increased U-boat production caused the Germans to finally ignore the political consequences of unrestricted U-boat warfare.

The U-boat war can be divided into four phases. Phase one, during which the Germans deployed their U-boats in a purely military role, lasted from 4 August 1914 to 3 February 1915. Phase two, from 4 February to 18 September 1915, was Germany's first attempt at an unrestricted anti-shipping offensive. It was at best a faltering attempt that collapsed completely in the wake of the *Lusitania* incident on 7 May 1915. Phase three covered the period from 19 September 1915 to 30 January 1917 and included the so-called "lost opportunity of 1916." During this sixteen-month period U-boats operated under stringent restrictions that severely limited their effectiveness in the anti-shipping role. Nevertheless, the U-boats in the Mediterranean, operating almost exclusively under the Prize Regulations, scored significant successes against Allied shipping. Phase four opened on 31 January 1917 and ended on 11 November 1918. During the last phase the U-boats finally fought an unrestricted war against commercial shipping. But by then it was too late to affect the outcome of the war.

Throughout the war, the Royal Navy led their allies in antisubmarine warfare (ASW) development and made by far the greatest ASW effort. But the British were slow to start a serious ASW campaign, and British ASW did not really become effective until 1917. The fact that the British were slow in developing a serious ASW capability lends credence to the argument that political indecision cost Germany the war in 1916.

Until the Germans opened their unrestricted campaign in January 1917, British surface ships relied heavily on ramming and gunfire to attack U-boats. Ramming was a potentially useful tactic until the boat went below thirty feet, and gunfire was only effective against surfaced U-boats. Despite its limited effectiveness, the British extended the ramming tactic to their merchant ships. The most dramatic result of the so-called Admiralty Ramming Order was the Capt. Charles A. Fryatt Affair in which the Germans executed Fryatt for attempting to run down U-33 with SS *Brussels* on 28 March 1915. The ramming tactic remained in effect throughout the war and played a role in at least twenty-five U-boat sinkings.[2]

Gunfire played a role in sinking U-boats on twenty-five occasions. But the gun's principal effect was to permit armed merchant vessels to escape in over 60 percent of the instances in which U-boats encountered them under the Prize Regulations. The gun also played a large role in rendering the Prize Regulations unworkable.

In addition to ramming and gunfire, the British relied on passive defenses such as mines and nets. The Royal Navy laid thousands of mines across the Dover Strait, in the Hoofden[3] off the Belgian coast, and off Helgoland. But until the end of 1917 British mines were inefficient because they were equipped with unreliable detonators. Most U-boat losses attributed to mines occurred after November 1917 when the British introduced the very effective H2 mine. At least twenty-three U-boats were lost to Allied mines and the number may be as high as forty-three.

The British deployed antisubmarine nets throughout the war, but they were nearly useless. The British had two types of nets: indicator nets and mine nets. Indicator nets were usually towed behind a herring drifter, and all mine nets were placed in fixed, anchored positions. The indicator nets were supposed to fold around the U-boat so that the wire strands fouled the propellers. At the same time chemical indicators ignited and produced flame and smoke that told the surface patrols exactly where the U-boat was. The surface patrols were then supposed to remain on the scene until the U-boat was forced to surface when its batteries went dead. The surface patrols could then ram the U-boat or sink it with gunfire. There was only one instance in which the scheme worked during World War I.

Some indicator nets were in fixed anchored positions, and U-boats did occasionally foul them. Most of the time the U-boats simply crossed the nets on the surface or went under them. When they did hit a fixed net, they nearly always tore completely through it. On the few occasions when the net did foul the propellers, the U-boat waited for dark, surfaced, and the crew cut away the net.

Mine nets were simply nets that had small mines attached to the panels. The idea was that the net would fold around the U-boat, thus bringing the mines in contact with the steel hull where they would explode and sink the U-boat. The British laid explosive nets off the Flanders coast hoping to catch the U-boats as they departed and returned to Zeebrugge and Ostend. There is evidence to suggest that the explosive nets may have sunk three U-boats, but the same evidence suggests that those three boats might have hit conventional mines.

Throughout the war the British deployed armed decoys, sometimes called Q-ships, to trap the U-boats. For the ploy to work, the U-boats had to comply with the Prize Regulations. The idea was that the armed decoy, disguised as a tramp steamer or a sailing ship, with its large caliber guns cleverly hidden, would lure the surfaced U-boat within range and then destroy it with overwhelming gunfire. The ruse included specially trained panic parties who abandoned the ship, lending realism to the scene.

The plan worked well at first, but as the war progressed the U-boat captains developed tactics against it. Long-range gunfire was one technique the U-boats used, and a submerged torpedo attack was another. Typically, after pounding the target at long range with his deck gun, the U-boat captain would approach submerged and examine the decoy carefully through his periscope. If he saw nothing suspicious, he surfaced and completed the attack under the Prize Regulations. If the decoy had done a good job of hiding its guns, the U-boat got a very nasty surprise when it surfaced close alongside the decoy. Decoys were dangerous, but the fact is that for every U-boat the decoys sank, the U-boats sank five decoys.

The British built three large antisubmarine barriers during the war. The first barrier they completed was the Dover net and mine barrier that extended across the Dover Strait from Goodwin Sands to Dunkirk. Its purpose was to prevent U-boats from passing through the Dover Strait to the English Channel and the western approaches. The barrier was utterly useless. The fixed, anchored net was impossible to maintain in the strong tidal currents present in the Dover Strait and whales, debris, and wrecks regularly fouled it. The mines that the British laid to support it dragged their anchors and fouled the net, making it unsafe for the British net tenders to maintain the barrier. To make matters worse, U-boat captains used the barrier as a navigation aid.

The second barrier was very successful. The enormous Folkestone to Cape Gris Nez deep mine barrage became operational in December 1917 and was intended to completely close the Dover Strait to U-boats. Two features made the barrier successful. The first was the availability of the H2 mine in large numbers. The second was the British tactic of illuminating the barrier at night and patrolling it heavily around the clock. The result was that U-boats were forced to dive as they approached the barrier, which forced them into the minefield. Because the mines were laid in a ladder pattern down to two hundred feet, any U-boat attempting to pass through the barrier would almost certainly hit a mine. For a time in early 1918 UB-boats continued to pass through the barrage, but with increasing losses. The British continued to lay new mines until by October 1918 the Dover Strait was effectively closed.

The third barrier was the joint American-British effort to seal off the North Sea with an enormous minefield that stretched from the Orkneys to Bergen, Norway. Known as the Northern Mine Barrage, it was a huge undertaking that featured the superior British H2 mine and the newly developed American Mark VI mine, both of which exhibited tendencies to explode prematurely. Despite the teething problems with the mines, the Northern Mine Barrage was a formidable barrier. Although not completed before the end of the war, its size made it almost unmanageable. But it did destroy at least five boats. More important, combined with the Folkestone to Gris Nez deep mine barrage in the Dover Strait, the presence of the enormous Northern Mine Barrage had a devastating effect on the morale of U-boat crews.

In the Mediterranean the British, Italians, and French joined forces in an effort to close the Otranto Strait with a mobile net defense and surface patrols. The effort was largely a waste of time because U-boats exiting or entering the Adriatic simply passed beneath the barrier on their way to and from the base at Cattaro. The barrier scored a few successes, but it was never a serious threat to the U-boats. After the Americans arrived in 1918, the French and Italians tried to lay a fixed mine net across the strait, but it too proved to be ineffective. The Americans provided purpose-built sub-chasers equipped with hydrophones, radio-telephones, and depth charges to patrol the barrier, but they scored no successes. The water was too deep for mines and even with nets that reached down 180 feet, the U-boats were able to slip under them.

During 1916, when U-boat activity was confined largely to the Mediterranean, the British introduced the hydrophone and the depth charge. The hydrophone was a passive listening device that picked up the engine, motor, and propeller noises that the U-boats produced. The practical range was limited to about three miles. The hydrophone operator could determine the direction from which the sounds were coming, but he could not accurately estimate range or depth. Three hydrophone vessels working together could, under the right conditions, fix a U-boat's position with fair accuracy. The British and the Americans were unable to overcome the hydrophone's technical deficiencies, and it remained only marginally useful during the war.

The depth charge was another matter. With the depth charge the British had a true U-boat killing weapon, and one that seriously demoralized U-boat crews. But in 1916 the British produced so few depth charges that they could issue them only in small numbers to selected vessels. Destroyers received not more than four while trawlers were limited to two. Most patrol vessels received none.

To be really effective, depth charges have to be dropped in large numbers over a wide area. Dropping one or two, or even four, rarely resulted in a U-boat's destruction, although there were exceptions. Saturation depth charging increased after June 1917 and was standard procedure in 1918. When the Americans entered the war they brought with them destroyers that carried over one hundred depth charges equipped with an automatic release rack. The number of depth charges carried climbed steadily until even subchasers had twelve aboard in racks. With the introduction in 1918 of the American Y-gun and the British Thornycroft depth charge thrower, a depth charge attack became a truly awesome event. Depth charges sank at least twenty-seven U-boats and damaged three times that number.

As the U-boat war unfolded, the Germans made continuous improvements in their designs and introduced new types. By the end of the war they were operating four different types: U-boat, UB-boat, UC-boat, and U-cruiser. Each type ostensibly had a specialized mission, and to some degree that remained true throughout the war. But as each type evolved, their missions began to overlap.

The first type, the U-boat, was designed as an oceangoing boat with a fairly long range. The U-boats' original mission was to act as scouts ahead of the High Sea Fleet, and to patrol picket lines in the North Sea. The Germans hoped that their U-boats would be able to torpedo Grand Fleet battleships and cruisers as the Grand Fleet approached the German coast. If the U-boats did their jobs, they would reduce the Grand Fleet's strength to a level at which the High Sea Fleet could engage it on a more equal basis.

When the Germans started deploying U-boats in an anti-shipping role, they found that they needed greater range and greater firepower. Originally, U-boats were not armed with deck guns, and one of the first new features to appear in the second U-boat generation was a single deck gun, usually a 75-mm to 88-mm. As the war progressed the caliber increased to 105-mm and many U-boats were armed with two deck guns, one forward of the conning tower and one aft. Diving time also became critical as the war progressed and U-boats grew larger. In 1914 a U-17–class boat could take as long as three to five minutes to get completely under.[4] The Germans quickly saw that safety depended on the ability to dive quickly and they soon developed a rapid venting system that reduced diving time to as little as thirty seconds.

The need for longer range, heavier armament, and more torpedoes resulted in larger designs. U-9, made famous when Kapitänleutnant Otto Weddigen sank three *Cressy*-class light cruisers in an hour on 21 September 1914, was just 189 feet long and displaced 611 tons submerged. U-135, laid down just two years later, was 275 feet long and displaced

1,534 tons submerged. Crew size aboard the U-boats remained fairly constant at four officers and twenty-eight or thirty-two crewmen.

To shorten construction time and costs, the Germans designed a boat for limited operations in the Hoofden and along Britain's east coast. Designated UB, the "B" simply indicated that it was the follow-on to the basic U-type. Commonly called a coastal-class boat, UB-boats entered service in 1915. The first designs, UB-1 to UB-17, required just four months to build, had no deck gun, and had only two bow torpedo tubes with one torpedo for reload. UB-boats were very small, only ninety-three feet long, and displaced 142 tons submerged. The crew consisted of one officer and thirteen men.

The second-generation boats, UB-18 to UB-47, were larger, had longer range, and were more heavily armed. They were 122 feet long and displaced 292 tons submerged. All carried a single deck gun mounted forward of the conning tower, and the size varied from 50-mm to 88-mm. All the second series UB-boats had two bow torpedo tubes with four to six reloads. The crew consisted of two officers and twenty-one men.

The third-generation boats, UB-48 to UB-249, were 183 feet long, displaced 649 tons submerged, and carried a crew of three officers and thirty-one men. Armament consisted of a single deck gun mounted forward of the conning tower that varied in size from 88-mm to 105-mm, and four bow torpedo tubes with ten reloads. The Germans modified some of the UB-boats to carry mines, but their primary mission throughout the war was to attack shipping.

For minelaying, the Germans designed and built the UC-type boats that began entering service in 1915. Like UB-boats, UC-boats went through three design series. Minelaying was their primary mission, although the later boats also conducted anti-shipping operations. They laid their mines by dropping them from the forward, vertical chutes while submerged. It was dangerous work and at least seven UC-boats were destroyed when their own mines exploded during dropping.

The first series, UC-1 to UC-15, was 112 feet long, displaced 183 tons submerged, and carried twelve mines in six vertical chutes. They had no deck gun and no torpedo tubes. The crew consisted of one officer and thirteen men.

The second series, UC-16 to UC-79, varied from 162 to 172 feet long and displaced from 493 to 511 tons submerged. This series carried eighteen mines in six vertical chutes. Because this series also attacked shipping, they carried a single deck gun forward of the conning tower. Nearly all of the guns were 88-mm, but starting with UC-65 some carried 105-mm guns. The entire series was equipped with two forward torpedo tubes and one stern tube, with seven reloads. The crew consisted of three officers and twenty-three men.

The third series, UC-80 to UC-192, was slightly larger and slightly better armed than the previous series, but they carried fewer mines. The UC type III series boats were all about 186 feet long and displaced about 560 tons submerged. They had a crew of three officers and twenty-nine men. They were armed with either an 88-mm or a 105-mm gun mounted forward of the conning tower, and three torpedo tubes, two in the bow and one in the stern. There were seven reloads. They carried only fourteen mines in six chutes forward of the conning tower.

The Germans also built twenty U-boats as large, oceangoing minelayers. The first were U-71 to U-80 and they entered service in 1916. They were only three feet longer than the UC type III series boats, but they were much larger, displacing 832 tons submerged. They had a crew of four officers and twenty-eight men. The big U-minelayers were armed with two deck guns, usually one 88-mm gun mounted forward and a 105-mm gun mounted aft. They all had one deck-mounted torpedo tube forward on the starboard side between the casing and the pressure hull, and one aft on the port side. There were four reloads that were stored between the casing and the pressure hull. The U-boat had to be surfaced in order for the crew to reload the tubes.

The U-minelayers carried thirty-eight mines that were discharged through two horizontal stern chutes. Instead of dropping the mines the way the UC-boats did, the U-minelayers trailed their mines out the stern as they moved forward. They could lay their mines while surfaced or submerged.

The second group of U-minelayers, U-117 to U-126, entered service in 1918. They were 270 feet long, displaced 1,468 to 1,512 tons submerged, and had a crew of four officers and thirty-six men. Depending on how they were configured, these boats could carry from forty-two to seventy-two mines. Forty mines were carried inboard and were discharged through two stern chutes. An additional thirty could be stored between the casing and the pressure hull and launched over the stern from deck-mounted chutes.

The last type of U-boat was the U-cruiser, a type that included the former *Deutschland*-class boats, U-151 to U-157, and the purpose-built boats, U-139 to U-194, of which only four were completed. The U-cruisers were intended for operations virtually anywhere in the world, but they spent most of their time off the east coast of the United States and around the Azores.[5]

Wartime U-cruiser losses were U-154 and U-156. Both were former *U-Deutschland*–class boats that were planned to have been part of a fleet of eight U-boat freighters designed to break the British blockade and reestablish trade with the United States. The first of the freighters completed was *U-Deutschland* (U-155), which made two trips to the United States in 1916. The second boat, *U-Bremen,* disappeared without a trace on its maiden trip in August 1916, following the *U-Deutschland*'s return from its second U.S. trip. The remaining six hulls—U-151 to U-154, U-156, and U-157— were completed as war boats and designated U-cruisers because of their size and range.

As war boats the *Deutschland*-class cruisers were mediocre performers. Slow, underpowered, and difficult to handle, they accomplished little. They were 213 feet long, had an enormous 29-foot beam, and displaced 1,875 tons submerged. All the boats except U-155 had two bow torpedo tubes with eighteen reloads, and carried two deck guns. The deck guns carried by all except U-155 were one forward-mounted 88-mm and one aft-mounted 150-mm. U-155, having been completed as a freighter, was converted to a war boat; its six torpedo tubes were mounted in pairs, port and starboard, each deflected 15 degrees from the keel line. Both deck guns were 150-mm.

By the end of the war there were six separate U-boat commands that controlled the activities of the several U-boat types.[6] The initial command was *Die U-Boote der Hochseeflotte,* which literally translates as "U-boats of the High Sea Fleet." Korvettenkapitän Hermann Bauer held the command and the title, *Führer der U-Boote,* which was abbreviated FdU. Bauer held the command until Kapitän zur See Andreas Michelsen relieved him on 4 June 1917. Michelsen, who held the temporary rank of Kommodore, was given the new title of *Befehlshaber der U-Boote.* Although Befehlshaber simply means commander, the term connoted greater authority in this sense than Führer.

The High Sea Fleet boats operated in the English Channel, the western approaches, the Irish Sea, along Britain's east and west coasts, and in the North Sea. The oceangoing minelayers assigned to the High Sea Fleet also operated in the Arctic Ocean. The High Sea Fleet's boats passed through the Dover Strait to reach their operations areas until Bauer ordered them to use the northern route around Scotland and down Britain's west coast on 15 April 1915. The longer route involved two weeks of travel time, which reduced time in the operations areas to about a week. Bauer, who was overly impressed with the British ASW capability accepted the lost time as an operational necessity. Bauer's north-about order remained in effect until February 1917.

After the German army had captured Bruges, Zeebrugge, and Ostend, the Germans established the *Marinekorps Flandern* under Vizeadmiral Ludwig von Schröder. The boats assigned to the *Marinekorps Flandern* were organized in a subordinate command called the *U-Boote des Marine-korps,* which translates as "U-boats of the Naval Corps." The boats assigned to the Flanders command were almost exclusively UB- and UC-boats. The command, which operated from Bruges, Zeebrugge, and Ostend, was established on 29 March 1915 with Korvettenkapitän Karl Bartenbach commanding. His official title was *Führer der U-Boote Flandern,* abbreviated FdU Flandern, and he held the command throughout the war.

The Marinekorps was an independent command and its UB- and UC-boats did not coordinate their activities with Bauer's High Sea Fleet boats. The Flanders boats operated off Britain's east coast and in the Dover Strait, the English Channel, and the Irish Sea. The type III UB-boats also operated in the western approaches.

The third U-boat command was an independent command in the Mediterranean theater, known as the *Mittelmeer Division* (Mediterranean Division), under Vizeadmiral Wilhelm Souchon, whose headquarters were in Constantinople (present-day Istanbul). Initially Souchon's command consisted of the cruiser SMS *Goeben* and the light cruiser SMS *Breslau,* which ostensibly had been turned over to the Turkish navy and renamed *Jawus Sultan Selim* and *Midilli,* respectively. On paper, Admiral Souchon took his orders from the Turkish navy, but in fact his superiors were in the Admiralstab in Berlin.

In March 1915 Souchon asked the Admiralstab to send him some U-boats to help defend the Dardanelles. The British had just launched their Gallipoli campaign in an attempt to knock Turkey out of the war, and Souchon wanted the U-boats to attack British warships and troop transports that were supporting the British campaign. In response to his request, the Admiralstab directed Bauer to send U-21 to Constantinople.

U-21 departed Wilhelmshaven on 13 March, and at the same time the Admiralstab dispatched three UB-boats by rail to Pola where they were to be reassembled. Next, the Admiralstab sent three UC-boats by rail and in August they sent four U-boats—U-33, U-34, U-35, and U-39—to join Admiral Souchon's Mittelmeer Division.

It soon became apparent to the Germans that basing U-boats in Constantinople was a bad idea because the Dardanelles was a choke point. Instead, the Germans established U-boat bases at Pola and Cattaro on the Adriatic, and created a new command called *Deutsche U-Halbflotilla Pola* under the command of Kapitänleutnant Hans Adam. As the Germans shifted their anti-shipping efforts to the Mediterranean during 1916, they sent more U-boats of all types to Pola and Cattaro. Some of those boats were detached and sent on to Constantinople for short periods.

Deutsche U-Halbflotilla Pola was the fourth U-boat command and it became the third largest. Kapitänleutnant Adam commanded the unit until 17 November 1915 when the unit became a full flotilla and Korvettenkapitän Kophamel took over. On 9 June 1917 the command was again upgraded and became identified by the title of its new commanding officer, *Führer der U-Boote Pola* (FdU Pola). Kapitän zur See Püllen took command with the temporary rank of Kommodore, holding the position until 29 December 1917 when Kapitän zur See Grasshoff took command.

U-boats based at Pola and Cattaro conducted operations throughout the Mediterranean. They ranged from Gibraltar to Port Said and hunted targets off Corsica, Sardinia, Sicily, Crete, and Cyprus. Some UC-boats were converted to cargo and troop carriers so that they could deliver weapons and agents to North Africa. The significant feature of the U-boat war in the Mediterranean was that it was conducted almost entirely according to the Prize Regulations.

The fifth separate command was in the Baltic where Prinz Heinrich von Preussen was the supreme commander. This was a small operation because the U-boats had few targets and the operating season was fairly short. The command was officially the *U-Boote der Ostseestreitkräfte,* which translates as "U-boats of the Baltic Armed Forces," but was commonly known as the *U-Flotilla-Kurland.* The boats operated in the middle and eastern Baltic, the Gulf of Bothnia, and the Gulf of Finland. The command accomplished little during its relatively brief existence. It was disbanded on 10 December 1917 following the Russian Revolution.

The sixth separate command, established on 27 March 1917 under the command of Korvettenkapitän von Koch, was the *U-Kreuzer-Flotilla,* or U-cruiser flotilla. Initially this long-range group consisted of the seven converted *Deutschland*-class boats, U-151 to U-157. In 1918 eight more U-boats were assigned to it and the command's name was changed to *U-Kreuzer-Verband,* which literally translates as "U-cruiser organization." Of the eight new assignments, four were conventional U-boats and four were specially designed U-cruisers. The U-cruisers operated off the east coast of the United States and Canada, around the Azores and Gibraltar, off the west coast of Africa, and in the Canary Islands.

There was one technical feature common to all types of U-boats that essentially remained unchanged throughout the war. Regardless of the type of boat—U, UB, or UC—the maximum rated depth was officially fifty meters (165 feet). Boats of all types went deeper than that, some intentionally and many unintentionally, and survived. Below 165 feet the hull started to fail, rivets popped out, seals failed, and water entered the boat through dozens of unseen places. In those situations, nearly every U-boat captain blew the ballast tanks and brought his boat to the surface.

Another feature common to many U-boats was their propensity to suddenly drop by the stern. This unnerving behavior could occur whether the boat was surfaced or submerged. *U-Deutschland* experienced the behavior during its second return to Germany on 9 December 1916. Approaching Helgoland, its diesel engines suddenly stopped and the boat started sinking by the stern. The stern down angle became so great that escape from the boat would have been impossible, and Kapitän zur See Paul König seriously believed that his boat was lost. The crew worked eleven hours before they were able to bring the stern back to the surface.

En route to Constantinople from Cattaro on 4 May 1915, UB-8 was running on the surface. On the conning tower were the watch officer, the helmsman, and a lookout. Suddenly the stern dropped and the watch officer barely had enough time to close the conning tower hatch before the boat went completely under and the three men on watch found themselves swimming. Inside UB-8 the situation was serious. Water was pouring in through the partially closed hatch and the boat was sinking rapidly by the stern. Oberleutnant zur See Ernst von Voigt closed off the inner hatch to the central control room and ordered the tanks blown. UB-8 rose to the surface. Von Voigt restarted the diesel engines, came about, and started a search for his three missing crewmen. He recovered the watch officer and the helmsman, but the lookout, Obermatrose Karl Rausch, had drowned.[7]

The causes of the sudden loss of buoyancy in the stern were never explained, probably because there was no specific cause that was common to every case. U-boats of all types suffered from a variety of mechanical and technical problems that were due in part to shoddy workmanship and the Germans' forced reliance on inferior materials for construction. The poor workmanship stemmed from a lack of skilled labor and the poor-quality materials were a direct result of the British blockade. Several unexplained losses, those classified as *verschollen,* were probably due to some technical or material failure that sank the boat.

Verschollen means missing or presumed dead. The Germans commissioned 435 boats during World War I; 203 were lost to all causes, and at one time nearly all of them were classified as verschollen. Rudolph Firle, Ernst von Gagern, Walter Gladisch, Otto Groos, Hermann Lorey, Heinrich Rollmann, Arno Spindler, and Ernst von Gagern worked from 1919 to 1963 writing Germany's official history of the war at sea. In the process they accounted for 113 of the 170 boats lost to enemy action, although in several cases the accounting was at best a faint possibility. Their collective efforts are the postwar German study frequently referenced in the text.

In their postwar study the German historians explained the losses of 113 U-boats to enemy action, and 33 to non-enemy action. Those lost to non-enemy action included boats that were stranded, scuttled, or suffered some sort of accident, and at least six minelaying submarines that blew up on their own mines in enemy waters. Of the boats that were lost to enemy action, survivors provided positive identification for fifty of the lost boats, British divers identified fifteen U-boats, and observed or physical evidence identified another sixteen. In thirty-two cases, the German historians based their conclusions on circumstantial evidence. In some cases the circumstantial evidence is such that there is no doubt about the boats' identities. But in many of the thirty-two cases the circumstances are such that there was no way to identify the boat beyond "possible." Upon completion, fifty-seven boats remained verschollen. But the fact is that the number was much greater than fifty-seven and humans demand answers so the bean counters tied up the loose ends with "solid possibilities."

The boats described in this book are limited to those that were front-line boats. The school boats that sank are not included, nor are the four UB-boats that the Germans turned over to the Austrians in 1915–1916 and the one they turned over to Bulgaria in 1916. *U-Bremen,* although a navy boat despite all the propaganda to the contrary, is not included because at the time it was not intended for a military role; *U-Bremen's* disappearance in November 1916 remains a mystery.

The entries are in alphanumerical order for each of the sixty-seven U-boats, seventy-four UB-boats, and sixty-two UC-boats. Readers should refer to the maps as needed to place the action. First, known facts are detailed. Excerpts from official reports, commanding officer reports, and firsthand accounts are presented whenever available. Additional information is given and discussed to substantiate or reject conjectures or rumors. Source information follows each entry.

Notes

1. Groos, *Der Krieg in der Nordsee,* 1:251.

2. For a complete account of antisubmarine warfare in World War I see Messimer, *Find and Destroy.*

3. "Hoofden" appears throughout this book. Hoofden is the German geographical term for the body of water that lies between the North Sea and the Dover Strait. It is bounded on the north by a line that runs roughly from Great Yarmouth to Amsterdam. The Dutch and Belgian coasts form the eastern boundary and Great Britain forms the western boundary. The southern boundary is roughly a line from Ramsgate to Ostend. The geographical term is used in this book because it plays such an important part in the account, and it is more specific. There are four maritime areas that make up the waters off Britain's east and south coasts. From north to south they are the North Sea, the Hoofden, the Dover Strait, and the English Channel.

4. Spindler, *Der Handelskrieg mit U-Booten,* 1:171–172.

5. All the foregoing technical information and design details are found in Gröner, *Die deutschen Kriegsschiffe,* 1:342–375; Herzog, *Deutsche U-Boote,* 45–66; and Rössler, *The U-Boat,* 38–87.

6. Spindler, *Der Handelskrieg mit U-Booten,* 2:1–13; 3:1–11; 4:7–20; 5:1–2.

7. *Records,* T-1022, Roll 77, PG61734, "KTB UB-8."

14

PART 1

U-Boats U-5 to U-156

U-5

Date Lost:	December 1914
Commander:	Kapitänleutnant Lemmer
Location:	Hoofden, off the Flanders coast
Position:	51°23' N, 3°11' E (possible)
Disposition:	Verschollen

U-5 departed Zeebrugge on 18 December 1914 for picket duty off the Belgium coast. U-5 did not return.

Additional Information

The British had laid a large minefield on 2 October 1914 that U-5 passed through to reach its picket station; there is a strong possibility that U-5 hit a British mine. Until November 1917 British mines were unreliable and U-boats regularly passed through British minefields unscathed. Nevertheless, U-boat captains never entered a minefield with a cavalier attitude, and passage through a minefield was a stressful experience.

Sources

Gibson and Prendergast, *The German Submarine War,* 17.
Groos, *Der Krieg in der Nordsee,* 3:46–47.
Records, T-1022, Roll 13, PG61504.
Spindler, *Der Handelskrieg mit U-Booten,* chart, 2:61.

U-6

Date Lost:	15 September 1915
Commander:	Oberleutnant zur See Reinhold Lepsius
Location:	North Sea, off Norway
Position:	58°55' N, 5°10' E
Disposition:	Torpedo

British submarine E-16 torpedoed U-6 in the afternoon of 15 September 1915 off the Norwegian coast near Udfire Island. There were five survivors.

Oberleutnant zur See Beyer, U-6

I saw a periscope 150 to 200 meters away and immediately turned hard to starboard. At that moment I saw two torpedo wakes. The first torpedo passed forward, but the second hit at the officers' room. Those of us on the conning tower were knocked down and I was knocked unconscious. When I awoke it was dark and wet. I was under water, fouled in either the radio antenna or the flag halyards. I freed myself and rose to the surface. I found four other swimmers including the chief engineer who had been in the control room. The British submarine E-16 picked us up.

Source

Records, T-1022, Roll 13, PG61505, "Gefechtsbericht des Oberleutnant zur See Beyer von U-6."

U-7

Date Lost:	21 January 1915
Commander:	Kapitänleutnant Georg König
Location:	German Bight, off the Dutch coast
Position:	53°43' N, 6°2' E
Disposition:	Torpedo (German)

On 20 January 1915 U-7 departed Ems en route to Zeebrugge where it was to become a part of the Flanders command, which the Germans called the Marinekorps. On that same day bad weather and heavy seas had forced Kapitänleutnant Bruno Hoppe in U-22 to leave his picket station off the British coast and return to Ems. On 21 January both boats were in sight of one another off the Dutch coast north of Ameland, which is one of the West Frisian Islands.

U-22 flashed a recognition signal challenge to U-7 but received no reply. Hoppe tried to close on U-7, but U-7 turned away and opened the distance. Hoppe now became suspicious and the heavy seas prevented him from recognizing the design features that identified U-7 as a German boat. For example, Hoppe did not see the tall ventilator over the engine room that was unique to all the boats that were equipped with Körting engines. The fact that the boat Hoppe was pursuing did not dive puzzled him, but he thought that it might be having problems with its diving controls. He sent another recognition signal that went unanswered.

Hoppe ordered the torpedoes in both bow tubes made ready and maneuvered to make a surface torpedo attack. He sent one more challenge, and when there was no reply he fired both torpedoes at nine hundred meters. One torpedo either missed or failed to explode, but the other torpedo hit U-7 just forward of the conning tower, sinking it almost instantly. When U-22 picked up the only survivor Hoppe learned that he had killed his best friend, Georg König.

Additional Information

The German navy did not hold Hoppe responsible for the accident and he continued in command of U-22 until 6 September 1916; he then took over the newly commissioned U-83. Hoppe and his entire crew were lost on 17 February 1917.

Sources

Groos, *Der Krieg in der Nordsee,* 2:181.
Records, T-1022, Roll 23, PG61506 (U-7); T-1022, Roll 24, PG61540 (U-22).

U-8

Date Lost:	4 March 1915
Commander:	Kapitänleutnant Alfred Stoss
Location:	English Channel, between Dungeness and Tréport
Position:	50°41' N, 0°6' E
Disposition:	Indicator Net, Explosive Sweep, Gunfire, Scuttled

U-8 departed Ostend on 4 March 1915 in company with U-20 for operations in the English Channel. Shortly after noon on 4 March HMS *Viking* sighted U-8 five nautical miles east-northeast of the Varne buoy, and opened fire, forcing U-8 to dive. The sea was calm with a light fog.

The drifter *Ma Freen* was stationed near the Varne when at 1230 its crew saw the pellets that marked its net moving eastward at four knots. *Ma Freen* reported the contact to HMS *Cossack,* whose captain passed the information on to Capt. C. D. Johnson, commanding the destroyers at Dover. Johnson left Dover in HMS *Maori* at 1330 and joined HMS *Viking* in pursuing the visual contact.

About an hour later the drifter *Roburn* saw an indicator buoy moving eastward. An hour later the destroyers spotted a periscope. *Viking* fired its explosive sweep without result. An hour later *Maori* saw the periscope farther down the channel and at 1700 HMS *Ghurka* exploded its sweep across the projected track. U-8 shot to the surface stern-first at an almost vertical angle. *Ghurka* and *Maori* fired at it and scored two hits on the conning tower. The submarine's crew and officer abandoned the sinking U-8 and were taken prisoners. U-8 sank approximately twenty-three nautical miles southwest of the Varne Bank Lightship.

The Official British Report

For thirty minutes the destroyers followed surface disturbances that indicated a U-boat's submerged passage moving northwest. At 1522 a periscope was sighted one mile north of the Varne buoy. The disturbances turned westerly and continued on the new course for fifteen minutes, before turning ESE. At 1550 *Viking* fired her sweep. The disturbances continued for about 150 yards and disappeared completely 4 1/2 miles northeast of the Varne buoy.

At 1555 the periscope was again seen. The destroyers *Cossack, Ghurka, Syren, Mohawk, Ure, Viking* and *Maori* were now involved in the hunt. At

1640 *Maori* sighted the periscope again and at 1710 *Ghurka* fired her sweep. Thirty seconds later a U-boat's stern rose above the surface at a 45° angle, and then the rest of the boat appeared on an even keel. The U-boat was immediately taken under fire. The crew abandoned the hulk, which sank quickly.

Kapitänleutnant Alfred Stoss, U-8

Departed Ostend 4 March 1915 en route the English Channel to attack shipping. The plan was to sink as much shipping as possible in the shortest possible time and return to Ostend to refuel and rearm. We sailed in company with U-20 [Kapitänleutnant Schwieger] until we reached the minefield off Ruytingen Bank. There we parted company. We crossed the minefield on the surface and immediately encountered a second, new, minefield that was extraordinarily thick.

Visibility dropped as heavy fog developed. I decided to remain on the surface for as long as possible in order to obtain an accurate position fix before entering the Dover Straits. Visibility deteriorated to the point that I decided to dive and lay on the bottom close to South Foreland. This proved impossible because of the rocky bottom and the very strong current created an alarming situation. We surfaced and proceeded on a westerly course, trimmed down, ready to dive, and running on electric motors.

An hour later visibility suddenly improved and we spotted a destroyer about 1.5 nautical miles away. We saw a second destroyer about four nautical miles away. The nearer destroyer turned toward us and came on at high speed, forcing us to dive.

We had been discovered at the entrance to the Dover Straits and behind us lay the minefield. We could not recross it on the surface because of the presence of the enemy. The tide was set to turn in an hour and flow in a westerly direction and we would be unable to make any submerged headway against it. Due to the rocky bottom and strong current, lying on the bottom was not an option.

The entire Dover destroyer flotilla had been mobilized against us and every time I showed my periscope to obtain a position a destroyer saw it. The weather was clear, the wind light and the sea calm. I decided not to use the periscope again and went down to twenty meters and made several course changes over a distance of about four nautical miles. Then I laid a course that would bring us abeam of Dungeness. During this time several destroyers passed directly over us and we heard the sounds of high-speed propellers.

At 1530 I heard a distant explosion. At 1600 first watch officer, Oberleutnant zur See Sauerland relieved Leutnant zur See Morgenroth on the diving controls and immediately reported a problem. The diving planes were not answering the controls and the controls felt "irregular." Oberleutnant zur See Sauerland suggested that we had fouled a net. I inspected the boat through the periscope, but saw nothing unusual or suspicious.

At 1730 I heard a faint but clearly audible noise that sounded suspicious. I went forward to the torpedo room to listen. At 1745 a tremendous explosion, accompanied by a brilliant white-yellow flash, shook the entire boat. The lights went out and only the emergency lights in the forward and after sections of the boat came on. All the lights in the central part of the boat were destroyed. Water poured in through several openings in the conning tower and flooded the control room. A fire broke out behind the starboard breaker panel and water poured through the main induction valve, cascading down on the electric motors.

An attempt was made to couple the port electric motor to both shafts, but the result was thick smoke and the odor of burning rubber, calcium, and sulfur. The main switch was immediately opened and the boat stopped. All electrical power failed. Oberleutnant zur See Sauerland reported that the diving controls were not functioning and the boat was starting to sink. The fire in the control room was spreading and the heavy flooding was forcing the bow down. We quickly went from 25° down angle to 50° and then 60° and the boat started sinking rapidly. Things started breaking loose and Oberleutnant zur See Sauerland ordered the crew to move to the stern to shift weight aft. The batteries toppled over, spilling acid that mixed with seawater and formed chlorine gas.

Leitender Ingenieur Pelz ordered the tanks blown with compressed air and U-8 started upward stern first, still 45° down by the bow. We broke surface with only the conning tower and after deck above the surface. Two British destroyers immediately opened fire, scoring two hits on the conning tower that wounded Obersteuermann Ryman and caused me flash burns. I ordered the crew to abandon ship through the conning tower hatch while Oberleutnant zur See Sauerland, Leitender Ingenieur Pelz and I scuttled the boat. The flooding valves were still open and I ordered Pelz to shut off the compressed air that was still blowing through the tanks. At the same time I opened the main induction valve. By the time we emerged from the conning tower, boats from the British destroyers were taking the crew off the stern as the U-8 settled deeper in the water. Moments after I stepped into a British boat, the U-8 sank beneath the surface.

Additional Information

The explosive sweep that sank U-8 was an enormous looped cable that the destroyers towed three hundred yards astern. The upper part of the loop had nine large floats that were submerged twenty-four feet below the surface and were held at that depth by a hydroplane device called a kite. Nine eighty-pound guncotton charges spaced one hundred feet apart were attached to the lower part of the loop, and they were held at about fifty feet below the surface. The charges either exploded on contact or an operator aboard the destroyer could detonate them electrically. The goal was to foul the U-boat so that the charges exploded or to place the charges close enough to the boat to damage it when the operator fired the charges electrically. The system rarely worked and there are several examples of U-boats being struck by the sweep without the charges detonating.

Sources

Records, T-1022, Roll 23, PG61507, "Official British Report on the Sinking of the U-8, 4 March 1914, Enclosure No. 1, letter British Naval Attaché, Berlin to Rear Admiral Arno Spindler, 25 October 1928" and Kapitänleutnant Alfred Stoss, "Gefechtsbericht über die Versenkung S.M. Unterseeboot U-8, Rotterdam den 15. Juli 1918."

U-10

Date Lost:	May or June 1916
Commander:	Kapitänleutnant Stuhr
Location:	Baltic Sea or Gulf of Finland
Position:	Unknown
Disposition:	Verschollen

On 27 May 1916 U-10 departed Libau in the Baltic to attack Russian warships in the waters north of Gotland, and simply vanished. The Germans did not know if U-10 had hit a floating Russian mine, or if a navigation error had put it in a German minefield. There was also the possibility that U-10 had suffered a diving accident.

Additional Information

Russian antisubmarine warfare measures were poorly developed and inefficient, but their mines were among the best in the world. The Russians made extensive use of defensive mines and laid enormous minefields across their harbor entrances and in the Gulf of Finland. Russian mines represented the most serious threat to German submarines operating in the Baltic.

Sources

Records, T-1022, Roll 31, PG61513.
Spindler, *Der Handelskrieg mit U-Booten,* 3:179.
Von Gagern, *Der Krieg in der Ostsee,* 3:33.

U-11

Date Lost:	December 1914
Commander:	Kapitänleutnant von Suchodoletz
Location:	Hoofden, Dover Strait, or English Channel
Position:	Unknown
Disposition:	Verschollen

U-11 departed Zeebrugge on 9 December 1914 for operations in the English Channel. There was no word of U-11 after that date and there were no survivors. A postwar German study failed to turn up any British action reports that could possibly explain the loss. It is possible that U-11 hit a mine or had a diving accident.

Additional Information

Bruges was the Germans' main naval base on the Flanders coast and the headquarters of the Marinekorps, an independent command that included the Flanders U-boat flotilla. Bruges lay eight miles inland and two canals connected the main harbor to the entrance harbors at Zeebrugge and Ostend. The U-boats based at Bruges used Zeebrugge and Ostend to refuel, rearm, and take on stores for their operations in the Hoofden, the Dover Strait, the English Channel, and the western approaches.

In September 2001, parts that were purported to have come from the wreck of U-11 appeared on eBay, an online auction firm. The seller, who identified himself only as stevo427, claimed that the parts had been removed from U-11's wreck off the Flanders coast. He did not reply to e-mail questions about the wreck's position, who discovered the wreck, or when the discovery was made. The parts consisted of what appeared to be water valves, one of which was stamped U-11, and a tank filler plate that was also stamped U-11.

Sources

Records, T-1022, Roll 31, PG61514.
Spindler, *Der Handelskrieg mit U-Booten,* 1:170.

U-12

Date Lost:	10 March 1915
Commander:	Kapitänleutnant Kratzsch
Location:	North Sea, north of Dogger Bank
Position:	56°7' N, 2°20' W
Disposition:	Ramming, Explosive Sweep

U-12 departed Helgoland on 4 March 1915 for operations off Britain's east coast. Off Aberdeen on 6 March, the trawler *Duster* spotted U-12. *Duster* was in the frustrating position of being unable to send a sighting report because it had no radio, but word was passed the next day upon meeting a radio-equipped steam yacht. On 8 March Auxiliary Patrol trawlers reported sighting U-12 in the morning and again that evening. In the meantime the British had deployed the 1st Destroyer Flotilla across the U-boat's path as it moved south. However, U-12 slipped through the search line on 9 March and made an unsuccessful torpedo attack on HMS *Leviathan* on that day. The fumbled attack alerted the 1st Destroyer Flotilla that their quarry was south of them and the chase was on.

The Official British Report

On 10 March 1915 at 0900 the trawler *Man Island* reported a U-boat at approximately 56°15' N, 1°56' W. The destroyers of the 1st Flotilla went to the area. At 1010 the destroyers *Acheron, Attack* and *Ariel* were steaming on a northeast course in line abreast at 1 nautical mile intervals. The wind was force 2, the sea calm, weather hazy. At 1010 HMS *Attack* spotted the U-12 two points to port steering northwest at almost right angle to the destroyer's course. The destroyer opened fire and went to full speed to attack. Two minutes later HMS *Ariel* saw the U-12 2 1/2 points to starboard at a distance of two nautical miles. All three destroyers turned to attack, and the U-boat dove. The *Ariel* saw the periscope four points to starboard, two hundred yards away. The *Ariel* turned toward the periscope, saw the conning tower just below the surface, and rammed the U-12 at an angle of 70 degrees. Two minutes later the U-boat surfaced and the destroyers took it under fire. The U-boat sank at 1030 and ten survivors were made prisoner. The *Ariel* was so badly damaged by the ramming that she had to be towed to port.

Steuermann Rath, U-12

We sighted destroyers to the south approaching at high speed. Dove, quickly reached trim at nine meters, and maneuvered to attack. A destroyer was five to ten meters off our port beam. The boat was just starting to dive deeper when a colossal explosion shook the entire boat and immediately the boat was rammed in the area of the conning tower. The blow rolled the boat 90 degrees starboard, blew out three rivets near the compass and destroyed the port breaker panel. Water poured through the periscope gland, the lights went out and the batteries shorted. The captain ordered the tanks blown with compressed air and the boat quickly gained the surface. The conning tower hatch could be opened only half way. The crew abandoned ship while three British destroyers fired into the boat.

Oberleutnant zur See Max Seeburg, U-12

I was asleep in my bunk when I was suddenly awakened by an alarm. I went immediately to the control room and met War Pilot Völker whose face was very pale. He said that destroyers had surprised us, and that the crew had been ordered forward to speed the dive. Visibility on the surface was from five hundred to one thousand meters. We were then at twenty-five meters and I heard Kapitänleutnant Kratzsch order the boat to rise to eleven meters and make two torpedo tubes ready for firing. As we approached eleven meters, Kapitänleutnant Kratzsch extended the periscope and immediately ordered the boat to dive quickly to twenty-five meters. Just as the periscope motor started running to retract the periscope I heard an ear-splitting noise of tearing metal. The boat rolled hard to starboard and dropped sharply by the bow. Immediately a tremendous explosion shook the boat.

Additional Information

Ten men escaped from the wreck and became prisoners of war. One of them, war pilot Völker, escaped from his British prison, made his way to Hull, and signed aboard the Swedish bark *Ironstrop* as an able bodied seaman. On 1 October 1915 U-16 stopped and examined *Ironstrop* in the North Sea. Völker reported himself to U-16's boarding officer and completed his escape by being taken aboard U-16. Völker did not survive the war. He was assigned as the war pilot aboard U-44 and went down with it on 12 August 1917.

Sources

Gibson and Prendergast, *The German Submarine War,* 33–34.

Records, T-1022, Roll 31, PG61516, "Übergang der stenographischen Aufzeichnung des Steuermannes Rath von *U-12*"; and "Brief, Kapitänleutnant a.D. Max Seeburg vom 22. November 1928 an Konteradmiral Arno Spindler: Verlust *U-12*."

Spindler, *Der Handelskrieg mit U-Booten,* 2:38–40, 247, "The Official British Report."

U-13

Date Lost:	August 1914
Commander:	Kapitänleutnant Arthur Graf von Schweinitz und Krain
Location:	North Sea
Position:	Unknown
Disposition:	Verschollen

Operations Order No. 1, dated 5 August 1914, directed ten U-boats to take stations in the North Sea and to attack units of the Royal Navy as the opportunity presented itself. Primary targets were heavy and light cruisers. U-13 was the sixth boat to depart on 6 August, and its course to its picket station was 322°(T) with orders not to go beyond 59° N. Once on their stations, the ten boats were to form a picket line with about seven nautical miles between each boat. U-13 did not return, and there is no clue as to its loss. U-15 was also lost during this operation.

Additional Information

During the first months of the war the Germans used their U-boats as pickets and their efforts were directed at attacking units of the Royal Navy. The anti-shipping campaign was a wartime development.

Sources

Groos, *Der Krieg in der Nordsee,* 1:77.
Spindler, *Der Handelskrieg mit U-Booten,* 1:170.

U-14

Date Lost: 5 June 1915
Commander: Oberleutnant zur See Hammerle
Location: North Sea, east of Aberdeen, Scotland, and north of
               Dogger Bank
Position: 57°16' N, 1°16' E
Disposition: Gunfire

In late April 1915 U-14 received a new captain and an almost entirely new crew. Kapitänleutnant Mühlau, the half-flotilla commander, was onboard as an observer when U-14 sailed on 31 May. U-14's assigned operations area was off the Firth of Forth but Mühlau ordered Oberleutnant zur See Hammerle to operate in the North Sea because he felt that Hammerle and his crew were too inexperienced to deal with the British antisubmarine measures off Britain's east coast.

On 5 June U-14 encountered the armed trawler *Oceanic II* on line with Peterhead. Hammerle fired a warning shot, and the trawler immediately returned fire. Outgunned, Hammerle attempted to dive, but a venting valve failure in the forward tank group caused the stern to sink while the bow remained on the surface. Several more armed trawlers arrived and fired at point-blank range into the exposed bow section. Hammerle brought the stern back to the surface and the crew abandoned the boat as it sank. The trawlers picked up the crew, except for Hammerle who went down with U-14.

Kapitänleutnant Mühlau, U-14

5 June 1915, eighty nautical miles, southeast of Peterhead. At 0745 a trawler hove into view and while the U-14 was heading toward her, the captain ordered scuttling charges brought up and the gun manned. The boat was running on one electric motor and one diesel engine.

At eighteen hundred meters the U-14 turned to port and fired two rounds across the trawler's bows. The trawler immediately returned fire with a gun of 5.0 to 7.5 cm. The captain ordered the helm hard over port to bring the trawler dead astern and shouted "Crash dive! Flood 1, 2, 12 and 13." As the gun crew hurried below, the diving orders and response were being shouted. I heard:

"Ready rapid venting valves."

"Rapid venting valves ready."

"Open rapid venting valves!"

"Rapid venting valves open."

"Tanks are flooding."

"Go to twenty meters."

We started our dive on an even keel, but as soon as we started going under the stern dropped down 8°. All available crewmen were ordered forward and we started pumping water forward. The forward diving planes were hard down and the after planes were hard up.

Leutnant zur See Ruppersberg went forward, found the vent valves to tanks 12 and 13 closed, and immediately opened them. He did that within thirty seconds after we started to dive. The boat continued to hang by her bow, and we were receiving several hits on the bow. None of the hits penetrated the pressure hull. The captain ordered the trim tanks flooded and the stern immediately dropped to a 20° down angle.

The captain ordered the after tanks blown and the boat came up on an even keel. But as soon as he ordered the rapid vents opened, the stern dropped down again. The captain again ordered the after tanks blown, and as the conning tower broke the surface he gave the order to continue blowing. He wanted to bring the boat up and restart the diving procedure. During that time the firing had ceased and there was nothing in view.

Suddenly the navigator who was on watch at the main periscope reported a trawler about to ram us. The captain ordered the port motor full astern and the helm hard over to starboard. He ordered the tanks flooded. The boat dropped by the stern and sank. The diving plane motor failed and the control was switched to manual. Then the anchor plate on the central bilge pump tore loose when we turned on the pump to move water out of the trim tanks. The captain ordered the trim tanks cleared with air pressure. The stern down angle diminished enough that the men who were forward acting as human ballast were able to return to their regular stations.

The boat was out of control and the captain made the decision to surface. The forward diving planes were hard up and one motor was full ahead. The boat reached the surface down by the stern and listing 10° to starboard. Her after section was awash up to the conning tower. The forward hatch was above the surface. The crew opened it and went out. While the crew abandoned the boat, the trawlers fired occasionally and ceased firing when the crew started jumping in the water. The trawlers picked up the entire crew except for the captain who remained aboard too long to escape.

Sources

Gibson and Prendergast, *The German Submarine War,* 45.

Records, T-1022, Roll 3, PG61519, "Unternehmung S.M. U-Boot *U-14* vom 31. Mai bis 5. Juni 1915 und Untergang des Bootes, Kapitänleutnant Mühlau, Rotterdam, 30. April 1918."

Spindler, *Der Handelskrieg mit U-Booten,* 2:125–26.

U-15

Date Lost:	9 August 1914
Commander:	Kapitänleutnant Richard Pohle
Location:	North Sea, east of Firth of Moray
Position:	58°22' N, 0°58' E
Disposition:	Ramming

Operations Order No. 1, dated 5 August 1914, directed ten U-boats to take stations in the North Sea and to attack units of the Royal Navy as the opportunity presented itself. Primary targets were heavy and light cruisers. U-15 departed Helgoland on 6 August with orders not to go beyond 59° N. When on their stations the ten U-boats were to form a picket line with about seven nautical miles between each boat.

Fog developed on the night of 8 August and blanketed the picket line the next morning. At 0227 on 9 August U-15 and U-18 made radio contact with each other. U-18 reported that at 0330 it had briefly spotted a cruiser with four stacks. U-15 replied that it was going to patrol in the middle of the North Sea on a line approximately 58° N.

On the morning of 9 August 1914 a lookout aboard the light cruiser HMS *Birmingham* spotted a U-boat on the surface, dead in the water. The men on *Birmingham*'s bridge could clearly hear what sounded like hammering coming from within the U-boat. Apparently it was broken down. *Birmingham* turned and went to full speed to ram. As the cruiser bore down on U-15, the U-boat got slowly under way, but it was much too late. *Birmingham* rammed U-15 just aft of the conning tower, cutting the U-boat completely in half. The severed pieces remained afloat only briefly and then sank with all hands.

Additional Information

During the night of 10–11 August, a German radio station at Poldhu picked up a message in clear English: "British Admiralty states one of the cruiser squadrons, main fleet, was attacked yesterday by a German submarine. None of HMS damaged. One enemy submarine, U-15 was sunk." This was the first and the last clue the Germans had as to what had happened. When the U-boats returned to Helgoland, U-13 and U-15 were missing. Like so many early scraps of information that surface after a

U-boat disappeared, the British radio transmission was only partly correct. U-15 had indeed been sunk, but it had not made an attack.

The fact that the British reported the U-boat's identity indicates that they had seen the hull number, either painted on the bow or on the conning tower. Otherwise they would have been unable to identify the boat so quickly.

Sources

Gibson and Prendergast, *The German Submarine War,* 3.
Groos, *Der Krieg in der Nordsee,* 1:76–77.

U-18

Date Lost:	23 November 1914
Commander:	Kapitänleutnant Heinrich von Hennig
Location:	Hoxa Sound, Orkney Islands
Position:	58°42' N, 2°48' W
Disposition:	Equipment Failure, Ramming, Scuttled

U-18 attempted to enter Scapa Flow through the Hoxa Sound gate on 23 November. Submerged at periscope depth, Kapitänleutnant Heinrich von Hennig followed a steamer through the boom and entered the Grand Fleet's anchorage only to discover that the fleet was not there. He went back through the gate, but as he was making his way down Hoxa Sound, a patrol boat spotted his periscope and the chase started. The trawler *Dorothy Gray* rammed the periscope, putting it out of commission. Next U-18's diving plane motor failed and the boat became unmanageable, plunging deep at one moment and shooting toward the surface in the next moment. At one point U-18 rammed the rocky seabed. Things got worse and von Hennig was forced to surface and scuttle his boat. British patrol boats picked up the entire crew.

Kapitänleutnant Heinrich von Hennig, U-18

In the night sky above Scapa Flow I saw several searchlight beams, which assured me that the fleet was there. In fact, as I later learned, they were taking on coal that night in preparation for a dawn departure. During the night I went over my plan for the following day, and it seemed to offer the prospect for success. The weather was not particularly good, but visibility was good and the tide would also be favorable. I planned to be off the entrance to Scapa Flow at still water with a fully charged battery. I assumed the narrowest part would be netted or mined and I expected strong antisubmarine measures, but they could not be any worse that those I had encountered in the English Channel.

At 0830 we dove to avoid a destroyer and by daylight we were in the north channel. At 1015 we were off Swona Island and the flood tide had set. At 1030 I approached the entrance to Scapa Flow at five knots. Ahead of us were some destroyers, steamers and fleet auxiliaries. I saw several coal ships and tankers lined up, stopped, spaced about five hundred meters. They were obviously assembled in front of the gate, preparing to enter Scapa

Flow. Slowly I took U-18 along the port side of the line and through the open gate. Once inside I found a point from which I could see the entire harbor, but it was empty.

I was now able to examine the gate defenses. Several buoys supported a net, and at each end there was an anchored net tender close to the shore, armed with small caliber guns and searchlights. The buoys were spaced forty meters apart with heavy timbers between them to prevent surface ships from crossing the barrier. The gate was at the north end of the barrier and there was no second net.

At 1220 I went back through the gate. Ahead were two destroyers, several other patrol vessels, and a few steamers that were queuing up to pass through the gate. At 1245 we were through the gate and in open water. I looked through the periscope and saw that the destroyers and patrol boats ahead of us were steaming at high speed and on constantly changing courses. Two destroyers were behind us, coming right up our keel line at high speed. Obviously we had been seen, probably because I had used the periscope more often than I wanted to due to the difficult navigation.

Propeller noises came from all sides. We ran at twenty meters and rose to periscope depth every ten to fifteen minutes to fix our position. At 1330, just as I was running up the periscope, the U-18 rolled over on her starboard side and then righted herself. The HMS *Garry* had rammed us on the port side and had carried away the after periscope. [Author's note: Von Hennig erroneously thought *Garry* was responsible; in actuality it was *Dorothy Gray*.] The remaining forward periscope was of limited usefulness. We went down to twenty meters and the propeller noises gradually diminished.

I plotted our position at two nautical miles from the entrance to Pentland Firth and twenty minutes from the area of strong currents. It was imperative that I obtain an accurate position fix. We rose to ten meters and I took a quick look around. Several destroyers were crossing our wake back and forth at high speed and dead ahead were several fishing boats.

Suddenly the bow dropped and the boat sank to forty meters. The diving plane motors had failed, and the problem was compounded when the reserve steering system jammed. It took enormous strength and effort to move the manual wheel, and the movement was very slow. In that water depth, with the strong currents and rocky bottom, there was no thought of setting the boat on the bottom. We had to make repairs under way.

Without the diving plane motors the boat went rapidly and repeatedly from sharply bow down to sharply stern down. It required enormous effort to make the corrections. We flooded and pumped, went ahead and back and shifted the crew from one end of the boat to the other. One minute we would be just below the surface and the next we were down to fifty or seventy-five meters. The deck plates in the conning tower buckled. Throughout the ordeal we could constantly hear propeller noises near us.

At 1330 the bow rammed the rocky seabed at fifty meters and the boat bounced back to the surface. Moments later the drifter *Dorothy Gray* rammed us in the stern. The boat went under again and the crew slowly corrected the diving plane problem. By the time we reached deep water the boat was again under control, but at 1420 the bilge pumps failed.

We again had problems controlling the boat, only this time the problems were more serious than they had been. The current drove the boat onto some rocks and the vertical rudder was bent and jammed. We were now unable to maneuver the boat, and I ordered the tanks blown with compressed air. We surfaced at 1430.

To the northwest, about five nautical miles away, was a group of fishing boats and to the south at about the same distance were several destroyers. After we surfaced I learned that the rudder was not repairable and I gave the order to scuttle the boat. At 1445 we opened the torpedo tubes and flooded the boat.

Oberheizer Otto Rohr, U-18

On the morning of 23 November 1914 we entered Scapa Flow at periscope depth. At noon a British destroyer discovered us and began hunting us. Because of the heavy sea we were often spotted and the destroyer HMS *Garry* rammed us. [Author's note: Rohr erroneously thought *Garry* was responsible; in actuality it was *Dorothy Gray.*] We dove. The boat sustained damage to the starboard side, but the pressure hull was undamaged. We tried to find deep water and struck the bottom with such force that the rudder was jammed hard to starboard. The grounding also damaged the starboard tanks. We then surfaced and remained on the surface for about two hours using compressed air. The destroyer was not in sight and we fired distress signals that attracted a fishing boat that was near, and she went to fetch the destroyer. In the meantime we threw the codebooks and secret papers overboard in a weighted bag, fired off the torpedoes and prepared to flood the boat. When the destroyer came within three hundred meters we flooded the boat and abandoned ship. Everyone was rescued except Ernst Missal who drowned.

Crew Member, U-18

An unidentified crew member sent a letter to his wife while he was a prisoner of war in Britain.

Dear Anny:

I hope you receive this letter that I have given to a man to take back to Germany. As you know from my earlier letter we left Helgoland on 17 November and on the 23rd we met our fate. Now I will tell you what happened.

Under cover of darkness we approached the British coast, and just before 0800 there was a British destroyer in our way. We crash dived and proceeded undisturbed under water. Our captain left the destroyer undisturbed because we had bigger fish to fry. Our captain had told us that were going to strike a blow for Germany such as had never before been done, so we were ready for something big. So we were all ready to do or die. Unfortunately, it did not come off, but that was not the fault of the crew.

We entered the British fleet base at Scapa Flow in the Orkney Islands, which is a navigation nightmare. Anyway, at 0800 we had gone under and were running at ten meters. The weather was good. The tension was terrific despite that we were not being disturbed, and the captain gave us regular reports of what he saw. After about three and a half hours we were inside and the captain could get a good look at the harbor. Suddenly he told us that the harbor was empty.

You can imagine our disappointment. We had imagined battle ships being torpedoed and rolling over. But now we had to get back out. We came about at 1230 and foresaw no difficulties. We did not want to have made the trip for nothing, so we decided to sink a destroyer on the way out. The torpedoes were made ready, but just before the shot was made, the periscope failed.

We went deep to work on the problem, but we had to rise again to get our bearings. The current there is very strong and it became critical for the captain to know where we were. But as we rose we heard propeller noises, so we had to remain deep. But in a short time the noises faded and we resumed rising. We had to get our bearings since we had spent so long without fixing our position. Just as we got to ten meters and the captain had run up the after periscope, there was a horrifying crash and screeching as though the entire conning tower had been ripped off. We had been rammed.

The boat rolled sharply to port and I thought that I was already dead. It seemed that the boat was going to roll completely over. Then it stopped and rolled back the other way and dropped sharply by the stern. The trim tanks were flooded, the motors went all ahead full, and we went deeper. We again had the boat under control.

We could not surface because the destroyer was still up there, so we had to remain under. But we had to take some bearings because we were right at the harbor entrance where the current was very strong and there were rocks all around us. If we could not fix our position, the current would sweep us onto the rocks.

The after periscope was broken, but the forward periscope was working again. We were just preparing to rise to periscope depth when we crashed into something. We had rammed the rocks. The boat again dropped by the stern and the propellers struck the bottom. Everything that was not nailed down went flying. The decks were strewn with wrenches, oil cans, lockers, ladders, tools and our noon meal. The torpedoes in the forward torpedo room, thankfully, remained in their tubes and did not come flying back inside.

We went astern, flooded and pumped to keep from going too deep or rising too high. But we could not regain control of the boat. The terrible current swept us along, the forward diving planes failed, and were kept receiving blows to port and to starboard. Sometimes the blows to the hull were so strong that we fell down. One minute the boat threatened to broach and the next she plunged to sixty meters, and finally the captain gave the order to blow the tanks with compressed air.

As soon as we were surfaced the captain opened the conning tower hatch and reported that there was nothing in sight. We were two miles off shore and our way to the open sea was clear. The captain ordered the men to repair the diving planes, but then came the word that the vertical rudder was jammed hard to starboard. Everyone pitched in to free the rudder, but it was hopeless. We had no choice but to scuttle the boat. We went over the side at 0310.

Sources

Groos, *Der Krieg in der Nordsee,* 3:14–20.

Records, T-1022, Roll 32, PG61526, "Bericht des Kommandanten von U-18, Kapitän-leutnant v. Hennig, über die letzte Unternehmung des Boots, 17.-23. November 1914"; "Aus der ausfürlichen Schilderung des Kommandanten von U-18, in welch Weise versucht wurde, das Boot weiter unter Wasser zu steuern, wird folgendes entnommen"; "Auszugsweise Abschrift von Frageboden, Wilhemshaven, den 29. September 1919, Oberheizer Otto Rohr"; and "Abschrift. Bericht eines in englischer Gefangenschaft befindlichen Obermaschinenmaaten über den Untergang von U-18, Dornchester, 31. Januar 1915."

U-20

Date Lost:	5 November 1916
Commander:	Kapitänleutnant Walter Kurt Schwieger
Location:	North of Point Blavands near Lyngvig, Denmark
Position:	56°33' N, 8°8' E
Disposition:	Stranded, Scuttled

On 2 November 1916 U-20 was homeward bound from the Irish Sea when it received a radio call from U-30 reporting that its diesel engines had broken down and a tow was needed. The following morning U-30 reported that both engines were back on line and no assistance was required, but since the boats were almost within hailing distance of each other they proceeded together toward Helgoland.

On 4 November they were five nautical miles north of Blavands Point, Denmark, where they lost their bearings in heavy fog, and the current set them ashore. Two hours later they got themselves off and U-30 found deep water, but U-20 again ran aground. The following morning, 5 November 1916, the torpedo boat B-109 tried to pull U-20 off the sand, but all attempts failed and the crew blew up U-20 with its own torpedoes. The Danes scrapped the hulk in 1925.

Sources

Herzog, *Deutsche U-Boote,* 88.
Records, T-1022, Roll 4, PG61536.
Spindler, *Der Handelskrieg mit U-Booten,* 3:248–49.

U-23

Date Lost:	**20 July 1915**
Commander:	**Oberleutnant zur See Hans Schulthess**
Location:	**North Sea, east of Firth of Forth**
Position:	**58°55' N, 0°14' E**
Disposition:	**Torpedo**

U-23 departed Ems on 17 July 1915 and three days later encountered the decoy trawler *Princess Louise,* which was towing the submerged submarine C-27. The trawler and the submarine were in telephone communication and when U-23 fired on *Princess Louise,* the trawler alerted C-27. The submarine cast off the tow, maneuvered into an attack position, and fired a torpedo that hit U-23 just abaft the conning tower. U-23 sank almost instantly, leaving four officers and six men in the water.

Oberleutnant zur See Hans Schulthess, U-23

> We fired a warning shot that caused the trawler to stop and swing out her boat. The lowering of the boat was very slow and we fired a second round. The trawler hoisted the Norwegian flag as the U-23 lay about two thousand meters away. There were no signs of suspicious behavior or armament aboard the trawler. Suddenly we saw a periscope 250 meters abeam and at the same moment the swell caused by two torpedoes being fired was observed. We turned hard to port at full speed to avoid the torpedoes. The first torpedo passed one meter astern, but the second struck us at the after gun mount, blowing some of the gun crew and the conning tower lookouts overboard. The U-23 sank very quickly, stern first, taking most of the crew with her. Some of the men from the gun crew, a few from the conning tower and two men who escaped from the control room were left swimming in the water. Several were wounded. The British submarine C-27 surfaced and started to pick up the survivors. The British boat was joined in the rescue by the trawler that had now set the British war flag.

Additional Information

This was the second and last time that the British successfully used the submarine and trawler combination as a trap. The first instance occurred on 23 June 1915 when the *Taranaki*–C-24 combination sank U-40. Following the destruction of U-23, the British made the mistake of allowing

U-23's crewmen to mingle with German civilians who were being repatriated. The German sailors told the civilians what had happened and the secret of the trawler-submarine traps was made known to the German navy.

Sources

Records, T-1022, Roll 24, PG61547.
Spindler, *Der Handelskrieg mit U-Booten,* 2:132–33.

U-26

Date Lost:	**August or September 1915**
Commander:	**Kapitänleutnant Freiherr von Berckheim**
Location:	**Eastern Baltic or Gulf of Finland**
Position:	**Unknown**
Disposition:	**Verschollen**

On 11 August 1915 U-26 and U-9 left Libau for operations in the eastern Baltic with orders to attack units of the Russian navy as the opportunity presented itself. On 22 August 1915 U-9 returned to Libau, but U-26 never returned. Kapitänleutnant Freiherr von Berckheim's orders were to operate off the south coast of the Gulf of Finland until 17 August. He was then to move on to Revel and then to Helsingsfors (Helsinki). U-26 had fuel and provisions for a four-week cruise; after that time the Germans listed U-26 as missing. The Germans believe that U-26 hit a Russian mine in the Gulf of Finland. Postwar investigation established that U-26 torpedoed the Russian naval transport *Petschora* (two thousand tons) on 25 August, and on the evening of 30 August HMS E-9 had sighted U-26 southwest of Dagerort.

Sources

Records, T-1022, Roll 33, PG61555.
Rollmann, *Der Krieg in der Ostsee,* 2:290.
Spindler, *Der Handelskrieg mit U-Booten,* 2:208–9.

U-27

Date Lost: 19 August 1915
Commander: Kapitänleutnant Bernhard Wegener
Location: Atlantic Ocean, fifty-five nautical miles west
                  of Bishop Rock
Position: 50°25' N, 8°15' E
Disposition: Gunfire

During World War I the Entente propaganda machine cranked out a steady stream of atrocity charges against the Germans, and especially against the U-boats. The fact was that most, if not nearly all, charges were unfounded. There were, however, instances in which both sides were guilty of violations of the rules of war, and the so-called *Baralong* Affair is a well documented case in which the British violated the rules of war.

U-27 departed Ems on 4 August 1915 for operations in the western approaches. The hunting was not particularly good but on 18 August Kapitänleutnant Bernhard Wegener, in strict observance of the Prize Regulations, stopped and sank four steamers totaling ninety-five hundred tons. On the 19 August, he stopped SS *Nicosian* (6,369 tons), which was carrying mules from the United States to Britain. Complying with the Prize Regulations, Wegener waited until *Nicosian*'s crew had taken to their boats and then his gun crew started shelling the mule carrier. While U-27's gun crew was firing into *Nicosian,* another steamer hove into view.

The newcomer was the British decoy vessel, *Baralong,* commanded by Lt. Cdr. Godfrey Herbert, RN. *Baralong*'s scruffy appearance and the presence of the American flag and American neutrality markers hid the fact that it was a heavily armed unit of the Royal Navy. Adding emotion to the developing drama was the fact that U-24 had torpedoed the White Star liner *Arabic* (15,801 tons) that morning with the loss of forty-four lives. To the Royal Navy crew aboard *Baralong,* the sinking of *Arabic* was an atrocity on the order of the 7 May 1915 torpedoing of the *Lusitania.*

U-27 was lying off *Nicosian*'s port quarter firing into it when *Baralong* hove into view. At the time, *Baralong* was displaying the international signal that it was going to rescue *Nicosian*'s crew. Wegener ordered his gunners to cease firing and took U-27 along *Nicosian*'s port side, intending to come around the bow and intercept the approaching steamer. As the

U-boat disappeared behind *Nicosian,* Herbert brought *Baralong* around on a parallel course along *Nicosian*'s starboard side.

At that moment the U-boat and the decoy were steaming on parallel courses with *Nicosian* between them. Before U-27 cleared *Nicosian*'s bow, *Baralong* dropped its American flag and neutrality markings, hoisted the Royal Navy white ensign, and unmasked its guns. When U-27 appeared from behind *Nicosian* the range was just six hundred yards and *Baralong*'s fire literally tore U-27 apart. U-27 rolled over and sank in less than a minute. The twelve men who got off alive were the men in the conning tower and the two gun crews. And that is where the *Baralong* Affair started.

According to four American witnesses, who were members of *Nicosian*'s crew, the British aboard *Baralong* opened fire on the swimmers with rifles and pistols. The Germans attempted to swim to *Nicosian* and get aboard by climbing up the falls. The British shot most of them in the water, but five or six managed to get aboard *Nicosian* and took refuge in the engine room. Herbert said that he was afraid that the Germans aboard *Nicosian* would scuttle it, so he sent Royal Marines aboard the steamer to hunt them down. The marines did their job efficiently and there were no German survivors from U-27. *Baralong* took *Nicosian* in tow.

Sources

Halpern, *A Naval History of World War I,* 301.
Records, T-1022, Roll 33, PG61556.
Spindler, *Der Handelskrieg mit U-Booten,* 2:255.

U-28

Date Lost:	2 September 1917
Commander:	Kapitänleutnant Georg Schmidt
Location:	Barents Sea, northeast of Kjelvik
Position:	72°24' N, 27°56' E
Disposition:	External Explosion

U-28 departed Ems on 19 August 1917 for operations in the Barents Sea. On 2 September 1917 at 1155 U-28 torpedoed the British SS *Olive Branch*, which was carrying ammunition to Russia. The steamer did not sink, so U-28 surfaced to finish the job with gunfire. U-28 got so close to its target that when the second round exploded in the ammunition it caused an explosion that destroyed U-28 along with *Olive Branch*. The only survivors of the incident were the crewmen from *Olive Branch* who had abandoned the steamer after it was torpedoed. They had rowed far enough away that they survived the explosion and reported the incident when they were rescued that same day. The British reported that the survivors from *Olive Branch* refused to take the survivors from U-28 into their boats, because the boats were already overcrowded. Apparently survivors from *Olive Branch* had enough time to identify U-28.

Sources

Records, T-1022, Roll 33, PG61559.
Spindler, *Der Handelskrieg mit U-Booten,* 4:272.

U-29

Date Lost:	18 March 1915
Commander:	Kapitänleutnant Otto Weddigen
Location:	North Sea, northeast of Peter Head
Position:	58°20' N, 0°57' E
Disposition:	Ramming

U-29 departed Ems on 4 March 1915 for operations in the Irish Sea. U-29 carried out anti-shipping operations under the Prize Regulations and started home on the northern route around Scotland. While en route to Ems, U-29 attacked a formation of British warships, and HMS *Dreadnought* rammed U-29, sinking it with all hands.

The Official British Report

On 18 March 1915 the 1st and 2nd Battle Squadrons of the Grand Fleet were steaming at fifteen knots in division columns on a zigzag course toward Scapa Flow. Behind them and on a slightly different course was the 4th Battle Squadron. The weather was clear and cold with excellent visibility. At 1315 HMS *Marlborough,* leading the port wing column, sighted a periscope and almost immediately a torpedo passed thirty yards astern of the HMS *Neptune,* the last ship in the port column. The 1st and 2nd Battle Squadrons turned twelve points to starboard and increased speed to seventeen knots.

At 1320 the 4th Battle Squadron had just turned and was passing astern the 1st and 2nd Battle squadrons when the *Marlborough* signaled "U-boat dead ahead of you." At 1328 HMS *Dreadnought,* the port wing ship, sighted a periscope twelve hundred yards to port and hoisted the red flag for "U-boat in sight." HMS *Dreadnought* increased to full speed and turned toward the periscope. The submarine's course changed frequently, but her base course was south.

At 1335 HMS *Dreadnought* rammed the submarine, apparently on her starboard side. The submarine's conning tower was not seen, but the bow came out of the water at a 30° angle exposing about thirty feet of the submarine's forward section. The number U-29 was painted on the bow and was clearly seen before the submarine sank.

The cruiser HMS *Blanche* remained on the scene and reported at 1510 that considerable debris, oil and clothing were on the surface. There were no survivors.

Sources

Records, T-1022, Roll 34, PG61560.
Spindler, *Der Handelskrieg mit U-Booten,* 2:35–36, "The Official British Report."

U-31

Date Lost:	January 1915
Commander:	Oberleutnant zur See Siegfried Wachendorff
Location:	Hoofden or German Bight
Position:	Unknown
Disposition:	Verschollen

U-31 departed Borkum on 31 January 1915 for operations in the Hoofden. U-31 did not return and there is no clue as to its fate.

Additional Information

U-31 earned a niche in history as the Phantom Submarine, a sort of submersible Flying Dutchman. The myth got its start in the official German history of the war at sea, *Der Krieg in der Nordsee,* published in 1923. Otto Groos wrote, "In August 1915 the U-31 was discovered completely undamaged, but with the entire crew dead, off Yarmouth. The British acquired valuable secret material from her, including her codebooks, ciphers, and mine charts. How this occurred has not been explained."

From that small entry the tale grew into a first class sea yarn in which U-31's departure date became Friday the 13th and thus was the cause of its undoing. The problem with that embellishment is that 13 January 1915 was a Wednesday and not a Friday. In any event, U-31 had departed on 31 January, not 13 January. Karl Adolf Georg Edgar Graf von Spiegel und zu Peckelsheim, better known to his friends as von Spiegel, told the tale to Lowell Thomas who included it in *Raiders of the Deep,* first published in 1928.

According to von Spiegel's version, U-31 disappeared in January 1915 and it showed up six months later adrift off Yarmouth where it grounded on a bar and the British found it. The British towed U-31 into an unnamed harbor, opened it up, and went inside. The boat was in perfect order except that the entire crew, officers and men, were in their bunks. The last entry had been made six months previously.

The explanation provided by Thomas in *Raiders of the Deep* was that Oberleutnant zur See Siegfried Wachendorff set U-31 on the bottom for the night and everyone went to sleep. Apparently Wachendorff was not too keen on watch keeping. Poison gas developed and the crew's sleep became eternal rest. The boat remained on the bottom until enough compressed air leaked into the ballast tanks to blow them and bring U-31 to the surface. From that point it was simply a matter of drifting about day and night through the most heavily patrolled waters in the world until finally winding up on the beach. Thomas was lucky that von Spiegel did not try to sell him the Brandenburg Gate.

Sources

Groos, *Der Krieg in der Nordsee,* 3:181–82.
Records, T-1022, Roll 34, PG61565.
Spindler, *Der Handelskrieg mit U-Booten,* 1:171.
Thomas, *Raiders of the Deep,* 172–73.

U-32

Date Lost:	**May 1918**
Commander:	**Kapitänleutnant Kurt Albrecht**
Location:	**Mediterranean, northwest of Malta**
Position:	**36°7' N, 13°28' E (probable)**
Disposition:	**Gunfire**

After being laid up in the yard at Pola from mid-October 1917 to 14 April 1918, U-32 went to sea for operations in the central and western Mediterranean. UB-48 exchanged signals with U-32 on 8 May 1918 while U-32 was following a convoy that was on a northwest course. According to the British, on that same day HMS *Wallflower* was escorting a convoy from Alexandria to Gibraltar and was forty nautical miles northwest of Malta at 36°7' N, 13°28' E when it sank a U-boat with gunfire. The boat was assumed to be U-32. There were no survivors.

Additional Information

A postwar German study concluded that *Wallflower* probably sank U-32 on 8 May 1918, based on the fact that UB-48 saw it in that area on that day.

Sources

Grant, *U-Boats Destroyed,* 131.
Records, T-1022, Roll 15, PG61569.
Spindler, *Der Handelskrieg mit U-Booten,* 5:151.

U-34

Date Lost:	October 1918
Commander:	Kapitänleutnant Johannes Klasing
Location:	Western Mediterranean
Position:	Unknown
Disposition:	Verschollen

U-34 departed Pola with U-63 and UB-48 on 16 October 1918 for operations in the Adriatic and the Tyrrhenian Sea. On 21–22 October the German High Command sent a general radio order for all U-boats to cease the anti-shipping campaign. On 25 October Kommodore Püllen, commander of the Mediterranean boats, sent a radio message to U-33 and U-34 authorizing them to return to Germany at once if they had sufficient fuel and supplies. No answer was ever received from U-34.

Additional Information

Since U-34 had been at sea for several days when Püllen sent the authorization to return to Germany, it is unlikely that it had sufficient fuel and supplies to make the trip home. But U-34 did not show up in Pola with the other boats to take on fuel and supplies. It is probable that U-34 disappeared sometime between its departure from Pola on 16 October and 25 October when the recall order went out.

A British report states that on 9 November 1918 the decoy vessel *Privet,* together with British motor launches, destroyed a U-boat with gunfire and depth charges. In that account U-34 was attempting to pass through the Strait of Gibraltar on the surface when two motor launches forced it to dive and depth charged it. Five minutes later U-34 surfaced very close to *Privet,* which opened fire and hit the conning tower. U-34 remained on the surface for three minutes during which *Privet*'s 12-pounder (3-inch) gun scored five more hits. After the U-boat dove *Privet* dropped seven depth charges. A short time later three dark objects, which might have been bodies, were seen on the surface but no closer investigation was made.

A postwar German study concluded that if U-34 had started home on 23 or 25 October, assuming it had sufficient fuel and stores for the trip, it would have cleared the Strait of Gibraltar long before 9 November. That same study concluded that it is more probable that the boat the motor launches and *Privet* attacked was either U-49 or U-51. Both boats passed through the Strait of Gibraltar on the night of 8–9 November and were depth charged, but came through unscathed.

Sources

Grant, *U-Boats Destroyed,* 133.
Records, T-1022, Roll 26, PG61575.
Spindler, *Der Handelskrieg mit U-Booten,* 5:196–97.

U-36

Date Lost:	24 July 1915
Commander:	Kapitänleutnant Ernst Graeff
Location:	Atlantic, northeast of Butt of Lewis, the Hebrides
Position:	59°10' N, 5°30' W
Disposition:	Gunfire

U-36 departed Helgoland on 17 July 1915 for operations near the Hebrides. On 24 July it captured the American square rigger *Pass of Balmaha* and sent it into Cuxhaven. That same afternoon U-36 stopped SS *Luise* and as the boarding party was throwing part of its cargo overboard, a lookout sighted another ship approaching. U-36 got under way and headed toward the steamer while flying the international "Stop" signal. The steamer that U-36 was approaching was the British decoy *Prince Charles.*

When U-36 opened fire and ordered *Prince Charles* to stop, Lieutenant Wardlaw complied and swung out his boats. The U-boat lay broadside to *Prince Charles,* six hundred yards off, and continued firing. Unable to draw in the U-boat closer, Wardlaw unmasked his port guns and opened fire. The first round hit twenty feet aft of the conning tower and the U-boat tried to dive. *Prince Charles* closed to three hundred yards and scored several hits; U-36 sank by the stern. *Prince Charles* picked up fifteen officers and men.

Kapitänleutnant Ernst Graeff

24 July 1915 in the afternoon U-36 stopped the Danish steamer SS *Luise* and was in the process of destroying part of her cargo when we sighted a steamer approaching. The distance was too great to make out her flag. U-36 proceeded toward the steamer and hoisted the international signal to stop and send across your papers. At three thousand meters we fired a round forward of her bow. The steamer stopped and swung out a boat.

As the U-36 closed with the steamer the steamer suddenly opened a heavy, accurate fire from hidden guns. We attempted to dive, but because the U-36 was not fitted with the new fast flooding valves our diving time was in excess of three minutes. During that time the steamer scored several hits on the pressure hull.

As the U-36 went completely under, water entered through several shell holes. We were unable to maneuver the boat for a submerged attack and were forced to blow the tanks with compressed air. As the U-36 regained the surface the crew abandoned her through the hatches and went over the side as the U-36 sank. One round hit the conning tower killing the helmsman and wounding Kapitänleutnant Graeff and the navigator. Throughout the abandon ship period the steamer continued to fire into the U-36.

The British did not cease firing when the U-36 sank, but continued firing into the swimmers with artillery and rifle fire. This firing lasted about fifteen minutes and stopped only when the SS *Luise* approached the scene and lowered a boat to pick up the swimmers. The British shifted their fire to her and moved in close to the freighter.

A half hour later the British ship returned, lowered a boat and picked up the survivors. The time lapse from the time the U-36 sank until the survivors were picked up was about forty-five minutes. During that time half the men who had safely abandoned the U-36 were killed by gunfire or drowned. The British also fired into the SS *Luise* because they thought she was a German resupply ship.

Additional Information

The German navy renamed the *Pass of Balmaha* the *Seeadler* and sent it to sea under Felix Graf von Luckner's command as a raider, operating in the Atlantic and the Pacific until wrecked in the Society Islands. Lowell Thomas made *Seeadler*'s wartime adventures famous in his 1927 book, *Count Luckner, the Sea Devil.*

Sources:

Chatterton, *Q-Ships and Their Story,* 13–16.
Records, T-1022, Roll 16, PG61581.
Spindler, *Der Handelskrieg mit U-Booten,* 2:118–20.

U-37

Date Lost:	April 1915
Commander:	Kapitänleutnant Wilcke
Location:	English Channel, Dover Strait, or Hoofden
Position:	Unknown
Disposition:	Verschollen

U-37 departed Helgoland on its first patrol on 20 March 1915 for operations in the English Channel. U-37 did not return.

Additional Information

There were several reports on U-37's activities before its disappearance. On 25 March U-37 attempted to sink the British SS *Delmira* under the Prize Regulations twenty-three nautical miles north-northeast of Cape d'Antifer on that same day SS *Lizzie* reported ramming a U-boat, but there was no confirmation. On 31 March the French patrol boat *Sainte Jehanne* spotted what was probably U-37 on the surface between Fécamp and Dieppe and tried to ram the U-boat as it dove. The next day U-37 sank SS *Emma* (1,617 tons) off Beachy Head and then torpedoed SS *Seven Seas* (1,194 tons) in the same area. That was the last sign of U-37 and the postwar examination of British naval records did not turn up any clue as to its fate.

Sources

Records, T-1022, Roll 16, PG61582.
Spindler, *Der Handelskrieg mit U-Booten,* 2:44–45.

U-39

Date Lost:	18 May 1918
Commander:	Kapitänleutnant Metzger
Location:	Cartagena, Spain
Disposition:	Bombed, Interned

U-39 departed Pola on 27 April 1918 for operations in the western Mediterranean. On 18 May at 1350 two French seaplanes caught U-39 on the surface. The U-boat crash dived. The airplanes dropped two bombs that exploded very close as U-39 reached twelve meters. Flooding in the after torpedo room caused the boat to drop sharply by the stern, and the diving controls failed. Sinking stern first and unable to control his boat, Kapitänleutnant Metzger blew the tanks and surfaced. The damage to the pressure hull and the loss of the after diving planes made it impossible for U-39 to dive, and Metzger laid a course for Cartagena, Spain. At 1700 two more French airplanes bombed the crippled U-boat, but the Germans drove them off with machine-gun fire. On the evening of 18 May 1918 U-39 entered Cartagena and was interned for the remainder of the war.

Sources

Records, T-1022, Roll 6, PG61588, "Kriegstagebuch des Kommandos SM U-39: Kapitänleutnant Metzger."

Spindler, *Der Handelskrieg mit U-Booten,* 5:157–58.

U-40

Date Lost: 23 June 1915
Commander: Kapitänleutnant Gerhardt Fürbringer
Location: North Sea, east of Firth of Forth
Position: 56°35' N, 1°2' W
Disposition: Torpedo

On the morning of 23 June 1915 U-40 stopped the decoy fishing trawler *Taranaki* east of the Firth of Forth. *Taranaki* was connected to the submerged C-24 with a combination tow cable and telephone line. When U-40 stopped the trawler, *Taranaki* telephoned the situation to C-24. But when C-24 tried to slip its tow the release mechanism failed. With one hundred fathoms of chain dangling from its bow, C-24 maneuvered to attack. Lt. F. H. Taylor was able to adjust the trim and avoided fouling the chain in the propellers. C-24 fired one torpedo that struck U-40 amidships, sinking the U-boat instantly and taking the crew that was inside with it. Only the men in the conning tower, Oberleutnant zur See Stobbe, Bootsmann Beizen, and the captain survived. The *Taranaki* picked up all three. This was the first use of the trawler and submarine combination.

Sources

Gibson and Prendergast, *The German Submarine War,* 46.
Records, T-1022, Roll 6, PG61589.
Spindler, *Der Handelskrieg mit U-Booten,* 2:130.

U-41

Date Lost:	24 September 1915
Commander:	Kapitänleutnant Klaus Hansen
Location:	Atlantic, near entrance to English Channel
Position:	49°10' N, 7°20' W
Disposition:	Gunfire

U-41 departed Helgoland on 14 September 1915 for operations off Britain's west coast. U-41 did not return. On 24 September U-41 was in the process of sinking SS *Urbino* with gunfire when the decoy vessel *Baralong* arrived. When U-41 moved in close to *Baralong,* the decoy opened fire and sank the U-boat. What followed became known as the second *Baralong* Affair, although in the absence of neutral witnesses the matter was a case of the Germans' version against the British version of what happened. The watch officer, Oberleutnant zur See Crompton, and Steuermann Godau reported on U-41's fate after their return from a British prisoner of war camp.

Oberleutnant zur See Crompton, U-41

On 24 September we were off the south Irish coast. At 0900 the British steamer *Urbino* was stopped thirty nautical miles southeast of the Scillies and was sunk with gunfire. The crew was given a half hour to leave the ship before we sank her. As the *Urbino* was listing heavily and burning, we spotted a smoke column.

The U-41 dove and maneuvered toward the steamer allowing it to pass forward of us at two hundred meters. The steamer was flying the American flag without any neutral identification marks on the side. Other than that shortcoming, there was nothing suspicious about the ship.

The U-41 surfaced and ordered the steamer to stop. The order was immediately followed and both vessels approached each other at slow speed on converging courses. At the signal to send across her papers the steamer sent the signal "Half" and swung out a boat. The U-41's forward gun crew manned their gun.

As the two ships came within three hundred meters of each other the steamer opened a heavy accurate fire. The firing started with rifle fire from all along the railing and was immediately joined with heavy caliber guns that were hidden forward and aft. The U-41 returned three rounds from the forward gun, all hits in the hull. Throughout the action the steamer continued to fly the American flag.

The captain ordered the gun crew to go below, but they continued firing and the navigator had to go forward to bring them in. The U-41 took several hits. The captain gave the order to dive and as the conning tower went under a round exploded against the conning tower view port. This round wounded me and I fell unconscious.

Steuermann Godau, U-41

Following my command to continue firing I saw that the number 2 loader, Obermaschinistenmaat Diekmann, had been blown overboard. I jumped down from the conning tower and assisted the gun crew. We fired a second round and I heard the diesel engines stop and the electric motors kick in. At that time we were receiving several hits along the hull between the forward diving plane and the gun mount.

We fired another round and I heard the rapid flooding valves open and I gave the command to go below. I had just closed the conning tower hatch when a round hit the conning tower. The explosion blew equipment off the bulkhead but did not penetrate the pressure hull.

We reached fifteen meters when the boat suddenly assumed a sharp bow-down attitude, started sinking quickly and could not be controlled with the diving planes. From forward came the shout that we were flooding forward in all compartments. The forward battery was cut out and the bilge pumps were started in the forward sections. The trim tanks were blown with compressed air, but despite the pumping and blowing the boat continued to sink and was down 25° to 30° by the bow.

The boat reached forty meters and the captain ordered all off watch crew to move aft and ordered air pressure in tanks 6 and 7. The boat continued sinking to eighty meters. The captain came into the conning tower and the boat started rising slowly, coming back to an even keel. As the conning tower broke the surface the steamer lay one hundred meters dead ahead, and the captain told me to open the hatch. The steamer was moving away and continued moving away until she was about three thousand meters distant.

The captain asked me how far out of the water we were and I told him that the ballast tank tops were just awash and he ordered the tanks blown clear with compressed air. In that moment the bow suddenly plunged down and the stern rose out of the water.

I was outside and jumped back to close the hatch because I thought we were diving. Before I could do that the wave washed me off the conning tower and I fell across the after gun. As I struggled in the water I saw the boat assume a vertical attitude and disappear below the surface. As I came back to the surface I was about thirty meters from the captain. Since I was heavily clothed I stripped to my under shorts and during that time I lost sight of the captain.

A while later I saw the steamer returning, and as she came within two hundred meters I could hear shouts for help. From the steamer came jeers, calls and whistling. The steamer passed within twenty meters of me, and the men along the rail threw things at me. I managed to swim away far enough to avoid the screws. The steamer was still flying the American flag.

A long time later I saw an empty lifeboat that had belonged to the *Urbino*. I swam to it and in a completely exhausted state, Lieutenant Crompton pulled me aboard. A while later the steamer returned and we started waving and whistling to attract her attention.

I saw a man standing in the bow who seemed to be directing the steamer's course with hand signals, right and left. The steamer did not slow and it became obvious that they intended to ram us. Just before she ran us down, we dove overboard and rode with the bow wave away from the screws.

After the steamer passed we returned to the badly damaged lifeboat, but it was kept afloat by an undamaged air tank. The steamer moved on for about five hundred meters and then came about, heading toward us again. Believing that they were going to ram us again, we donned two life vests that were in the boat and waited for their next move. Instead the steamer stopped and threw us a line.

Oberleutnant zur See Crompton, U-41

I came to in the water. Around me there was no sign of the *Urbino,* the U-41 or our crew. After I had been swimming for a while the steamer passed within sixty meters of me. I raised my arm and shouted, but the crew only threw things at me. Because I had no life vest, and my clothes were heavy, I shed my clothing and continued swimming.

Some time later an abandoned lifeboat from the *Urbino* drew near and I swam to it and climbed in. I heard Godau calling and when he reached the boat I hauled him aboard. We planned to rest a while and then set the sail. The weather was misty, the wind northwest 4, sea state 3 to 4 with occasional hail. Because I had lost a considerable amount of blood, I lay down in the stern and Godau lay down in the bow.

A while later we saw the steamer returning and we tried to signal her by waving and shouting. The steamer came toward us at high speed and I saw a man in the bow directing her course with hand signals. It was obvious that she intended to run us down, and as she came in to ram, we jumped into the bow wave and were carried clear of the screws.

The lifeboat was severely damaged but remained afloat on one air tank. We got into the wreckage as best we could, but the steamer soon came about and started toward us again. But this time she stopped and threw us a line. The boat went down at about noon and we were taken aboard the British decoy two hours later.

Additional Information

The British maintain that *Baralong* first picked up the *Urbino*'s crew and then returned to pick up the German survivors. They deny having run down the lifeboat.

Sources

Crompton, *Crompton U-41: Der zweite Baralong-Fall,* 47–54.

Records, T-1022, Roll 6, PG61590, "Bericht des Oberleutnants z.S. Crompton über die Vernichtung S.M. Unterseeboot U-41 und die Behandlung der überlebenden in Kriegsgefangenschaft."

Spindler, *Der Handelskrieg mit U-Booten,* 2:262–67.

U-44

Date Lost:	12 August 1917
Commander:	Kapitänleutnant Paul Wagenführ
Location:	Atlantic, north of Scotland
Position:	58°51' N, 4°20' E
Disposition:	Ramming

U-44 departed Wilhelmshaven on 17 July 1917 for operations in the North Channel in the Irish Sea. On the morning of 5 August 1917 U-44 encountered the British decoy vessel *Chagford* 120 nautical miles northwest of Tory Island and Kapitänleutnant Paul Wagenführ torpedoed it, causing serious damage. Then U-44 surfaced eight hundred yards away to finish the job with gunfire, but as the U-boat came up *Chagford*'s gunners opened fire and hit it. The U-boat dove. Wagenführ torpedoed *Chagford* two more times before it finally sank.

On 8 August, while headed home, U-44 met the outbound U-84 off the northern tip of the Hebrides. Wagenführ briefed Kapitänleutnant Walter Roehr on the conditions and British antisubmarine measures in the Irish Sea and along Britain's east coast. Wagenführ also told Roehr that *Chagford*'s round had holed the pressure hull and that seawater had gotten to the batteries and was producing chlorine gas. Wagenführ added that the conditions inside the hull prevented U-44 from diving.

U-44 sent a radio message on the evening of 11 August 1917 reporting that it was off the Norwegian coast, ten nautical miles west of Utsire, and it would arrive off the Lyngvig Lighthouse on 13 August at about 0600. U-44 added that it had sunk sixty-four hundred tons.

The 3rd Light Cruiser Squadron, operating off Bergen, picked up Wagenführ's transmission. Although they could not read the coded message, the strength of the radio signal alerted the squadron that a U-boat was in the immediate area. The next morning the destroyer HMS *Oracle* sighted U-44 six or seven miles away. At 0607 the U-boat dove. Six minutes later it reappeared three miles away and then dove again only to reappear a few moments later. *Oracle* turned toward the U-boat and at 0615 U-44's bow appeared a half a mile away to starboard. *Oracle* opened fire, and turned to ram. At 0617 the destroyer rammed U-44 squarely between the conning tower and the stern at twenty-seven knots, and passed over it. The

U-boat's bow appeared briefly above the surface at a 45-degree angle. The collision severely damaged *Oracle*'s bow below the waterline.

Sources

Chatterton, *Q-Ships and Their Story,* 288–89.
Grant, *U-Boats Destroyed,* 62–63.
Records, T-1022, Roll 7, PG61596.
Spindler, *Der Handelskrieg mit U-Booten,* 4:264–65.

U-45

Date Lost:	12 September 1917
Commander:	Kapitänleutnant Erich Sittenfeld
Location:	Atlantic, north of Malin Head, Ireland
Position:	55°48' N, 7°30' W
Disposition:	Torpedo

U-45 departed Helgoland on 5 September for operations off Britain's west coast. Minesweepers escorted U-45 in company with U-54 and U-88 through the minefields. U-45 took the northern route around the Shetlands. On 12 September the British submarine D-7 caught U-45 on the surface off the north Irish coast and sank it with one torpedo. There were two survivors: FT-Obergast Pustelnik and Oberheizer Babbel. Both had been lookouts atop the conning tower. Unfortunately neither man made a report on what happened.

Sources

Records, T-1022, Roll 7, PG61958.
Spindler, *Der Handelskrieg mit U-Booten,* 4:267.

U-47

Date Lost:	28 October 1918
Commander:	Kapitänleutnant Bünte
Location:	Pola
Position:	44°52' N, 13°50' E
Disposition:	Scuttled

On 21 October 1918 the Admiralstab sent a worldwide order that all U-boats that were ready for sea were to return to Germany. On 23 October the Germans began evacuating Pola and Cattaro. U-47 was one of ten boats that either could not make the trip home or was not ready for sea. The Germans destroyed these ten boats during the period 28 October to 1 November 1918 at Cattaro, Fiume, Pola, and Trieste.

Additional Information

U-47 was in the yard at Pola from 9 December 1917 to 14 July 1918. In August 1918 Kapitänleutnant Erich Gerth attempted to take U-47 back to Germany, but engine problems ended the trip after two days. In September Kapitänleutnant Bünte tried his luck, but again engine problems forced U-47 to return to Pola. After a brief attempt in October to operate off Brindisi the U-boat was back in Pola with more engine problems and the Germans scuttled it on 28 October.

Sources

Records, T-1022, Roll 18, PG61602.
Spindler, *Der Handelskrieg mit U-Booten,* 5:197–98, 226–28.

U-48

Date Lost:	24 November 1917
Commander:	Kapitänleutnant Edeling
Location:	Goodwin Sands, Dover Strait
Position:	51°11' N, 1°31' E
Disposition:	Stranded, Gunfire, Scuttled

U-48 departed Ems on 22 November 1917 for operations off Britain's west coast. When he entered the Dover Strait, Kapitänleutnant Edeling waited until the moon set before crossing the Dover-Dunkirk barrier on the surface. While he was waiting, the strong current set U-48 to the west side of the Goodwin Sands, and at 0430, approximately two nautical miles east-northeast of Gull Lightship, U-48 ran aground at high water. At dawn British patrols found the stranded U-boat.

Several drifters and the destroyer HMS *Gypsy* brought U-48 under heavy fire. U-48's gun crew returned the fire, but resistance was hopeless. Edeling ordered charges set in the forward and after torpedo rooms. The crew abandoned the boat, which then blew up. Enemy fire killed Edeling and eighteen men.

Oberleutnant zur See Erhard-Friedrich Maertens, U-48

Kapitänleutnant Edeling went aground on the Goodwin Sands at high water and soon after we grounded the tide began to fall. We blew the tanks and took off ammunition, but all our attempts to get off by lightening the boat failed.

At dawn several armed drifters and an old destroyer came into view. The U-48 opened fire with the forward 10.5-cm gun and the boat was prepared for demolition. Despite the short range and the solid platform provided by the grounded boat, our gunnery was not good. The drifters and the destroyer returned fire and the U-48 suffered several hits. The gun was destroyed, the gun captain was killed and the gun layer was seriously wounded.

I was in charge of preparing the demolition charges. We rigged four torpedo warheads forward and three aft and placed scuttling charges in the control room. When the forward gun was knocked out the crew went into the water and we blew up the boat. While the crew was leaving the ship, the British ceased firing for a while and then opened fire with machine guns and small arms on the swimmers. This was when most of the casualties occurred. Seventeen men were rescued.

Sources

Records, T-1022, Roll 18, PG61604, "Abschrift aus Fragebogen. Oberleutnant zur See Friedrich Maertens von U-48"; "Abschrift aus Fragebogen. Heizer Höpfner"; and "Abschrift aus Fragebogen. Adam Weber."

Spindler, *Der Handelskrieg mit U-Booten,* 4:419–20.

U-49

Date Lost:	11 September 1917
Commander:	Kapitänleutnant Richard Hartmann
Location:	Atlantic, 350 nautical miles west of English Channel
Position:	46°17' N, 14°42' W (probable)
Disposition:	Ramming

U-49 departed Wilhelmshaven on 30 August 1917 for operations in the western approaches and south to Cape Ortegal, Spain. U-49 did not return and there were no survivors.

Additional Information

At 2055 on 11 September 1917 the SS *British Transport* was at 46°17' N, 14°42' W, when a lookout heard an odd sound. *British Transport* turned to starboard, and as it was turning, the lookouts saw two torpedo wakes coming toward the steamer from the starboard side. Both torpedoes missed. As *British Transport* completed its turn the bridge crew saw a U-boat dead ahead just before it disappeared below the bow. A heavy blow and the sounds of tearing metal immediately followed. As *British Transport* continued forward, the U-boat appeared astern. Shouts were heard and then all was silent and no more was seen of the U-boat. A postwar German study concluded that *British Transport* probably ran down U-49.

Source

Spindler, *Der Handelskrieg mit U-Booten,* 4:269–70.

U-50

Date Lost:	September 1917
Commander:	Kapitänleutnant Berger
Location:	German Bight
Position:	Unknown
Disposition:	Verschollen

U-50 departed Wilhelmshaven on 30 August for operations in the western approaches. Minesweepers escorted U-49 and U-50 through the German minefields to a point north of Terschelling at 53°57.5' N, 4°55' E. Once the escorts left, Kapitänleutnant Berger's orders were to pass through the British minefields submerged. On 31 August U-50 radioed that it would use the northern route around Scotland, and that was the last anyone heard from it.

Additional Information

On 23 September Berger's corpse washed ashore on Amrum, one of the North Frisian Islands off the coast of Schleswig-Holstein. German pathologists estimated that Berger had been in the water for up to four weeks. Given U-50's last reported position and the place where the captain's body washed ashore, the Germans concluded that U-50 hit a British mine somewhere in the German Bight as it headed north.

Source

Spindler, *Der Handelskrieg mit U-Booten,* 4:271.

U-51

Date Lost:	14 July 1916
Commander:	Kapitänleutnant Rumpel
Location:	Off German coast, near Wilhelmshaven
Position:	53°56' N, 7°55' E
Disposition:	Torpedo

On Friday 14 July 1916 seven U-boats—U-19, U-24, U-46, U-48, U-51, U-53, and U-64—were approaching the Ems mouth in an extended column. Coming from Helgoland, they were en route to Wilhelmshaven for overhaul and refitting. On that same morning Lieutenant Varley, RN, in command of the submarine H-5, was at periscope depth off the Ems mouth near the outer Jade Lightship. Varley was there in direct violation of his orders, but as things worked out he got off lightly. He sighted U-51 running on the surface and fired two torpedoes, one of which struck U-51 just aft of the conning tower. Two miles astern of U-51, Kapitänleutnant Hans Rose in U-53 witnessed the explosion accompanied by a water column and smoke. U-51 vanished.

U-51 sank in about seventy feet of water. Inside the hull eighteen men, including all the officers, took refuge in the forward torpedo room. Three men were sealed in the after torpedo room and the spaces between the two compartments were fully flooded. Surface vessels, destroyers and drifters, arrived on the scene almost immediately, but there was nothing they could do. The first men to escape were two machinists from the forward torpedo room, surfacing eleven hours after U-51 sank. The next three, who came from the after torpedo room, surfaced sixteen hours after U-51 sank. One of them, Maschinistenmaat Sobirey drowned before he could be pulled from the water.

U-Maschinist Msyk, U-51

We were en route the Jade from Helgoland. The off watch was eating their noon meal and the watertight doors were closed as usual. At 1145 there was a terrific explosion that those of us in the forward torpedo room assumed was either a mine or a torpedo. At the moment of the explosion the navigator had opened the watertight door to the control room so that he could go to the bridge. He saw a bright flash and immediately closed the door. The diesel engines stopped, the lights went out and the boat sank by the stern.

We tried to go to the control room, but the captain met us and ordered everyone into the forward torpedo room. The water was already up to our knees and there was an immediate danger that chlorine gas would develop and the circuits would short, causing a fire. The bilge was already full of water and the air pressure was rising slowly. This was particularly evident because the watertight door to the torpedo room was difficult to open.

The people in the forward torpedo room were the captain, the chief engineer, the navigator, the senior machinist, six petty officers, three radiomen, and five seamen. The water in the torpedo room was already a half meter deep, but rising slowly because we had already closed off the ventilation system. How quickly the battery compartment flooded I do not know, but we could already detect a trace of chlorine gas in the air.

Of the eighteen men in the forward torpedo room only six had rescue breathers. All the rescue breathers and emergency flashlights had been brought forward. The chief engineer tried to blow the tanks using the forward emergency controls, but it did not work. We discussed what to do and we agreed to wait for our rescue. At that time our morale was very good. But four hours later the air suddenly went bad.

Oxygen was released, those with rescue breathers donned them, and the others breathed through potash pellets. Compressed air was released in the compartment and raised the inside air pressure to 1.8 kg. Breathing became difficult and we became tired and slept off and on. Some men dropped their mouthpieces and started gagging. The air purification system and the auxiliary systems shut down as the electric power failed.

Earlier we had tapping communication with the after torpedo room. They said, "Here is Böttcher in the after torpedo room. Is help coming?" By now four or five people were already dead and at 2300 the air was so bad that one man said, "This is not going to work. We have to get out." Earlier the majority had rejected an attempt to escape because most did not have rescue breathers. But now the captain said that we had to try it. I stood on the ladder with Maschinist Pieper. We did not have rescue breathers, but we did have rubber life vests. We released the lugs and pushed open the hatch and in that moment I was knocked unconscious. I think that because the boat was listing the weight of the hatch caused it to close itself after we went out. The others were probably too weak to open it and were trapped inside.

U-Heizer Adolf Kössinger, U-51

I was with Böttcher and Sobirey in the after torpedo room when a tremendous explosion shook the boat and flames spurted through the speaking tubes. We tried to go forward to the control room but we could not open the watertight door. I climbed the ladder and tried to open the torpedo room hatch, but it would not open either.

The lights had gone out and we tried to turn on the emergency lights but the switch was not where it was supposed to be. The floor plates were torn up and I saw a faint light in the bilge. I went down and found an emergency flashlight that had turned itself on. Because the battery was wet the beam was very weak, but after I dried the battery, the light worked fine. With the flashlight we found the emergency lighting switch and turned on the emergency lights.

The water was already a meter over the deck plates and it was very hot, about 45°[C]. It appeared to be coming from the steering rudder motor. Water was also pouring in through the speaking tubes from the conning tower and the control room. We broke out the tool kit and took down the ladder and laid it across the berths and provisions, and sat on it so that we were out of the water. Then we tried to open the hatch with a hammer and chisel, but that did not work.

We found our rescue breathers and tried them to see if they were working, and they were. The air was still good so that we did not need them at that moment and we laid them aside. The water rose slowly and we were about a meter above the surface. We sat on the ladder and waited to be rescued, but the air pressure continued to rise and our breathing became more difficult.

Right after the explosion the pressure gauge registered 1 kg in our compartment, and now it showed nearly 2 kg. We had given up hope of being rescued and we opened the starboard ventilation valve to flood the torpedo room. We knew that each kilogram of pressure represented about ten meters depth and when the gauge showed 2.5 kg we figured we were down twenty-five meters.

In order to speed the flooding, Böttcher and I opened the hatch about 5 cm and a large amount of water poured in, but we had to close it because Sobirey pleaded with us not to drown him. He was already exhausted. After a long conversation he said he was ready to try and we opened the hatch again. But as soon as we opened the hatch he started crying and jabbering again, so we closed it. He was terrified and we opened and closed that hatch at least six times because he became nearly hysterical each time.

Finally the water was up to our necks and we donned our rescue breathers. Böttcher and I opened the hatch and I was blown out with the air bubble. Böttcher grabbed my ankle and I grabbed the anti-net wire. Then I reached down and helped the other two out. We all went up together and Böttcher and I were rescued ten minutes after we surfaced. It was about 0300 when the drifter pulled us out of the water.

U-Oberheizer Böttcher, U-51

I have nothing to add to Kössinger's report. I established communications with the forward torpedo room at about 1800. I tapped out Morse code with a hammer on the ventilation pipes. I asked if help was coming and they answered that it was on the way. I told them that our compartment was half flooded and asked them who and where they were. They sent back that they were three men and then said four men. After that I received no more replies.

When we went out of the boat Sobirey was nearly all in. As we went out I grabbed his head under my arm and we went up together. But as soon as we surfaced he panicked and grabbed my hair and tore my mouthpiece from me. We both went under and I shoved him away. He drowned despite that a seaman from the drifter dove in to save him.

Additional Information

On 28 July 1919 a British prize court awarded the British submarine H-5 a bounty of £175 for sinking U-51. The award was based on thirty-five crewmen at £5 per crewman aboard the U-boat. But U-51 had thirty-six men aboard. This is one of the rare instances in which a prize court underpaid the bounty.

Sources

Edwards, *We Dive at Dawn,* 275.

Records, T-1022, Roll 19, PG61609, "Auszug aus dem Kriegstagebuch des FdU"; "U-Maschinist Msyk vom U-51, Helgoland, den 22. Juli 1916"; "Ubootsheizer Adolf Kössinger, Wilhelmshaven, den 22. Juli 1916"; and "Oberheizer Böttcher, Wilhelmshaven, den 22. Juli 1916"; T-1022, Roll 71, PG61934, "Londoner Prisen-gerichtsverhandlungen wegen vierzehn deutscher U-Boote."

U-56

Date Lost:	November 1916
Commander:	Kapitänleutnant Hermann Lorenz
Location:	Barents Sea
Position:	Unknown
Disposition:	Verschollen

U-56 departed Kiel on 13 October 1916 on its first and last war patrol. The boat operated in the Barents Sea and was last heard from on 1 November 1916 when it landed the crew from SS *Ivanhoe* in Tanafjord on Norway's extreme northern coast.

Additional Information

There is an unsubstantiated report that Russian antisubmarine patrol vessels sank U-56 off the Lapland coast on 2 November 1916, but there are no details available. A postwar German study concluded that the report could be correct because U-56 was operating in that area at the time.

Sources

Records, T-1022, Roll 19, PG61618.
Spindler, *Der Handelskrieg mit U-Booten,* 3:251–52.

U-58

Date Lost: 17 November 1917
Commander: Kapitänleutnant Gustav Amberger
Location: English Channel, at entrance to St. George's Channel
Position: 51°32' N, 5°21' W
Disposition: Depth Charge

U-58 departed Helgoland on 12 November 1917 for operations south of Ireland. U-58 attacked a convoy escorted by USS *Fanning* and USS *Nicholson* on 17 November. Despite poor visibility Kapitänleutnant Gustav Amberger carried out a submerged attack. While he was making his approach, a lookout on *Fanning*'s bridge spotted the periscope. *Fanning* attacked, dropped one depth charge, and a few moments later *Nicholson* dropped another. The explosions knocked out U-58's electric motor that drove the diving planes and the U-boat became unmanageable. U-58 broached and *Fanning* dropped three more depth charges. The three explosions destroyed all electrical power and the manual diving plane controls. U-58 sank to fifty meters, where Amberger ordered the tanks blown. When U-58 surfaced both destroyers opened fire as the crew came out on deck. As U-58 sank, *Fanning* picked up the crew.

Kapitänleutnant Gustav Amberger, U-58

I observed a strongly protected convoy and maneuvered to attack. Due to heavy fog the convoy disappeared and we turned to the convoy's reciprocal course and passed under the escort. I maneuvered to regain a bow shot position. Suddenly a destroyer appeared out of the fog headed directly toward us.

"Go deep!" The destroyer passed directly over us and dropped a depth charge that shook the entire boat. Reports reported all compartments tight, but all diving controls inoperative. We were then at fifty meters. The boat rose suddenly and broke the surface despite our having flooded the trim tanks. Moments later we heard fast propeller noises and then two strong explosions close aboard.

Inside the boat everything flew apart. Simultaneously the diving planes, vertical rudder, all the depth gauges, the trim pumps and the bilge pumps failed. The boat assumed a sharp stern down attitude. The control room reported that the manual control had also failed and the down angle was

50°. The watch officer reported that it was impossible to control the boat submerged.

I gave the order to blow the tanks and the boat rose slowly. The boat came to the surface, bow down with the forward deck under water back to the conning tower. I gave the order to open the forward hatch to flood the boat. The Americans picked up the entire crew and the U-58 sank in eighty meters. Maschinist Glinder died of a heart attack after he was aboard the *Fanning* and Maschinistenmaat Baden drowned.

Oberheizer Grunert, U-58

Around 1630 a convoy appeared. The escorts were ten destroyers and six trawlers. Destroyers 37 and 52 interfered with our attack, and at one point we were so close to a destroyer that he had to go half speed astern on both motors. A destroyer spotted our periscope and dropped a depth charge at fifteen to eighteen meters depth. The blast destroyed the main and after diving planes and opened ballast tanks 1 and 2. The boat dropped by the stern, but we were able to come back to an even keel. A second depth charge exploded close to the forward diving planes and destroyed them. It was impossible to hold the boat at any level and we had to surface. The boat and all the secret documents sank in 150 meters of water.

Sources

Records, T-1022, Rolls 19–20, PG61621, "Kriegstagebuch U-58, Kapitänleutnant Gustav Amberger, 12–17. Dezember 1917" and "Bericht des Oberheizers Grunert von U-58."

Sims, *The Victory at Sea,* 154–57.

Spindler, *Der Handelskrieg mit U-Booten,* 4:409–10.

U-59

Date Lost:	14 May 1917
Commander:	Kapitänleutnant Freiherr von Fircks
Location:	German Bight
Position:	55°33' N, 7°15' E
Disposition:	Navigation Error, German Mine

U-59 departed Helgoland at 1100 on 14 May 1917 for operations along Britain's west coast. Two minesweepers escorted the U-boat with their sweeps deployed. What they failed to recognize was that after dark the current was setting them northward and they were outside the swept channel. At 2300 the group was approaching Horns Reef when one of the escorts discovered a mine and hoisted the warning signal. U-59 was one hundred meters astern and to starboard of the minesweeper and standard procedure was for the U-boats to hold their positions astern of the minesweepers until the mine was destroyed. Apparently the lookouts in U-59 did not recognize the signal in the low visibility so U-59 moved closer to hail the escort. As it approached the minesweeper U-59 hit a German mine and quickly sank. There were only four survivors.

Sources

Records, T-1022, Roll 20, PG61622.
Spindler, *Der Handelskrieg mit U-Booten,* 4:69–70.

U-61

Date Lost:	26 March 1918
Commander:	Kapitänleutnant Dieckmann
Location:	St. George's Channel, Irish Sea
Position:	51°48' N, 5°32' W (possible)
Disposition:	Depth Charge

U-61 departed Helgoland on 14 March 1918 for operations in the Irish Sea. On 17 March it rendezvoused with U-101 and delivered a reserve valve that U-101 needed. That was U-61's last known position.

Additional Information

On 26 March 1918 the British P-boat P-51 sighted a surfaced U-boat in St. George's Channel off Milford Haven and attempted to ram. A steering casualty foiled the attempt and the U-boat dove, but P-51 repaired the problem in time to drop one depth charge near the spot where the U-boat went under. After the depth charge exploded the U-boat was seen momentarily on the surface and then disappeared. A postwar German study concluded that because P-51 did drop a depth charge and U-61 could have been in that area at that time, it is possible that P-51 sank U-61.

Sources

Records, T-1022, Roll 34, PG61625.
Spindler, *Der Handelskrieg mit U-Booten,* 5:17–18.

U-64

Date Lost:	17 June 1918
Commander:	Kapitänleutnant Robert Moraht
Location:	Mediterranean, west of Sicily
Position:	38°7' N, 10°27' E
Disposition:	Depth Charge, Ramming

On 9 June 1918 U-64, together with U-73 and UC-52, departed Cattaro on the Adriatic to support an Austrian surface raid on the Otranto Strait barrier. The raid was canceled on 10 July and U-64 undertook a patrol into the western Mediterranean to the coast of Spain.

On 17 June 1918 U-64 encountered a convoy that was going from Marseille to Malta and torpedoed SS *Kandy* (4,921 tons). Immediately following the torpedo shot, U-64 broached. Heavy seas caused a delay in regaining trim and getting under, so the escorts *Lychnis* and *Partridge II* were able to get a good location fix on the U-boat. The escorts conducted a standard depth charge attack, saturating the area with 120 depth charges.

The escorts were so fast that U-64 had barely reached periscope depth when the depth charging began. The explosions sprung the deck hatches so that they partially opened and could not be closed, and the forward and after compartments flooded.

Kapitänleutnant Robert Moraht, U-64

The depth charges exploded very close, and one apparently landed directly on the after deck. The noise was indescribable. The lights went out and the air was filled with objects that had been blown from their places. The boat dropped sharply down by the stern. We switched to emergency lighting and I called for reports from all compartments. Water was entering through both deck hatches and several other places. None of the pumps were working, the electric motors had stopped and we could not get the boat back on an even keel. The boat was sinking and the depth gauge showed sixty meters when I ordered the tanks blown and we surfaced.

Moraht surfaced and *Lychnis* rammed U-64, rolling it on its beam ends. Water poured in through the open hatches and sunk the U-boat. Kapitänleutnant Moraht reported:

I opened the hatch and waved my hat to show that we were surrendering. We were being fired at and one of the escorts was coming right at us, obviously intending to ram us. I shouted down to the control room for full speed but the order could not be carried out and he rammed us forward of the conning tower. The boat rolled to port and sank. I found myself swimming and had to shed my heavy sea clothes.

The two officers and two seamen on the conning tower survived, but the only man to escape from inside the hull was Obermatrose Karl Metze who somehow managed to go out through the forward hatch after the boat had been rammed and was sinking.

Obermatrose Karl Metze, U-64

On 17 June 1918 my U-boat was engaged with British surface units in the Mediterranean. During the engagement my U-boat sank and all my comrades went down with her. The deck hatches would not close and the water poured in through them flooding the entire boat. I was the only one who got through the forward hatch and reached the surface. I was in the water for about twenty minutes.

Source

Records, T-1022, Roll 36, PG1631, "Kapitänleutnant Robert Moraht" and "Abschrift, Karl Metze."

U-65

Date Lost: 29 October 1918
Commander: Kapitänleutnant Gustav Siess
Location: Pola
Position: 44°52' N, 13°50' E
Disposition: Scuttled

On 21 October 1918 the Admiralstab ordered all U-boats that were ready for sea to return to Germany, and the Germans began evacuating Pola and Cattaro on 23 October. U-65 was one of ten boats that either could not make the trip home or was not ready for sea. The Germans destroyed these ten boats during the period 28 October to 1 November 1918 at Cattaro, Fiume, Pola, and Trieste.

Additional Information

U-65 made its last patrol from 26 August to 22 September 1918, and was heavily depth charged on 2 September. Either because of damage sustained during the depth charging, or because the boat needed a major overhaul, U-65 went into the yard at Pola for extensive repair and overhaul. When the order to evacuate the base arrived, the work was not complete and the yard crew blew up U-65 in Pola on 29 October 1918.

Sources

Records, T-1022, Roll 36, PG61633.
Spindler, *Der Handelskrieg mit U-Booten,* 5:226–27.

U-66

Date Lost:	September 1917
Commander:	Kapitänleutnant Mühle
Location:	North Sea, Atlantic, or Irish Sea
Position:	Unknown
Disposition:	Verschollen

U-66 departed Emden on the morning of 2 September 1917 for operations in the North Channel. On 3 September shortly after noon it sent a position report in the North Sea that put it beyond the British minefields. After that there was no further word from U-66.

Additional Information

The British suggest that U-66 may have hit a mine in one of the older fields off Dogger Bank. Another British explanation, although not supported by details, is that a combined effort of destroyers, submarines, and net tenders operating west of Dogger Bank destroyed it sometime between 1 and 11 October. The postwar German study offers no possible explanation for U-66's loss.

Sources

Chatterton, *Beating the U-Boats,* 96.
Gibson and Prendergast, *The German Submarine War,* 209.
Grant, *U-Boats Destroyed,* 51.
Records, T-1022, Roll 37, PG61637.
Spindler, *Der Handelskrieg mit U-Booten,* 4:277.

U-68

Date Lost:	22 March 1916
Commander:	Kapitänleutnant Ludwig Güntzel
Location:	Atlantic, off Dingle in Southern Ireland
Position:	51°54' N, 10°53' W
Disposition:	Gunfire, Depth Charge

U-68 departed the Ems on 16 March 1916 for operations off Britain's west coast. This was U-68's first war patrol. On 22 March, while en route to the operations area, U-68 encountered the British decoy vessel *Farnborough* (Q-5). The *Farnborough,* commanded by Lt. Cdr. Gordon Campbell, was armed with five 12-pounders (3-inch), two 6-pounders (57-mm), and a machine gun.

At 0640 on 22 March a lookout aboard *Farnborough* sighted a U-boat on the surface about five nautical miles off its port side. The decoy held its course and speed. Twenty minutes later a torpedo passed close across the bow, but *Farnborough* continued holding its course and speed. Twenty minutes later U-68 surfaced one thousand yards dead astern of *Farnborough,* moved off to its port quarter, and fired a round forward of its bow.

Farnborough stopped, blew off steam, and put out a boat. U-68 moved to within eight hundred yards and fired a round that fell short. *Farnborough* immediately opened fire from three 12-pounders, firing twenty-one rounds, rapid fire. The rounds scored several hits on U-68 and it slowly sank. As the U-boat went under, Campbell steamed across the spot and dropped a depth charge. U-68's bow rose above the surface back to the conning tower at a sharp angle. *Farnborough's* gunners fired five more rounds into the conning tower and the boat sank stern first. There were no survivors.

Additional Information

A postwar German study concluded that *Farnborough* probably did sink U-68, although no positive identification was made at the time. The study was not kind to Kapitänleutnant Ludwig Güntzel. The study pointed out that by 1916 the U-boat captains had specific instructions on how they were to deal with ships that flew neutral flags. The instructions directed the captains to first examine the vessel through the periscope, looking for guns and to be sure that the flag and neutral markings were proper and looked genuine. The captains were also to consider the course and speed of the ship. Was it going in the right direction, or was it wandering aimlessly around various headings?

The instructions directed the captains to surface at a safe range and fire the warning shot. From the safe distance the captains were supposed to observe the lowering of the boats as the crew abandoned ship. Did the procedure appear to be genuine? Then they were to dive again, and move in close to the stopped ship for a very close inspection through the periscope. If he was satisfied, the captain was to surface so that his boat was least exposed to fire from hidden guns.

In the case of U-68, the report said, the captain had ignored everything that had been learned in 1915 about decoys and had done everything wrong.

But Kommodore Hermann Bauer, commander of the U-boats assigned to the High Sea Fleet, was more generous in his assessment. He pointed out that Güntzel was a new captain who was out on his first operation, and that, contrary to normal practice, the navy had not sent him to sea under an experienced captain to show him the ropes.

Despite *Farnborough*'s action report, on 28 July 1919 a British prize court awarded the British submarine H-5 a bounty of £180 for sinking U-68, based on the rate of £5 per crewman aboard the U-boat. There were no details included in the award statement, and H-5 is not on the postwar list of Entente submarines that sank a U-boat.

Sources

Bauer, *Als Füher der U-Boote im Weltkrieg,* 358.

Records, T-1022, Roll 37, PG61641; T-1022, Roll 71, PG61934, "Londoner Prisenger-ichtsverhandlungen wegen vierzehn deutscher U-Boote."

Spindler, *Der Handelskrieg mit U-Booten,* 3:106–7, 119–20.

U-69

Date Lost:	July 1917
Commander:	Kapitänleutnant Wilhelms
Location:	North Sea or Atlantic
Position:	Unknown
Disposition:	Verschollen

U-69 departed Emden on 9 July 1917 for operations off Ireland. The boat used the northern route and made its last position report on 11 July at 0230 when it was thirty-five nautical miles south of Lindesnes (The Naze) on Norway's southern tip. There was no further word from U-69 and its fate is unknown.

Additional Information

Two British sources say that HMS *Patriot* sank U-69 on 12 July in position 60°25' N, 1°32' E. According to the account, *Patriot* was working with a kite balloon when the observer spotted a surfaced U-boat at 0700. The U-boat dove and the hunt lasted until noon. *Patriot* dropped two depth charges that brought up thick brown oil. But the Germans say their postwar study makes that unlikely.

Sources

Chatterton, *Beating the U-Boats,* 76.
Gibson and Prendergast, *The German Submarine War,* 191.
Records, T-1022, Roll 37, PG61643.
Spindler, *Der Handelskrieg mit U-Booten,* 4:279.

U-72

Date Lost:	1 November 1918
Commander:	Oberleutnant zur See Bohm
Location:	Adriatic, north of Cattaro
Position:	Unknown
Disposition:	Scuttled

When the Admiralstab ordered all U-boats that were ready for sea to return to Germany on 21 October 1918, U-72 was waiting to be repaired in the Pola yard. Although there since 17 June waiting to have its diesel engines repaired, the yard had been unable to get the parts needed. U-72 was a particularly valuable boat because it was one of only ten large mine-layers, U-71 through U-80, that the Germans built during the war. When the Germans began evacuating Pola and Cattaro on 23 October U-72 was one of ten boats that either could not make the trip home or was not ready for sea. The Germans made frantic efforts to find a way to repair its engines, even trying to cannibalize parts from the other boats that were being left behind. Their efforts failed and on 1 November 1918 U-72's maintenance crew scuttled it in deep water north of Cattaro.

Source

Spindler, *Der Handelskrieg mit U-Booten,* 4:353; 5:208, 226–28.

U-73

Date Lost:	30 October 1918
Commander:	Kapitänleutnant Meusel
Location:	Pola
Position:	44°52' N, 13°50' E
Disposition:	Scuttled

On 21 October 1918 the Admiralstab ordered all U-boats that were ready for sea to return to Germany, and the Germans began evacuating Pola and Cattaro on 23 October. U-73 was one of ten boats that either could not make the trip home or was not ready for sea. The Germans destroyed these boats during the period 28 October to 1 November 1918 at Cattaro, Fiume, Pola, and Trieste.

Additional Information

U-73 was a big oceangoing minelayer with a history of engine problems that forced it to break off operations and return to Cattaro on 4 and 18 August. The Germans sent U-73 to Pola for an engine rebuild but the work was not completed by the time the order to evacuate Pola was issued. On 30 October the Germans sank it off the entrance to Pola.

Sources

Records, T-1022, Roll 30, PG61651.
Spindler, *Der Handelskrieg mit U-Booten,* 5:209, 226–28.

U-74

Date Lost:	27 May 1916
Commander:	Kapitänleutnant Erwin Weisbach
Location:	North Sea, off Britain's east coast at Stonehaven
Position:	57°10' N, 1°20' E
Disposition:	Gunfire

U-74 departed Helgoland on 13 May 1916 to lay mines off the Firth of Forth, and did not return.

Additional Information

Apparently U-74 had engine problems because just before noon on 27 May a lookout aboard the trawler *Sea Ranger* spotted a sail and smoke to the north. *Sea Ranger* led *Kimberly, Oku,* and *Rodino* to investigate. The four trawlers discovered that the strange sailing vessel was a U-boat and they opened fire. U-74 tried to dive, but moments after it went under it reappeared on the surface listing heavily to port. Two of the trawlers tried to ram the U-boat but it maneuvered clear and in so doing passed within eight feet of *Kimberly. Kimberly* fired into U-74 at point-blank range, blowing holes in the hull and causing it to sink stern first. There were no survivors.

Sources

Records, T-1022, Roll 20, PG61652.
Spindler, *Der Handelskrieg mit U-Booten,* 3:180–83.

U-75

Date Lost: 13 December 1917
Commander: Kapitänleutnant Schmolling
Location: Off Dutch coast, near Terschelling
Position: 53°59' N, 5°24' E
Disposition: Mine

U-75 departed Helgoland on 13 December 1917 to lay mines in the Hoofden. Two minesweepers escorted U-75 through the German minefields to a point where the picket vessel *Nordstern* was anchored. This was the outer limit of the German minefield and from that point U-75 proceeded alone. The escorts and *Nordstern* returned east. Fifteen minutes later U-75 hit a British mine and sank in less than three minutes. Despite the short time it took for the U-boat to go down, most of the crew had time to escape. While they were in the water they fired flares that attracted *Nordstern*'s attention, but the extremely cold water killed most of them before *Nordstern* returned. The enlisted navigator, Steuermann Schadebrodt, was one of the few lucky ones reached in time.

Steuermann Schadebrodt, U-75

> I was in the officers' room working on the chart. The captain was in his cabin. Immediately following the explosion the after torpedo room flooded and we used compressed air to clear the space. That probably kept the boat afloat a little longer. The boat sank in three minutes, which was enough time for everyone to get up on deck and to fire a flare. The *Nordstern* arrived to pick us up thirty minutes later.

Source

Records, T-1022, Roll 20, PG61653, "Steuermann Schadebrodt teilte heute über den Untergang von U-75 an 13. Dezember 1917 aus seiner Erinnerung Folgendes mit."

U-76

Date Lost:	27 January 1917
Commander:	Kapitänleutnant Bender
Location:	Barents Sea, on Norway's north coast
Position:	71° N, 23° E
Disposition:	Ramming, Scuttled

U-76 departed Helgoland on 9 January 1917 to lay mines along the Murmansk coast. During the night of 21–22 January an unidentified, darkened steamer accidentally rammed it, tearing a hole in the pressure hull that resulted in serious flooding. No longer able to dive, the question remaining was could U-76 steam thirteen hundred miles on the surface to Helgoland? Shortly after starting home on diesel-electric drive, both diesel engines quit.

On 27 January U-76 was being driven onto the rocks at Söröy Island. Kapitänleutnant Bender decided to use what was left of the batteries to find a place where he could land his crew and scuttle the boat. At 1500 he made the international distress signal and attracted the attention of the fishing cutter *Alia* that came alongside and took off the crew. Bender, his chief engineer, and the first machinist opened the valves and sank the boat. Leaving U-76, the chief engineer fell into the water and drowned. After a short internment in Norway, the entire crew was released and returned to Germany.

Kapitänleutnant Bender, U-76

Because of the snow flurries we did not see the steamer until she was three thousand meters away. She was approaching from port. We turned 30° to starboard, went to full speed, and dove. While we were going under the steamer rammed us just aft of the conning tower and the engine room was taking water quickly. I blew the tanks and surfaced. The steamer was just five hundred meters away and was proceeding as though nothing had happened. I don't know if she was just a normal steamer or an auxiliary, but I'm sure she had no idea that she had rammed a U-boat.

The deck from the conning tower back to the after gun was a shambles. The gun was lying on its side and both port side fuel tanks had been ripped open. Both the port side, forward compressed air tanks had been torn loose, and the air pipe from diving tank number 1 to the main exhaust mast was cut. Both ready ammunition lockers were destroyed and loose rounds were scattered about. The pressure water line to the starboard outer fuel bunker was damaged and not working. There was a deep depression in the top of the pressure hull and there were many popped rivets and open seams. The after part of the conning tower casing was twisted to starboard and the anti-net wire was broken.

We were able to pump out the engine room, but we were unable to complete our mission. We were unable to dive and we were trailing a very large oil slick. We had ten tons of fuel in the port outer fuel bunker. My first intention was to find a safe place where we could effect enough repairs to make it home on the surface. We got under way and ran on both diesel engines for twelve hours, and then we switched to diesel-electric to save fuel. In order to determine exactly where all the leaks are, we had to remove both port fuel tanks from above the port diesel engine. The job took us all day to complete and we plugged the popped rivets with wooden plugs and we caulked the open seams. Following those repairs, the boat took very little water so long as we remained on the surface.

The sea motion was causing the after deck gun to shift. This threatened to do further damage to the remaining compressed air tanks. The forward, starboard fuel tank had ten tons of fuel but we could not use it because of the damage to the piping. Our situation at that time was that running as we were on diesel-electric, we had enough fuel to last fourteen days. We had to go thirteen hundred nautical miles, but our average speed was just four knots. I decided to put into a fjord and make additional repairs.

We anchored in twelve meters and cleared away the damage on the after deck. The gun was thrown overboard, and we rigged an emergency pipe to the starboard outer fuel tank. The loose compressed air tanks and deck plates were lashed in place and we plugged more leaks. The port trim tank continued to leak and there was nothing we could do about it. It was taking water at the rate of one ton per day.

Shortly after we got under way the diesel engines developed problems and had to be shut down. The problem stemmed from weak engine mounts that allowed the engines to vibrate. The result was that cylinders 1 and 2 loosened. The vibrations also sheared the bolts that held the exhaust flange in place and that allowed the engine room to fill with exhaust fumes. We were unable to clear the fumes from the engine room because the ventilation blowers had been destroyed by water. The engine room crew had to wear gas masks while working in the engine room if the engines were running. While repairs were made to the engines, we ran on electric power.

We got one engine back online, but we could run it only on four cylinders. In order to save electric power we shut down all nonessential machinery. Because we had lost our ventilation system, the air inside the boat quickly became foul. We rigged a wind scoop through the conning tower hatch to move some air through the engine room. We managed to run the port diesel engine for an hour and a half on four cylinders, but we had to shut it down when smoke developed. We found that a crankshaft bearing and a cross-head had come loose.

As darkness came on bearings showed that the wind and sea were driving us toward the rocks. We were about ten nautical miles offshore and had enough battery remaining to run eight hours. There was no hope that we would have one of the diesel engines back online in less than twenty hours. The compressed air tanks had broken loose again and their movement was popping more rivets so that we were now taking some water in the electric motor room. Given the little electrical power we had, there was no hope of pulling away from the coast, and any attempt to do so would only delay by several hours the time until we would go on the rocks, and that would be at night.

Even if we could have gotten the diesel engine back online, there was no hope of reaching Helgoland. We could not eliminate the vibrations and the engine could only be used to charge the battery. For those reasons I decided to use what electrical power remained to reach a place where I could put the crew ashore and scuttle the boat.

We laid a course for Söröy Island. We spotted a fishing boat close to land and fired a distress flare. We also hoisted the international signal for vessel in distress. The fishing boat came over to us and sent his boat across, but the seas were too high to transfer the crew. We moved in closer to the shore and completed the transfer.

The chief engineer, first machinist and I remained aboard to scuttle the boat. We flooded the mine tanks, opened the deck hatches and all the watertight doors. The diving tank flooding valves were opened and the main ventilation valve. We went out through the forward hatch. The boat flooded slowly and dropped by the stern. The chief engineer jumped from the deck to the fishing boat's cutter, but missed and fell between the U-76 and the cutter. Despite the fact that he was wearing a rubber life vest, he did not come up. The U-76 sank in Skarsfjord.

The *Alia* took the crew to Hammerfest where we were confined in the local Social Democratic Union Hall. The Norwegians in Hammerfest treated us very well and saw to all our needs. I sent a telegram to the German ambassador reporting our presence and asking that he arrange for our release as shipwreck survivors. I added that he could tell the Norwegian government that we had engaged a British auxiliary cruiser fifty to sixty nautical miles off the coast and had been damaged by gunfire. [Author's note: The claim of engaging a British cruiser was not true.] We managed to reach the coast in sinking condition and were rescued by a Norwegian fishing cutter that responded to our distress signal. At the time of our rescue we were outside Norwegian territorial waters and were brought ashore in the rescuing vessel. [Author's note: This also was not true.]

The captain of the fishing cutter swore that our U-boat sank because of damage and not because we scuttled her. He swore that we were outside the Norwegian territorial waters when he rescued us. For rescuing us and as hush money I have given him a thousand Kroner and five hundred Kroner for each of his crew. The Norwegian government released us since we were shipwrecked sailors and we traveled by train and by ship to Sassnitz and then on to Kiel.

Sources

Records, T-1022, Roll 20, PG61654, "Kriegstagebuch SM U-76, 9–27. Januar 1917."
Spindler, *Der Handelskrieg mit U-Booten,* 3:278–79.

U-77

Date Lost:	July 1916
Commander:	Kapitänleutnant Erich Günzel
Location:	North Sea
Position:	Unknown
Disposition:	Verschollen

U-77, one of the big oceangoing minelayers, departed Helgoland on 5 July 1916 to lay mines on the east coast of Scotland off Kinnaird Head. There was no further word from U-77, but the British swept up a U-boat mine on 26 July off Kinnaird Head. There is a good possibility U-77 was blown up by one of its own mines.

Additional Information

There are several factors that may have played a role in U-77's loss. A new boat, it had joined the High Sea Fleet's 1st Half Flotilla at Helgoland on 29 June 1916, and this was Kapitänleutnant Erich Günzel's first command. It is also true that the big minelayers suffered from chronic engine problems that also troubled U-72, U-73, and U-74. Also, minelayers, especially the UC-boats, sometimes blew up on their own mines. A postwar German study found no explanation for U-77's loss.

Sources

Records, T-1022, Roll 21, PG61655.
Spindler, *Der Handelskrieg mit U-Booten,* 3:183.

U-78

Date Lost:	28 October 1918
Commander:	Kapitänleutnant Johann Vollbrecht
Location:	North Sea, off the Danish coast
Position:	56°2' N, 5°8' E
Disposition:	Torpedo

U-78, one of the big oceangoing minelayers, departed Helgoland on 25 October 1918 to lay mines off Britain's east coast in support of a planned final sortie by the High Sea Fleet. On 28 October the British submarine G-2 torpedoed U-78 southwest of the Skagerrak. The British identified U-78 through debris and clothing that came to the surface. There were no survivors.

Sources

Records, T-1022, Roll 21, PG61657.
Spindler, *Der Handelskrieg mit U-Booten,* 5:270.

U-81

Date Lost:	1 May 1917
Commander:	Kapitänleutnant Raimund Weisbach
Location:	Western approaches off Ireland's southern coast
Position:	51°25' N, 13°5' W
Disposition:	Torpedo

U-81 departed Borkum on 17 April 1917 for operations off Britain's west coast. On 1 May U-81 torpedoed SS *Dorie*. The British submarine E-54 was in the area, and its captain, Cdr. Robert H. T. Raikes, RN, heard the explosion. He investigated and soon sighted *Dorie* dead in the water and down by the head.

An hour later Raikes saw a U-boat surface. At 1711 E-54 fired both bow tubes at a range of four hundred yards. One hit U-81 midway between the conning tower and the stern, sinking it in less than thirty seconds. E-54 surfaced and picked up the seven survivors.

Kapitänleutnant Raimund Weisbach, U-81

On 17 April 1917 I sailed in command of U-81 from Emden for operations off the west coast of Ireland. On 1 May I made a submerged torpedo attack on a sugar steamer. The torpedo struck forward but the steamer did not sink. After thirty minutes I surfaced to complete the ship's destruction with gunfire. The steamer sank very slowly.

In the meantime, I moved among the lifeboats to determine the cargo, ship's name and destination. While we were returning to the steamer, which was about twelve nautical miles away, we spotted a periscope three hundred meters off our starboard beam. We saw a torpedo wake at the same moment and I ordered full speed and tried to turn to avoid the torpedo. The torpedo struck aft followed by a tremendous explosion that sank the U-81 in mere seconds. The men on deck leapt into the water. Fifteen minutes later a British submarine, E-54, surfaced and picked up seven men. The E-54 took us to Queenstown.

Obermatrose Herbert Hoeck, U-81

After torpedoing a British steamer we were torpedoed by a British submarine that we had not observed in the area. The first warning came when we saw the periscope and the torpedo wake to port. The captain ordered all ahead full, but the torpedo struck before the engines could respond. The U-81 sank in five seconds.

Sources

Edwards, *We Dive at Dawn,* 292–93.

Gibson and Prendergast, *The German Submarine War,* 181.

Records, T-1022, Roll 8, PG61662, "Abschrift aus Frageboden, Wilhelmshaven, den 27. October 1919, Kapitänleutnant Weisbach" and "Abschrift: Obermatrose Herbert Hoeck."

Spindler, *Der Handelskrieg mit U-Booten,* 4:98–99.

U-83

Date Lost: 17 February 1917
Commander: Kapitänleutnant Bruno Hoppe
Location: Western approaches off Ireland's southern coast
Position: 51°34' N, 11°23' W
Disposition: Gunfire

On 31 January 1917 U-83 departed Helgoland and passed through the Dover Strait for operations in the western approaches. On 17 February, west of the south tip of Ireland, U-83 torpedoed a steamer flying the Norwegian flag with the name *Norge* painted on the hull. The tramp was decoy vessel *Farnborough*. The torpedo hit the ship at the No. 3 hold, blowing a huge hole in the hull. The captain, Lt. Cdr. Gordon Campbell, saw the U-boat's periscope a short time later off the starboard quarter about two hundred yards away. The U-boat passed along the starboard side only about thirteen yards away and in water so clear that Campbell could clearly see the hull beneath the surface. Just ten feet below the surface Kapitänleutnant Bruno Hoppe was examining *Farnborough* carefully before surfacing. He saw no sign of armament.

U-83 passed around the bow and surfaced three hundred yards off the port bow. At 1005 the U-boat was off *Farnborough*'s port beam when *Farnborough* opened fire. The range was point blank and the results were catastrophic for U-83. The first round struck the conning tower, killing Hoppe instantly. U-83 sank quickly and at least eight Germans were seen in the water, but *Farnborough*'s boat was able to pick up only two survivors, the watch officer, Leutnant zur See Boenicke, and the navigator, Pfützer, who was badly wounded. The navigator died the following day.

Additional Information

Farnborough was itself in bad shape. The engine room, boiler room, and after holds 3 and 4 were flooding rapidly. The ship was down by the stern and sinking. A distress call brought HMS *Buttercup,* and most of *Farnborough*'s crew transferred to it. Campbell and twelve men remained aboard to attempt salvage and to rig the tow. At 1700 the sloop started towing *Farnborough* toward Bantry Bay. *Farnborough* sank during the night but was later salvaged and repaired; it ended the war as a cargo carrier.

Sources

Chatterton, *Q-Ships and Their Story,* 193–98.

Records, T-1022, Roll 9, PG61665, "Friedrich Boenicke, an Marine Archiv, Berlin, 23. Juni 1929."

Spindler, *Der Handelskrieg mit U-Booten,* 4:100–101.

U-84

Date Lost:	26 January 1918
Commander:	Kapitänleutnant Walter Roehr
Location:	Southern entrance to St. George's Channel
Position:	51°53' N, 5°44' W (possible)
Disposition:	Ramming

U-84 departed Ems on 1 January 1918 for operations in the Bay of Biscay. On 6 January U-84 reported that it was in the western approaches to the English Channel. This was the last anyone heard from U-84. According to the British, on 26 January P-62 rammed a U-boat in St. George's Channel. There were no survivors.

Additional Information

There is no confirmation that U-84 was in fact the U-boat sunk on 26 January, nor is it even certain that a U-boat was sunk on that day. A postwar study of U-boat losses concluded that U-84 could have been in that area if it had completed operations off the French coast and was headed home. U-84's orders were to use the northern route for its return, which means that it could have entered the Irish Sea. The German postwar study concluded that it is possible that P-62 rammed and sank U-84, but the evidence is circumstantial.

Sources

Records, T-1022, Roll 9, PG61666.
Spindler, *Der Handelskrieg mit U-Booten,* 5:40–41.

U-85

Date Lost:	12 March 1917
Commander:	Kapitänleutnant Petz
Location:	English Channel, off Plymouth
Position:	50°2' N, 4°13' W
Disposition:	Gunfire

U-85 departed Ems on 6 March 1917 for operations in the Irish Sea. On the afternoon of 12 March, twenty nautical miles southeast of Start Point, U-85 attacked the British decoy vessel *Privet* (Q-19). The torpedo missed, and U-85 surfaced and opened fire at twenty-four hundred yards. *Privet* stopped and U-85 closed the range to eighteen hundred yards and continued firing, scoring several hits. *Privet* got under way and opened fire at two thousand yards, scoring two hits. U-85 ceased firing and dove, but immediately surfaced; *Privet* scored several more hits that sank U-85. There were no survivors.

Additional Information

HMS *Orestes* took *Privet* in tow, but the decoy sank just off Plymouth Sound. A postwar German study concluded that *Privet* sank U-85 on 12 March.

Sources

Chatterton, *Q-Ships and Their Story,* 170–71.
Records, T-1022, Roll 37, PG61667.
Spindler, *Der Handelskrieg mit U-Booten,* 4:103–4.

U-87

Date Lost:	25 December 1917
Commander:	Kapitänleutnant Freiherr von Speth-Schülzburg
Location:	St. George's Channel, off Cardigan
Position:	52°56' N, 5°7' W
Disposition:	Ramming, Depth Charge, Gunfire

U-87 departed Wilhelmshaven in company with U-100 on 8 December 1917 for operations in the English Channel. U-87 did not return and there were no survivors.

Additional Information

According to the British, P-56 was escorting a six-ship convoy when a lookout spotted a periscope 150 yards away. P-56 dropped two depth charges that exploded and forced the U-boat to surface. P-56 rammed the U-boat midway between the conning tower and the stern, cutting the boat in two. The stern section sank immediately, but the forward section remained afloat for a short time and the crew on P-56 could see men inside the U-boat. There were no survivors. P-56 was heavily damaged as a result of the collision. A postwar German study concluded that given the time and location, the U-boat could only have been U-87.

Sources

Records, T-1022, Roll 38, PG61670.
Spindler, *Der Handelskrieg mit U-Booten,* 4:421.

U-88

Date Lost:	September 1917
Commander:	Kapitänleutnant Walter Kurt Schwieger
Location:	Hoofden, Dover Strait, or English Channel
Position:	Unknown
Disposition:	Verschollen

U-88, together with U-45 and U-54, departed Helgoland on 5 September 1917. Minesweepers escorted the three U-boats through the German minefields to a point north of Terschelling at 53°57.5' N, 4°5' E. At that point the three U-boats dove and no further word was received from U-88.

Additional Information

U-54 reported that while submerged on 5 September from 2232 to 2327 it encountered mines and could hear the cables scraping along the hull. During that time U-54 recorded two heavy explosions. A postwar German study concluded that U-88 probably hit a British mine, but there was no way to establish exactly when and where that happened. Kapitänleutnant Walter Kurt Schwieger had previously commanded U-20, when it was stranded and scuttled on 5 November 1916.

Sources

Records, T-1022, Roll 38, PG61671 (U-88); T-1022, Roll 28, PG61615 (U-54).
Spindler, *Der Handelskrieg mit U-Booten,* 4:274.

U-89

Date Lost:	13 February 1918
Commander:	Kapitänleutnant Bauck
Location:	North Channel of Irish Sea
Position:	55°38' N, 7°32' W (probable)
Disposition:	Ramming

U-89 departed Wilhelmshaven on 4 February 1918 for operations in the St. George's Channel in the Irish Sea. On 10 February it reported that it was off Peterhead. This was the last anyone heard from U-89.

Additional Information

According to the British, the cruiser HMS *Roxburgh* was escorting a convoy when a lookout spotted a surfaced U-boat. The cruiser rammed it in position 0020 in 55°38' N, 7°32' W. On 28 July 1919 a British prize court awarded *Roxburgh* a bounty of £210 for sinking U-89, based on the rate of £5 per crewman aboard the U-boat. The Germans' postwar study concluded that *Roxburgh* probably sank U-89.

Sources

Records, T-1022, Roll 38, PG61672; T-1022, Roll 71, PG61934, "Londoner Prisenger- ichtsverhandlungen wegen vierzehn deutscher U-Boote."
Spindler, *Der Handelskrieg mit U-Booten,* 5:31.

U-92

Date Lost:	September 1918
Commander:	Kapitänleutnant Günther Ehrlich
Location:	North Sea, or off Britain's west coast
Position:	Unknown
Disposition:	Verschollen

U-92 departed Wilhelmshaven on 3 September 1918 for operations of Britain's west coast. British countermeasures, especially mining, forced Kapitänleutnant Günther Ehrlich to pass through the Kaiser Wilhelm Canal (present-day Kiel Canal) and enter the North Sea through the Kattegat and the Skagerrak. On the evening of 9 September U-92 reported that it was through the Little Belt; after that nothing more was heard from U-92.

Additional Information

The British reported an explosion in the western section of the Northern Mine Barrage on 9 September that may have been U-92 hitting a mine. But spontaneous explosions were a common occurrence in the Northern Mine Barrage. Nevertheless, the fact that U-92 could have been in that area at the time makes it possible that it was the cause of the explosion.

Sources

Records, T-1022, Roll 38, PG61675.
Spindler, *Der Handelskrieg mit U-Booten,* 5:311–12.

U-93

Date Lost:	January 1918
Commander:	Kapitänleutnant Helmut Gerlach
Location:	English Channel or Bay of Biscay
Position:	Unknown
Disposition:	Verschollen

U-93 departed Ems on 29 December 1917 for operations in the English Channel between the Channel Islands and Penmarch, using the Dover Strait route to get there. On 5 January U-93 exchanged recognition signals with UC-17 thirty nautical miles west of Penmarch, which is on the southern coast of Brittany at the top of the Bay of Biscay. That was U-93's last confirmed position.

Additional Information

The British SS *Braeneil* reported that at 0415 on 7 January 1918 it rammed a U-boat off the Lizard in position 49°59' N, 5°12' W. There is no doubt that *Braeneil* hit something because its stem was heavily damaged and the ship went into dry dock for repairs. Some British historians believe that *Braeneil* sank U-93, but the Germans are not so sure. The Royal Navy attributed U-93's loss to a British mine, while the Germans thought a decoy might have sunk it. Some sources say that *Braeneil* sank U-95 instead of U-93, but in any event U-93's disappearance played a role in closing the Dover Strait to the U-boats.

Korvettenkapitän Hermann Bauer closed the Dover Strait to fleet U-boats on 12 April 1915 because he believed, incorrectly, that British antisubmarine measures in the strait were too effective and losses would be too high. He ordered boats to use the northern route around Scotland or around the Shetlands to reach their operations areas in the Irish Sea and the English Channel.

Bauer's prohibition remained in effect until the opening of the unrestricted anti-shipping campaign in February 1917, when it became important that the U-boats reach their operations areas as quickly as possible to allow the maximum time on station. Going north around Scotland took ten days away from the time they could spend in their operations areas, and Bauer canceled the two-year-old prohibition as an operational necessity.

But Bauer's orders canceling the prohibition were vaguely worded and most U-boat captains continued to use the northern route throughout 1917. The unexplained losses of U-83, U-87, U-93, and U-95 in January 1918 caused Kommodore Andreas Michelsen, who replaced Bauer on 5 June 1917, to reinstate the prohibition. The result was that U-boats used the longer northern route for the remainder of the war.

Sources

Records, T-1022, Roll 38, PG61676.
Spindler, *Der Handelskrieg mit U-Booten,* 4:428; 5:43.

U-95

Date Lost:	January 1918
Commander:	Kapitänleutnant Prinz
Location:	English Channel or Dover Strait
Position:	Unknown
Disposition:	Verschollen

U-95 departed Ems on 27 December 1917 for operations in the western approaches to the English Channel. Using the Dover Strait route to reach its operations area, U-95 reported being in the channel on 30 December. On 31 December U-95 sank the Norwegian SS *Vigrid* (1,617 tons). After that there was no further word of U-95.

Additional Information

U-95's loss has been attributed to two sources. One source claimed that SS *Braeneil* rammed the U-boat on 7 January and another source said U-95 hit a mine in the Folkstone–Gris Nez deep mine barrage on 19 January. The Germans believe that the more likely of the two possibilities is that U-95 hit a mine, but the fact is that no one knows what happened.

Sources

Records, T-1022, Roll 38, PG61678.
Spindler, *Der Handelskrieg mit U-Booten,* 4:428; 5:45.

U-99

Date Lost:	July 1917
Commander:	Kapitänleutnant Max Eltester
Location:	North Sea
Position:	Unknown
Disposition:	Verschollen

U-99 departed Helgoland on 12 June 1917 for operations in the North Sea between the Shetlands and Norway. On 6 July U-99 torpedoed the destroyer HMS *Itchen,* which was escorting a convoy bound for Norway. What happened to U-99 after that is unknown; U-99 did not return and there were no survivors.

Additional Information

The British submarine J-2 reported sighting a surfaced U-boat at 0750 in position 58°0' N, 3°5' E on 7 July. J-2 fired a four-torpedo spread. The range was four to five thousand yards and an explosion was heard, but not seen.

On 12 July a British hunting group equipped with a kite balloon was operating near the area where HMS *Itchen* had gone down. They reported that in the early morning they sighted a surfaced U-boat that immediately dove. The destroyers dropped depth charges but were unable to see any specific results. At noon that same day the hunting group reported a strong underwater explosion followed by large amounts of oil coming to the surface.

Another report made its way into popular postwar literature. Reportedly, the British SS *Valeria* (5,865 tons) rammed a submerged object off the southwest coast of Ireland at 0400 on 20 June in position 52°20' N, 12°28' W. According to the account, U-99 surfaced and *Valeria*'s gunners hit the U-boat with the first shot. Two more shots, which exploded at the base of the conning tower, sank U-99. In a variation of the tale, only the conning tower appeared above the surface and *Valeria*'s gunners fired three rounds, the first at one hundred yards and the third at five hundred yards. All three rounds were hits and the U-boat sank. The problem is that U-99 was nowhere near the southwest coast of Ireland on 20 June and on 6 July it torpedoed HMS *Itchen* in the North Sea.

A postwar German study concluded that it was possible for U-99 to have been in either place on the dates and times the actions of 7 and 12

July occurred, but there was no way to positively determine which location. The place and time of U-99's loss is unknown.

Sources

Chatterton, *Beating the U-Boats,* 74.
Gibson and Prendergast, *The German Submarine War,* 185.
Records, T-1022, Roll 9, PG61682.
Spindler, *Der Handelskrieg mit U-Booten,* 4:255–56.

U-102

Date Lost:	September 1918
Commander:	Kapitänleutnant Kurt Beitzen
Location:	Atlantic, off Ireland's west coast or North Sea
Position:	Unknown
Disposition:	Verschollen

U-102 departed Helgoland on 1 September 1918 for operations in St. George's Channel in the Irish Sea. On 20 September U-102 reported that it was starting home from a position 170 nautical miles west of the Scillies. No further word was heard from it.

Additional Information

One British source says that U-102 hit a mine in the Northern Mine Barrage a week after leaving Helgoland, but that is not feasible because on 20 September it was west of the Scillies. Another source simply says that U-102 hit a mine in the barrage in September. It is possible that it hit a mine in the Northern Mine Barrage during its homeward trip, which would have been near the end of September.

Sources

Chatterton, *Beating the U-Boats,* 152.
Gibson and Prendergast, *The German Submarine War,* 321.
Grant, *U-Boats Destroyed,* 106.
Records, T-1022, Roll 10, PG61685.
Spindler, *Der Handelskrieg mit U-Booten,* 5:292–93.

U-103

Date Lost:	12 May 1918
Commander:	Kapitänleutnant Klaus Rücker
Location:	Western entrance to the English Channel
Position:	49°16' N, 4°51' W
Disposition:	Ramming

U-103 departed Helgoland on 3 May 1917 to conduct operations in the western approaches. During the night of 12 May just before 0400 U-103 sighted SS *Olympic* (46,359 tons) on an easterly course. *Olympic* was carrying nine thousand U.S. soldiers to France and had three American destroyers as escorts. Kapitänleutnant Klaus Rücker elected to make a night surface attack on the steamer. During U-103's approach, *Olympic* fired on the U-boat and turned toward it to ram. Rücker gave the command to crash dive. As the boat reached the ten-meter mark, *Olympic* rammed it on the port side at the conning tower. The boat rolled over on its beam ends and the men and equipment inside were hurled against the starboard side. The lights went out and someone quickly switched on the emergency lighting. Water poured into the conning tower, control room, and the engine room, and the boat plunged stern down to fifty meters. The electric motors stopped and chlorine gas began to develop. As the boat reached its maximum rated depth, Rücker ordered the tanks blown and the boat started rising slowly. U-103 came to the surface with its after deck awash and the crew poured out through the forward and conning tower hatches. Thirty-six men went over the side and USS *Davis* picked up twenty-seven.

Obermatrose Heinrich Lüpertz, U-103

On 12 May 1918 just before 0500 we were running on the surface from the French coast toward the English Channel. It was dark. Astern and to port we saw a large dark shadow that had three stacks. Both stern tubes were cleared for firing. The two rounds fell close aboard, knocking out the lights. The boat submerged stern first and was almost immediately rammed. The lights went out and we closed the watertight door between our compartment and the control room. When the emergency lights came on the depth gauge in the forward torpedo room showed fifty meters and water was entering around the port torpedo tube. The tanks were blown and as soon as we were on the surface the crew got out. The steamer continued on. About an hour later an American destroyer picked up all but nine men who had drowned.

Sources

Records, T-1022, Roll 10, PG61686, "Abschrift vom Frageboden, Wilhelmshaven den 29. September 1919, Obermatrosen Heinrich Lüpertz."
Spindler, *Der Handelskrieg mit U-Booten,* 5:23.

U-104

Date Lost:	25 April 1918
Commander:	Kapitänleutnant Bernis
Location:	St. George's Channel
Position:	51°59' N, 6°26' W
Disposition:	Ramming, Depth Charge

U-104 departed Helgoland on 10 April 1918 for operations in the English Channel. On the night of 24–25 April the *Flower*-class sloop HMS *Jasmine*, under the command of Cdr. S. A. Geary-Hill, RN, rammed and depth charged U-104 in the Irish Sea. Visibility was excellent with a calm sea and a full moon so the lookouts aboard *Jasmine* easily spotted a surfaced U-boat a half mile away at 0145; there was no doubt about its identity. The officer of the deck, Lt. Marshall Reay, ordered full speed and turned toward the U-boat to ram it.

U-104 dove. *Jasmine* passed over the spot and dropped four depth charges just as the boat went under. The depth charges exploded along U-104's starboard side, causing enormous damage and flooding the engine room. The stern dropped and U-104 plunged stern first to fifty meters. The electric motors stopped.

Some of the crew escaped into the forward torpedo room and closed the watertight door. In the meantime, Kapitänleutnant Bernis attempted to blow the tanks, but the after tanks were destroyed so only the forward tanks were vented. The bow up angle became nearly vertical and the bow rose until it was ten meters below the surface.

Water was entering the forward torpedo room through the speaking tubes and piping through the bulkhead. The air pressure inside the compartment had risen to the point that when Maschinistenmaat Karl Eschenberg tried to open the hatch, it popped open and the out-rushing air blew him through the opening. He was the only man to reach the surface. *Jasmine* picked him up and remained in the area for thirty minutes without finding anyone else.

Additional Information

On 14 August 1919 a British prize court awarded HMS *Jasmine* a bounty of two hundred pounds for sinking U-104. The award was based on forty crewmen at five pounds per crewman aboard the U-boat. But U-104 had only thirty-six crewmen aboard. So the prize court overpaid the bounty.

Sources

Chatterton, *Beating the U-Boats,* 112–13.
Chatterton, *Danger Zone,* 334–35.
Records, T-1022, Roll 10, PG61688, "Abschrift, Protokoll, Dortmund den 26. I. 1920, ehemalige U-Masch.Mt. Karl Eschenberg"; T-1022, Roll 71, PG61934, "Londoner Prisengerichtsverhandlungen wegen vierzehn deutscher U-Boote."
Spindler, *Der Handelskrieg mit U-Booten,* 5:24.

U-106

Date Lost:	7–8 October 1917
Commander:	Kapitänleutnant Hufnagel
Location:	German Bight
Position:	Unknown
Disposition:	Verschollen

U-106 departed Emden on 8 September 1917 for operations in the Irish Sea. U-106 did not return and there were no survivors.

Additional Information

On 6 October U-106 reported that it was off St. Abbs Head and expected to arrive off Terschelling on the morning of 7 October. It requested that minesweeper escorts be on hand to lead it through the German minefields. At 0200 on 7 October U-106 reported that it would arrive off Terschilling on the morning of 8 October. At 1514 and again at 1911 4th U-Flotilla headquarters directed U-106 to use a different rendezvous because the British had laid a new minefield off Terschelling. In both cases U-106 replied that it had not understood the transmission. No further word was heard from U-106. It is probable that it hit a mine in the newly laid British minefield in the approximate position 54°50' N, 6°0' E.

Sources

Records, T-1022, Roll 11, PG61690.
Spindler, *Der Handelskrieg mit U-Booten,* 4:431.

U-109

Date Lost:	26 January 1918
Commander:	Kapitänleutnant Ney
Location:	Dover Strait
Position:	50°54' N, 1°32' E (probable)
Disposition:	Mine

U-109 departed Ems on 24 January 1918 for operations in the St. George's Channel. Kapitänleutnant Ney had the choice of using the northern route or the Dover Strait route. U-109 did not return.

Additional Information

At 0800 on 24 January the trawler *Beryl II* was patrolling the Folkestone–Gris Nez deep mine barrage when it spotted a U-boat on the surface off Gris Nez and opened fire. The U-boat dove; at 1015 an explosion occurred in the barrage. The Germans' postwar study concluded that if Ney did use the Dover Strait route, he would have been off Gris Nez at about that date and time. Because no other boats were operating in the Gris Nez area around that date, they concluded that U-109 was the boat that was destroyed.

Sources

Records, T-1022, Roll 11, PG61693.
Spindler, *Der Handelskrieg mit U-Booten,* 4:48–49.

U-110

Date Lost:	15 March 1918
Commander:	Korvettenkapitän Karl Kroll
Location:	Atlantic, off Ireland's northern coast
Position:	55°49' N, 8°6' W
Disposition:	Technical Problem, Depth Charge, Gunfire

U-110 had been on patrol for two weeks. On 14 March 1918 a problem developed with the after diving planes that forced Korvettenkapitän Karl Kroll to return to Wilhelmshaven. En route home he torpedoed SS *Amazon,* which was able to get off a distress call before going down. The destroyers HMS *Moresby* and HMS *Michael* answered *Amazon*'s distress call and found U-110 on the surface. The U-boat dove and the destroyers depth charged it. U-110's after diving planes malfunctioned, causing it to plunge to more than one hundred meters. The pressure hull failed and water poured into the boat. Kroll blew the tanks and surfaced. The destroyers opened fire on U-110 and sank it. Only the chief engineer and three seamen were rescued.

Sources

Gibson and Prendergast, *The German Submarine War,* 292.

Records, T-1022, Roll 11, PG61694, "The Prize Court, Destruction of German Auxiliary Cruiser and Submarines: Bounty."

Spindler, *Der Handelskrieg mit U-Booten,* 5:49–50.

U-154

Date Lost:	11 May 1918
Commander:	Korvettenkapitän Gercke
Location:	Atlantic
Position:	36°51' N, 11°50' W
Disposition:	Torpedo

On 16 February 1918 U-153 and U-154 departed Warnemünde for joint operations off Dakar on the northwest coast of Africa. While the two U-boats were carrying out their joint mission, the Admiralty sent the British submarine E-35, under the command of Lieutenant Commander D'Oyly-Hughes, to Gibraltar to hunt U-boats. On 7 May British radio intercepts disclosed that U-154 and U-62 would rendezvous 180 nautical miles west of Cape St. Vincent. An alternate position thirty miles west was also designated. The British ordered E-35 to cover the primary position and J-1 to cover the alternate spot.

E-35 reached the rendezvous position on 11 May. A gale was blowing and there was a long breaking swell. At 1600 D'Oyly-Hughes saw a large object rise up on a particularly high swell and then disappear in the trough. He maneuvered E-35 to close on the object that he now identified as a very large U-boat moving slowly away from him. D'Oyly-Hughes followed the U-boat and at 1817 fired a torpedo that passed under the U-boat. Apparently the lookouts did not see the torpedo wake because of the heavy sea.

At 1822 D'Oyly-Hughes fired two torpedoes at a range of four hundred yards. Both torpedoes hit and the results were instantaneous and catastrophic. U-154's after magazine exploded, creating a shock wave that knocked out E-35's lights. A tremendous water column, accompanied by smoke and flame, rose two hundred feet. When the water column had collapsed and the smoke had cleared there was no sign of U-154.

When U-154 exploded, U-153 was on the surface four nautical miles away. Kapitänleutnant Adolf Franz recorded in his log that there was a bright flash, a high water column, and a cloud of black smoke. After that there was nothing left of U-154. Moments later a submarine of the British E or H class surfaced, remained there for two or three minutes, and then dove. U-153 also dove.

According to D'Oyly-Hughes there were three swimmers in the water when he surfaced, but the presence of U-153 made it impossible to remain surfaced long enough to pick them up. As a result, there were no survivors from U-154.

Sources

Edwards, *We Dive at Dawn,* 251–54.

Records, T-1022, Roll 64, PG61708, "Kriegstagebuch U-153, von 17.11.17 bis 3.6.18"; T-1022, Roll 64, PG61709 (U-154).

Spindler, *Der Handelskrieg mit U-Booten,* 5:237–38.

U-156

Date Lost:	September 1918
Commander:	Kapitänleutnant Feldt
Location:	North Sea
Position:	Unknown
Disposition:	Verschollen

U-156 departed Kiel on 16 June 1918 to lay mines off New York and to attack shipping off the North American coast from Halifax to Boston. On 19 July the armored cruiser USS *San Diego* sank after hitting one of the mines U-156 had laid off Fire Island, and that tonnage was added to that of twenty-two other ships to total forty-one thousand tons for the trip. U-156 started its homeward bound trip on 1 September. On 20 September it met U-139 off northern Scotland. On 24 September U-156 notified Kiel that it was northwest of the Shetlands, expected to pass through the Northern Mine Barrage on 25 September, and be off the Skagen Lightship on 27 September. It did not keep that date and it probably hit a mine in the Northern Mine Barrage.

Sources

Records, T-1022, Roll 22, PG61713.
Spindler, *Der Handelskrieg mit U-Booten,* 5:258–59.

PART 2

UB-Boats UB-3 to UB-129

UB-3

Date Lost:	May 1915
Commander:	Oberleutnant zur See Siegfried Schmidt
Location:	Eastern Mediterranean or Aegean
Position:	Unknown
Disposition:	Verschollen

UB-3 departed Cattaro on 23 May 1915 for temporary assignment in Smyrna (present-day Izmir) in Turkey. UB-3 did not return.

Additional Information

Because of its limited range, an Austro-Hungarian destroyer towed UB-3 through the Otranto Strait and cast off the tow off the island of Kérkira. That was the last anybody saw of UB-3. The route would have been south along the Ionian Islands and then around the south end of Peloponnesos and through the Cyclades. UB-3 would then go north in the Aegean Sea and hook around Khios and Karaburun into Izmar Bay. If everything went well, it should have arrived in Smyrna on 28 or 29 May with about half its fuel left. The Germans received a radio transmission from UB-3 when it was eighty nautical miles off Smyrna, but the transmission was so broken up that the entire message could not be understood. There were no minefields in the area and there were no indications that it might have been destroyed as a result of enemy action. The probable cause of UB-3's disappearance was an unexplained technical problem.

UB-3 was a type I UB-boat. The type I UB-boats, UB-1 through UB-17, were small, single screw, single hull boats designed to be built quickly and used in relatively confined areas that did not involve long-range patrols. They were ninety-three feet long and their surface displacement ranged from 127 to 147 tons. A single, sixty horsepower diesel engine provided their surface propulsion. They were armed with two bow torpedo tubes and carried two torpedoes, but had no deck gun. They were very maneuverable underwater and they could dive in twenty seconds. Their maximum rated diving depth was fifty meters, about 165 feet, and they could remain submerged for ten hours at four knots. The crew consisted of one officer and thirteen enlisted men.

The type I UB-boats assigned to the Mediterranean were shipped in sections by rail and assembled in Pola. UB-3 was shipped by rail from

Germany to Pola on 15 April 1915. Assembly time was about two weeks. The boats that were sent on to bases in Turkey were towed from Cattaro to a point outside the Otranto Strait; they then proceeded under their own power.

Sources

Gröner, *Die deutschen Kriegsschiffe,* 1:362.
Herzog, *Deutsche U-Boote,* 56.
Records, T-1022, Roll 39, PG61726.
Rössler, *The U-Boat,* 39–40.
Spindler, *Der Handelskrieg mit U-Booten,* 2:195, 198.

UB-4

Date Lost:	**15 August 1915**
Commander:	**Oberleutnant zur See Karl Gross**
Location:	**North Sea, off British coast at Cromer**
Position:	**52°43' N, 2°18' E**
Disposition:	**Gunfire**

UB-4 departed Zeebrugge on 13 August 1915 for operations off Yarmouth, and on 15 August it encountered the armed sailing smack *Inverlyon* near the Smiths Knoll spar buoy. The weather was hazy and *Inverlyon* was operating among genuine fishing vessels when UB-4 rose to the surface close to it. Oberleutnant zur See Karl Gross called across to it to abandon ship, and stopped thirty yards away. *Inverlyon* hoisted the battle flag and its Royal Navy gun crew opened fire with a 3-pounder (47-mm) gun, killing Gross and blowing his body overboard. No longer under command, UB-4 drifted within ten yards of *Inverlyon's* stern. UB-4 took four more hits and sank by the bow at an 80° angle. There were no survivors, but items recovered from the water identified the boat as UB-4.

Sources

Chatterton, *Fighting the U-Boats,* 137–38.
Records, T-1022, Roll 39, PG61727.
Spindler, *Der Handelskrieg mit U-Booten,* 2:213.

UB-6

Date Lost:	12 March 1917
Commander:	Oberleutnant zur See Steckelberg
Location:	Dutch coast
Position:	51°53' N, 3°58' E
Disposition:	Stranded, Interned

UB-6 departed Zeebrugge on 10 March 1917 for operations off the Maas Lightship. On the morning of 12 March Oberleutnant zur See Steckelberg made a navigational error that caused him to enter Dutch territorial waters and run firmly aground in the mouth of the Maas River. On 18 March the Dutch interned the boat and the crew.

Additional Information

The Germans protested, but the Dutch pointed out that UB-6 was a fully armed and equipped warship at sea on a war patrol when it ran aground inside Dutch territorial waters. The fact that its grounding was the result of a navigational error did not constitute a vessel in distress, which would have allowed the Dutch to release the boat and the crew. UB-6 and its crew remained in Holland for the duration of the war; in 1919 the Germans surrendered the U-boat to France. The French scrapped UB-6 at Brest in 1921.

Sources

Records, T-1022, Roll 77, PG61732.

Spindler, *Der Handelskrieg mit U-Booten,* 4:108–9.

UB-7

Date Lost:	October 1916
Commander:	Oberleutnant zur See Lütjohann
Location:	Black Sea
Position:	Unknown
Disposition:	Verschollen

UB-7 was part of the Mittelmeer Division headquartered in Constantinople (present-day Istanbul). The UB-boat departed Varna on 27 September for operations off Sevastopol and was never heard from again.

Additional Information

In June 1917 a captured Russian pilot told the Germans that a Russian airplane bombed UB-7 off the Chersones Lighthouse in position 44°30' N, 33°15' E, but he provided no specifics and no corroboration. UB-7 was the first U-boat that disappeared in the Mediterranean theater without a trace. The Germans sorely felt the loss because the Mediterranean division's senior radio officer, Oberleutnant zur See Heinke, was aboard UB-7 as an acting watch officer.

Sources

Chatterton, *Fighting the U-Boats,* 196.
Gibson and Prendergast, *The German Submarine War,* 135.
Lorey, *Der Krieg in den türkischen Gewässern,* 1:287.
Records, T-1022, Roll 77, PG61733.
Spindler, *Der Handelskrieg mit U-Booten,* 3:178.

UB-10

Date Lost:	5 October 1918
Commander:	Oberleutnant zur See Stüben
Location:	Zeebrugge
Position:	51°21' N, 3°12' E
Disposition:	Scuttled

By mid-September 1918 the war situation had turned against the Germans. On 26 September the French and British launched an offensive along the entire front and the Germans began falling back. On 29 September the Germans began evacuating Flanders and dismantling their naval facilities at Bruges, Zeebrugge, and Ostend. Boats that could not be made ready for return to Germany under their own power were either blown up in Bruges, Ostend, or Zeebrugge, or taken out to sea and scuttled.

Additional Information

UB-10 was one of the early type I UB-boats; in 1918 it was worn out. On 12 September 1918 the Germans decommissioned it because it had not undergone a major overhaul in a long time and was no longer capable of conducting war patrols. On 2 October 1918 a maintenance crew scuttled UB-10 off the Zeebrugge Mole.

Sources

Records, T-1022, Roll 78, PG61739.
Spindler, *Der Handelskrieg mit U-Booten,* 5:106, 149.

UB-12

Date Lost:	19–31 August 1918
Commander:	Oberleutnant zur See Schöller
Location:	Hoofden or Dover Strait
Position:	Unknown
Disposition:	Verschollen

UB-12 departed Zeebrugge on 19 August 1918 to lay mines in the Downs. It did not return.

Additional Information

The Germans had converted UB-12 to a minelayer. A British source says it hit a British mine off Helgoland in August 1918, but that is not possible because UB-12's route from Zeebrugge to the Downs would not have taken it anywhere near Helgoland. A postwar German study noted that on 18 August 1918 there were no new British mines in UB-12's operations area. However, the study concluded that the most likely explanation of its disappearance is that it either hit a British mine or was blown up by one of its own mines that malfunctioned while being laid. There is also the possibility that UB-12 suffered a diving accident related to its conversion.

Sources

Gibson and Prendergast, *The German Submarine War,* 318.
Records, T-1022, Roll 80, PG61745.
Spindler, *Der Handelskrieg mit U-Booten,* 5:133.

UB-13

Date Lost:	24 April 1916
Commander:	Oberleutnant zur See Metz
Location:	Off Flanders coast or in Hoofden
Position:	Unknown
Disposition:	Verschollen

UB-13 departed Zeebrugge on the evening of 23 April 1916 for operations off the Thames mouth, and was never seen again.

Additional Information

The British had laid an explosive net during the early hours of 24 April in position 51°33' N, 2°45' E. Explosive nets were conventional antisubmarine nets that had two electro-contact mines attached to each panel. When a U-boat struck the net, the panel separated and folded around the boat, bringing the mines in contact with the hull. The U-boat's hull provided the ground that completed the electrical circuit and exploded the mine. There is a possibility UB-13 was destroyed when it fouled the net and exploded the attached mines. It may also have hit a mine in one of the many British minefields that were laid off the Flanders coast.

Sources

Records, T-1022, Roll 80, PG61747.
Spindler, *Der Handelskrieg mit U-Booten,* 3:122.

UB-16

Date Lost:	10 May 1918
Commander:	Oberleutnant zur See Vicco von der Lühe
Location:	Hoofden
Position:	52°6' N, 2°1' E
Disposition:	Torpedo

UB-16 departed Zeebrugge on 6 May 1918 for operations in the Hoofden. At 1850 on 10 May homeward-bound E-34 sighted it on the surface off Harwich. At first the British captain, Lieutenant Pulleyne, thought the other boat might be British because it was so close to home, but he took no chances and dove. Through his periscope he identified the still-surfaced boat as German, and maneuvered to attack. At 1915 he fired two torpedoes at four hundred yards. One torpedo hit UB-16 in the bow but did not explode; the other torpedo hit the U-boat below the conning tower and sank it almost instantly. Five minutes after UB-16 went down, E-34 surfaced and pulled Oberleutnant zur See Vicco von der Lühe out of the oil-covered water. Von der Lühe was the only survivor and he died in a British prisoner of war camp of influenza on 1 March 1919. He made no report on UB-16's loss.

Sources

Edwards, *We Dive at Dawn,* 299.
Records, T-1022, Roll 65, PG61753.
Spindler, *Der Handelskrieg mit U-Booten,* 5:107.

UB-17

Date Lost:	March 1918
Commander:	Oberleutnant zur See Branscheid
Location:	North Sea or Hoofden
Position:	Unknown
Disposition:	Verschollen

UB-17 departed Zeebrugge on 11 March 1918 for operations in the Hoofden and never returned.

Additional Information

One postwar account says that two British seaplanes bombed a U-boat on 12 March in the North Sea. Although a possible explanation, there are no details to support it. Another account says that the destroyer HMS *Onslow* destroyed UB-17 on 25 February 1918 south of Portland. The problem with that account is that UB-17 was berthed in Zeebrugge on 25 February. A postwar German study also discounted the possibility that HMS *Thruster,* HMS *Retriever,* and HMS *Sturgeon* sank UB-17 at 2125 on 11 March in position 57°7' N, 2°43' E because UB-17 did not depart Zeebrugge until thirty minutes after the attack reportedly took place.

Sources

Grant, *U-Boats Destroyed,* 121.
Records, T-1022, Roll 66, PG61757.
Spindler, *Der Handelskrieg mit U-Booten,* 5:108.

UB-18

Date Lost:	8–9 December 1917
Commander:	Oberleutnant zur See Niemeyer
Location:	Western entrance to English Channel
Position:	49°17' N, 5°47' W (probable)
Disposition:	Ramming

UB-18 departed Zeebrugge on 1 December 1917 for operations in the western entrance to the English Channel. On 4 December UB-18 exchanged recognition signals with U-84. After that there was no further word from UB-18.

Additional Information

According to one British source, shortly after midnight on 8 December the armed trawler *Ben Lawers* sighted a surfaced U-boat and rammed it just aft of the conning tower. The U-boat sank immediately, and the trawler was heavily damaged. Two other British sources say that on 17 November 1917 UB-18 hit a mine off the Start Point in approximately 50°26' N, 3°30' W. That is obviously wrong because UB-18 did not set out on its last patrol until two weeks later.

A postwar German study noted that there is no doubt that *Ben Lawers* did ram something, and the ramming did occur in UB-18's operations area. On the basis that no returning U-boats reported being rammed in that area, and the fact that it was possible for UB-18 to have been there at that time, the study concluded that *Ben Lawers* probably rammed and sank UB-18.

UB-18 was the first of the type II UB-boats, which included UB-18 through UB-47. Like the type I UB-boats, the type II UB-boats were transported by rail in sections to their bases where they were assembled. Type II UB-boats were bigger, faster, and more heavily armed than type I boats. Type II UB-boats were 122 feet long and had a surface displacement of 263 to 279 tons. Twin diesel engines that developed 284 horsepower provided the surface propulsion. They were armed with two bow torpedo tubes and carried four to six torpedoes. They also carried either a 50-mm or an 88-mm deck gun. Although less maneuverable underwater than type I boats, they could dive in twenty to thirty-three seconds. Maximum rated diving depth was fifty meters, about 165 feet, and they could remain submerged for nine hours at five knots. The crew consisted of two officers and twenty-one enlisted men.

Sources

Chatterton, *Beating the U-Boats,* 100.
Gibson and Prendergast, *The German Submarine War,* 226.
Gröner, *Die deutschen Kriegsschiffe,* 1:363.
Herzog, *Deutsche U-Boote,* 56.
Records, T-1022, Roll 52, PG61760.
Rössler, *The U-Boat,* 50–51.
Spindler, *Der Handelskrieg mit U-Booten,* 4:440–41.

UB-19

Date Lost:	**30 November 1916**
Commander:	**Oberleutnant zur See Noodt**
Location:	**English Channel**
Position:	**50°0' N, 2°48' W**
Disposition:	**Gunfire**

UB-19 departed Zeebrugge on 22 November 1916 on its first patrol with a new captain. It sank four steamers and one sailing vessel with explosive charges under the Prize Regulations. UB-19 did not return from its patrol.

Additional Information

On 30 November the British decoy vessel *Penshurst* (Q-7) was thirty-nine nautical miles southwest of Portland Bill. At 1350 a lookout spotted a conning tower five miles to southward. *Penshurst* proceeded on a southwesterly course at slow speed, and the U-boat slowly overhauled it. As the distance narrowed UB-19 fired a warning shot. *Penshurst* turned away, and UB-19 began firing steadily. After receiving several hits, the decoy slowed and swung out its boats at 1612; instead of stopping *Penshurst* turned toward the French coast. UB-19 was within one thousand yards and it sheered out to port, passed down *Penshurst*'s port side, and crossed the decoy's stern at five hundred yards.

Up to that point Oberleutnant zur See Noodt did not seem to be suspicious of *Penshurst,* but as he crossed its stern he could see that there was no name painted on the stern and the ship was an overall warship gray color. He further noted that the lifeboats had stopped rowing and were motionless on the water.

Now suspicious, Noodt gave the order to dive as UB-19 came up on *Penshurst*'s starboard quarter. *Penshurst*'s gunners opened fire at a range of just 250 yards, scoring several hits on the U-boat before it got under. Massive flooding forced Noodt to blow the tanks and bring UB-19 back to the surface. *Penshurst*'s gunners continued a murderous fire that holed UB-19's hull in several places. The U-boat sank without returning fire. Eight men were killed and *Penshurst* picked up fifteen, including the wounded captain.

On 28 July 1919 a British prize court awarded *Penshurst* a bounty of £115, based on the rate of £5 per crewman, for sinking UB-19.

Sources

Chatterton, *Q-Ships and Their Story,* 113–16.

Records, T-1022, Roll 52, PG61760; T-1022, Roll 71, PG61934, "Londoner Prisenger-
ichtsverhandlungen wegen vierzehn deutscher U-Boote."

Spindler, *Der Handelskrieg mit U-Booten,* 3:288–89.

UB-20

Date Lost:	28 July 1917
Commander:	Oberleutnant zur See Hermann Glimpf
Location:	Off Flanders coast
Position:	Unknown
Disposition:	Verschollen

On 17 June 1917 the British bombed Bruges and one of the bombs exploded alongside UB-20, doing extensive damage that put the U-boat in dry dock until 27 July when UB-20 went down to Ostend. On 28 July 1917 it left Ostend at noon for a four-hour test run and never came back.

Additional Information

On 3 September 1917 Oberleutnant zur See Hermann Glimpf's body washed ashore on the Jutland coast. A British account says that two British seaplanes bombed UB-20 on either 29 or 30 July 1917. That is unlikely because UB-20 was only supposed to have been out for four hours on 28 July; it should have been back in Ostend on 29 and 30 July. Because the British laid extensive minefields off the Flanders coast in 1917 a postwar German study concluded that UB-20 probably hit a British mine near Thornton Ridge, but that was just an educated guess.

But poor Glimpf, his crew, and his boat became undeserved World War I legends much like the phantom U-31. The myth persists even today. According to one popular account, UB-20 was aground off the North Hinder Lightship where two British seaplanes bombed it and it went down with all hands. Exactly how a U-boat that is firmly aground in shallow water could sink with all hands is not explained. But that is not where the tale ends. According to the same account, Glimpf had taken UB-20 to sea without authorization for an impromptu day of boating and partying. Among his party guests were several army officers and their girlfriends.

Lowell Thomas used this story in his book, *Raiders of the Deep,* first published in 1928, and added a few strokes of his own. In Thomas's account, German Army Headquarters suddenly realized that several of its officers were missing and went looking for them. The army discovered that the missing officers had gone boating with the convivial Glimpf and that Glimpf had put to sea without orders on an undersea joy ride. Thomas tried to work around the problem of UB-20 being grounded. In his account, the U-boat was in water too shallow to dive and half the crew was sick with influenza. Unable to maneuver, UB-20 made an easy target and went down like a rock.

In September 2001, a seller, who identified himself as stevo427, offered what he claimed were parts from UB-20 on eBay, an online auction firm. The parts, mounted as a display on a board, consisted of a battery connector and three pieces of copper tubing. No identifying marks were visible on any of the items. The seller did not reply to an email request for information on the wreck's location, who found it, and when the wreck was found. Other than the parts, the only additional information the seller provided was that the wreck had been found off the Flanders coast.

Sources

Chatterton, *Beating the U-Boats,* 77.
Gibson and Prendergast, *The German Submarine War,* 192–93.
Records, T-1022, Roll 52, PG61761.
Spindler, *Der Handelskrieg mit U-Booten,* 4:297.
Thomas, *Raiders of the Deep,* 235.

UB-22

Date Lost:	19 January 1918
Commander:	Oberleutnant zur See Wacker
Location:	German Bight
Position:	54°27' N, 6°35' E
Disposition:	Mine

UB-22 departed Helgoland on 19 January 1918 for operations off Britain's east coast. Two minesweepers, with their sweeps deployed, escorted UB-22 to a point fifty-five nautical miles northwest of Helgoland where they turned around. UB-22 proceeded a short distance beyond the turnaround point and suddenly detonated several mines in rapid succession. There were no survivors.

Additional Information

S-16, one of the minesweeper escorts, returned to hunt for survivors and also struck a mine. S-16 sank with all hands, as did two more escorts that entered the minefield to hunt for survivors. The minefield that destroyed UB-22 and its escorts was an example of British offensive mining that became very efficient after November 1917. In 1918 the British were using the reliable and efficient H2 mine, which had a 300-pound charge. The H2 mine was a copy of the German E mine.

Sources

Records, T-1022, Roll 52, PG61761.
Spindler, *Der Handelskrieg mit U-Booten,* 5:51.

UB-23

Date Lost:	28 July 1917
Commander:	Oberleutnant zur See Heinz Niemer
Location:	Coruna, Spain
Disposition:	Depth Charge, Interned

On 26 July 1917, while UB-23 was in the western entrance to the English Channel, off Falmouth, Oberleutnant zur See Heinze Niemer torpedoed an unidentified steamer. While he was maneuvering at periscope depth to attack, HMS P-60 spotted UB-23's periscope, ran across UB-23's track, and dropped two depth charges. The explosions knocked out the auxiliary machinery, damaged the diving controls, opened seams, and popped rivets. Water rose steadily inside the boat and the batteries became almost useless. Shortly before 2300 Niemer blew the tanks and surfaced. Unable to dive, UB-23 could not return to Flanders through the Dover Strait, and it lacked the fuel to attempt the northern route. Niemer laid a course for Coruna, Spain, and arrived there 28 July 1917. The Spanish government interned UB-23 and its crew for the remainder of the war.

Sources

Records, T-1022, Roll 55, PG61768, "Führer der Unterseebooten Flandern, 7.11.17." Spindler, *Der Handelskrieg mit U-Booten,* 4:297–98.

UB-26

Date Lost:	5 April 1916
Commander:	Oberleutnant zur See Smiths
Location:	Entrance to Le Havre harbor
Position:	49°28' N, 0°2' W
Disposition:	Net, Depth Charge, Scuttled

UB-26 departed Zeebrugge on 30 March 1916 on its first war patrol for operations off Le Havre, France. UB-26 made two attempts to enter the harbor. On the first attempt fog reduced visibility so that accurate navigation was impossible, and on the second attempt a mirror flat sea and strong surface patrols prevented entry.

On 5 April conditions were perfect. Oberleutnant zur See Smiths entered the anchorage only to find it empty. He then hoped to ambush a steamer as it entered the harbor, but at that point the surface patrols forced him to dive to twenty meters. When he rose to periscope depth, his partially extended periscope struck a patrol vessel's rudder and moments later the port propeller fouled a net, putting the port electric motor out of service.

Smiths set UB-26 on the bottom, planning to wait until dark when he could surface and clear away the net. The surface patrols alerted the French destroyer *Trombe* and it dropped two depth charges. The explosions opened pressure hull seams, destroyed controls, and started an electrical fire in UB-26. Smiths surfaced amid the patrols and two French destroyers; all opened fire on UB-26. Smiths and his crew scuttled the boat before they went over the side.

Oberleutnant zur See Smiths, UB-26

UB-26 departed Zeebrugge on 29 March 1916. That same day we passed through two minefields and were forced to dive to avoid two air attacks during which bombs fell fairly close. During the night we made a surface passage through the middle of the Dover Strait where we encountered twenty-five to thirty patrol craft with lights. We were forced once to dive but otherwise the trip went according to plan past Dieppe to Le Havre, and twice during the day we were in the anchorage area off Le Havre. Fog kept us concealed during one of the passes but on the second pass two destroyers saw us. The sea was mirror flat.

145

There was no fog during the night of 4–5 April and on the morning of 5 April we entered the Le Havre harbor in foggy weather at high water. There were hardly any steamers in the harbor. I attacked an in-bound four-thousand-ton grain carrier and had to dive to twenty meters to avoid four trawlers steaming toward me in line abreast. We steered various courses to avoid the trawlers. With the trawlers were two destroyers. I remained at twenty meters for twenty minutes and then rose to eleven meters. As we passed the thirteen-meter mark I extended the periscope; it struck something, broke the lens and made the periscope useless. We went back down to twenty meters.

Tried to maneuver close to the bottom by diving to twenty-five meters in twenty-seven meters of water. Through the conning tower ports and the second periscope I saw that we were fouled in a net. Stopped the motors and laid the boat on the bottom to await nightfall. My intention was to surface after dark, cut away the net and proceed out of the harbor.

Shortly after we lay on the bottom an explosion occurred aft of us that knocked out the lights, destroyed the compass, and shorted the batteries. Both oxygen bottles in the engine room were blown from the bulkhead, the after oil bunkers were breached and oil poured down on the starboard electric motor. The lines connecting the after compressed air holding tanks were smashed, making the tanks useless, and water was entering the engine room through the pressure hull.

We restored the lighting just before a second explosion that occurred near the forward hatch. The blow was so severe that the forward hatch was compressed to an oval shape, the forward torpedo doors and the port side hatch were sprung. The compressed air system was largely inoperative and the depth gauge was destroyed.

We attempted to get under way on the port motor. Moments later the propeller stopped, apparently fouled in the net. The decision was made to surface, scuttle the boat, and abandon her. Scuttling charges were prepared and I ordered the remaining compressed air be used to take us up.

As we broke surface we were surrounded by two destroyers and four trawlers that fired into us with artillery and rifle fire. Despite the heavy fire we suffered no casualties.

In an undated letter, Smiths wrote to his wife:

And now something about how I became a prisoner. On 5 April in the morning I wanted to attack a large grain carrier that was entering the Le Havre harbor. I had spent several days off the harbor entrance without success. Our chances were made worse by heavy fog and a mirror-calm sea that betrayed our periscope. I did not believe that there were minefields or nets in the harbor and assumed that my third entry into the harbor would be no problem. But as I entered I suddenly ran into an indicator net that was patrolled by four trawlers and two destroyers. The carbide buoys and floats gave the boat's exact location. At first I had no idea we were in a net until I saw the wires through the conning tower port. I decided to lay the boat on the bottom and wait for night. Suddenly there was a powerful explosion followed by a second. The boat was flooding aft, the batteries were afire, the compass destroyed and the lights out. The boat was lost. I blew the tanks, surfaced and the crew abandoned the boat. The boat sank immediately, but the French raised it three days later and towed her into Brest.

Obermaschinistenmaat Anwärter Ernst Look, UB-26

On 5 April 1916 between 1000 and 1030 we attempted to enter Le Havre harbor, submerged at twenty-seven meters. Unexpectedly we fouled a net and we could hear the net wires dragging along the starboard side of the hull. The motors continued to run and then we felt the boat gaining speed, which meant we were clear of the net. Then the starboard motor stopped and we found that the propeller was fouled in the net. That left us with just the port electric motor. Because the French destroyers were above us, we attempted to maneuver away using the port motor. A depth charge hit the forward part of the boat destroying all auxiliary power, knocked out the lamps and cut power to the motors and the bilge pumps. The boat was unable to maneuver and the captain ordered the tanks blown. We surfaced, scuttled the boat, and went over the side.

U-Maschinistenmaat Kurt Heckert, UB-26

UB-26 fouled a net on 5 April 1916 at the entrance to Le Havre harbor. The net fouled the propellers and the boat was unable to maneuver. Two destroyers and four trawlers depth charged the boat; that seriously damaged the boat and started electrical fires. Oberleutnant zur See Smiths ordered the tanks blown and the boat scuttled. We were all taken prisoner.

Additional Information

The French salvaged UB-26, renamed it *Roland Morillot*, and commissioned it in the French navy. On 23 October 1922 it encountered a severe storm off the west coast of Guernsey. Heavy seas battered the hull to the point that the pressure hull was compromised and the boat sank. The entire crew was rescued. The French again salvaged the boat and kept it in service until 3 January 1924 when they laid it up. The French scrapped it at Cherbourg in 1931.

Sources

Records, T-1022, Roll 55, PG61771, "Oberleutnant zur See Smiths, Bericht, 11. February 1920"; "Abschrift vom, Oberleutnant zur See Smiths, Brief an Seine Frau"; "Abschrift, U-Maschinistenmaat Kurt Heckert"; and "Obermaschinistenmaat Anwärter Ernst Look, Bericht, 15 February 1920; and London Times, 25 October 1922."

UB-27

Date Lost:	29 July 1917
Commander:	Oberleutnant zur See Freiherr von Stein zu Lausnitz
Location:	Off Britain's east coast at Cromer, north of Great Yarmouth
Position:	52°47' N, 2°24' E (possible)
Disposition:	Ramming, Depth Charge

UB-27 departed Zeebrugge on 22 July 1917 for operations in the Hoofden, and did not return.

Additional Information

On 29 July at 1057 HMS *Halcyon* spotted a periscope four hundred yards away. The destroyer passed over the spot at seventeen knots, felt a jar, and dropped two depth charges. Several hours later the British swept the area with grapples. They fouled something on the bottom in twenty-four fathoms that they believed to be the wrecked U-boat, but divers did not locate it. There is no certainty that *Halcyon* sank a U-boat on 29 July 1917; nor is it certain that it sank UB-27. A postwar German study concluded that because UB-27 could have been in that area at that time it is possible that *Halcyon* did sink UB-27.

Sources

Chatterton, *Beating the U-Boats,* 77.
Grant, *U-Boats Destroyed,* 62.
Records, T-1022, Roll 55, PG61772.
Spindler, *Der Handelskrieg mit U-Booten,* 4:298.

UB-29

Date Lost:	December 1916
Commander:	Oberleutnant zur See Platsch
Location:	English Channel, Dover Strait, or Hoofden
Position:	Unknown
Disposition:	Verschollen

UB-29, in company with UC-19, departed Zeebrugge on 27 November 1916 for operations in the English Channel. Both boats failed to return. Exactly what happened to them is not known, but there were several claims made about their destruction and the claims were often applied to both boats.

Additional Information

On the afternoon of 6 December 1916 the destroyer HMS *Ariel* spotted a U-boat a mile and a half away moments before the U-boat dove. *Ariel* deployed its explosive paravanes at thirty feet. The paravanes crossed the U-boat's estimated track, and the starboard paravane exploded. The explosion brought large amounts of heavy oil and debris to the surface. The action took place in position 49°41' N, 6°30' W.

On 14 July 1919, a British prize court awarded HMS *Ariel* £115 for the destruction of UB-29. The problem with this award is that on 7 December, the day following *Ariel*'s explosive sweep attack, UB-29 sank the Norwegian SS *Meteor* under the Prize Regulations. The *Meteor*'s crew recognized UB-29 by the number painted on the side of its bow. That same day UB-29 fired a torpedo at the Belgian SS *Keltier* that missed. UB-29 surfaced, stopped the ship, and sent a boarding party aboard to sink it with scuttling charges. The action occurred in position 49°29' N, 7°26' W; *Keltier*'s crew clearly saw UB-29's number painted on its bow.

Other evidence suggests that *Ariel* did not sink any U-boat on 6 December 1916. The explosive paravane was newly issued in 1916 and each use had to be reported. The paravane report form had four result options to check: Possibly Slightly Damaged; Probably Seriously Damaged; Probably Sunk; or Known Sunk. *Ariel*'s paravane report shows no results checked for the 6 December 1916 attack, thus implying that *Ariel*'s crew did not think the attack had been successful.

The destroyer HMS *Landrail* also made a claim for UB-29's destruction. Shortly after midnight on 13 December 1916 *Landrail* was patrolling south of Goodwin Sands when a lookout spotted the conning tower of a diving U-boat three hundred yards dead ahead. Apparently the U-boat had been surprised by the destroyer's sudden appearance and had crash dived. *Landrail* went to full speed, crossed over the spot, and dropped two depth charges. The explosions were followed by an upswelling of thick oil and debris. The action occurred in position 51°9' N, 1°46' E.

Because no one aboard HMS *Landrail* recognized the U-boat, and there were no survivors, there is no way to establish with certainty that the boat *Landrail* attacked was UB-29. The possibility exists that *Landrail* sank UB-29, but there is not enough circumstantial evidence to make that a probability. There is no doubt that UB-29 was lost at sea, but how it was lost remains unknown.

Sources

Chatterton, *Fighting the U-Boats,* 206.
Cornford, *The Paravane Adventure,* 277.
Records, T-1022, Roll 55, PG61776.
Spindler, *Der Handelskrieg mit U-Booten,* 3:292–93, 316–18.

UB-30

Date Lost:	13 August 1918
Commander:	Oberleutnant zur See Stier
Location:	Off Britain's east coast near Whitby
Position:	54°32' N, 0°35' W
Disposition:	Ramming, Depth Charge

UB-30 departed Zeebrugge at 2300 on 6 August 1918 for operations off Britain's east coast. UB-30 did not return.

Additional Information

On 13 August UB-30 attacked a convoy north of Whitby. The armed trawler *John Gillman* spotted a periscope at three hundred yards, rammed the submerged U-boat, and dropped two depth charges, one set for one hundred feet and the other set for eighty feet. The armed yacht *Miranda* arrived shortly thereafter and also dropped depth charges. Two hours later UB-30 surfaced near the trawlers *John Brook* and *Viola,* and they opened fire. No hits were observed, but UB-30 either sank or submerged. The trawlers dropped five depth charges and oil and air bubbles rose to the surface. Four days later divers identified the wreck as UB-30.

Sources

Gibson and Prendergast, *The German Submarine War,* 316.
Grant, *U-Boats Destroyed,* 128.
Records, T-1022, Roll 56, PG61777.
Spindler, *Der Handelskrieg mit U-Booten,* 5:111–12.

UB-31

Date Lost:	2 May 1918
Commander:	Oberleutnant zur See Braun
Location:	Dover Strait
Position:	51°6' N, 1°28' W
Disposition:	Mine

UB-31 was returning from operations in the English Channel. While making a night-time surface approach to the Folkestone–Gris Nez deep mine barrage on 2 May 1918, the armed drifters *Lord Leitrim, Loyal Friend,* and *Ocean Roamer* forced UB-31 to dive into the minefield and the U-boat hit a mine. British divers identified the wreck as UB-31.

Additional Information

The British laid the Folkestone–Gris Nez deep mine barrage in November and December 1917, and continually improved it. The barrage was composed of hundreds of H2 and H4 mines laid in a ladder pattern that formed a virtual wall of mines down to two hundred feet. In addition to strong patrols around the clock, the surface was brightly illuminated along its entire length at night. The object was to force U-boats to dive into the mine barrage where they would hit one of the mines.

Sources

Grant, *U-Boat Intelligence,* 97.
Records, T-1022, Roll 56, PG61780.
Spindler, *Der Handelskrieg mit U-Booten,* 5:113–14.

UB-32

Date Lost:	September 1917
Commander:	Oberleutnant zur See von Dittfurth
Location:	English Channel or Dover Strait
Position:	Unknown
Disposition:	Verschollen

UB-32 departed Zeebrugge on the morning of 10 September 1917 for operations in the English Channel and the western approaches. UB-32 did not return and there were no survivors.

Additional Information

A postwar German study produced two possible explanations for UB-32's loss. First, on 11 September ML-358 depth charged and sank it in the English Channel in position 50°23' N, 1°6' W. Second, on 22 September the British seaplane 8695 bombed and sank it east of the Dover Strait in position 51°45' N, 2°5' E. Postwar British historians credit seaplane 8695 with destroying UB-32, but they differ on where the attack occurred. Some place it east of the Dover Strait and others place it in the English Channel.

Sources

Chatterton, *Beating the U-Boats,* 81.
Gibson and Prendergast, *The German Submarine War,* 199.
Records, T-1022, Roll 57, PG61783.
Spindler, *Der Handelskrieg mit U-Booten,* 4:302.

UB-33

Date Lost:	11 April 1918
Commander:	Oberleutnant zur See Gregor
Location:	Dover Strait
Position:	50°56' N, 1°17' E
Disposition:	Mine

UB-33 departed Zeebrugge on 6 April 1918 for operations in the English Channel. Apparently Oberleutnant zur See Gregor was returning early, because on 11 April 1918 at 1800 UB-33 was southwest of the Varne approaching the Folkestone–Gris Nez deep mine barrage. It dove to evade a British drifter division, and UB-33's dive carried the U-boat into the deep mine barrage. It hit a mine and sank with all hands.

Additional Information

The drifter *Ocean Roamer* witnessed an explosion that was followed by large amounts of oil and debris rising to the surface. British divers visited the wreck of UB-33 on 29 May 1918 and recovered its codebooks and cipher keys, along with Gregor's body, which they removed from the conning tower.

Sources

Grant, *U-Boats Destroyed,* 84.
Records, T-1022, Roll 59, PG61786.
Spindler, *Der Handelskrieg mit U-Booten,* 5:115–16.

UB-35

Date Lost:	26 January 1918
Commander:	Oberleutnant zur See Stöter
Location:	Dover Strait
Position:	51°03' N, 1°46' E
Disposition:	Depth Charge

UB-35 departed Zeebrugge at 1515 on 17 January 1918 for operations in the English Channel. On 26 January as it was approaching the Goodwin Sands net, Oberleutnant zur See Stöter came up to periscope depth to locate the net buoys, and the destroyer HMS *Leven* saw the periscope. *Leven* dropped a string of depth charges along the U-boat's projected track and sank it.

Additional Information

Leven saw seven swimmers in the water but six sank before the destroyer could pick them up; the seventh man died shortly after pick up. The British identified the dead man as a member of UB-35's crew.

Sources

Chatterton, *Beating the U-Boats,* 118.
Gibson and Prendergast, *The German Submarine War,* 287.
Grant, *U-Boats Destroyed,* 81.
Records, T-1022, Roll 60, PG61791.
Spindler, *Der Handelskrieg mit U-Booten,* 5:116–17.

UB-36

Date Lost:	21 May 1917
Commander:	Oberleutnant zur See von Keyserlingk
Location:	Bay of Biscay
Position:	48°42' N, 5°14' W
Disposition:	Ramming

UB-36 departed Zeebrugge on the evening of 9 May 1917 to attack coal convoys going from Britain to Quessant. On 21 May Oberleutnant zur See von Keyserlingk torpedoed and sank the French coal carrier SS *Ferdinand A* (2,062 tons) off Ushant. Forty minutes later SS *Molière,* an armed steamer that was a part of the convoy, saw the wake of a torpedo and a periscope very close dead ahead. *Molière* rammed the submerged U-boat and the lookouts reported air bubbles rising as the steamer passed across the U-boat. *Molière*'s bow was heavily damaged.

Additional Information

Although the U-boat was never seen and there were no survivors, the Germans' postwar investigation concluded that *Molière* had sunk a U-boat and the victim had to be UB-36. The decision was based on UB-36's movements prior to the time *Molière* rammed the U-boat.

Sources

Records, T-1022, Roll 60, PG61794.
Spindler, *Der Handelskrieg mit U-Booten,* 4:121.

UB-37

Date Lost:	14 January 1917
Commander:	Oberleutnant zur See Günther
Location:	English Channel
Position:	50°7' N, 1°47' W
Disposition:	Gunfire, Depth Charge

UB-37 departed Zeebrugge on 2 January 1917 for operations in the English Channel. Radio reports from UB-37 showed that it was active and successful during the period 5–10 January in the western part of the English Channel. On 14 January UB-37 encountered the British decoy vessel *Penshurst* (Q-7).

Penshurst was steaming between the Isle of Wight and Alderney when a lookout spotted a U-boat coming toward them. Five minutes later the U-boat fired a round at a range of about three thousand yards that fell short. *Penshurst* stopped, blew off steam, and sent its panic party away in two boats. The U-boat continued to close the range, firing at intervals until the range was down to seven hundred yards.

The U-boat altered course and stopped port side to off *Penshurst*'s starboard bow and fired two rounds that hit the bridge. The explosion killed and wounded several men and did moderate damage. At 1624 *Penshurst* returned fire from its forward starboard 12-pounder (3-inch). The first round hit the U-boat at the base of the conning tower, exploding the ready ammunition, and causing a large explosion that blew chunks of the conning tower into the air. *Penshurst* continued firing until the U-boat sank by the stern. After the boat went under *Penshurst* got under way, crossed the spot, and dropped two depth charges that exploded and brought up large quantities of oil.

Additional Information

A postwar German study concluded that *Penshurst* had sunk UB-37 although no one identified the U-boat and there were no survivors. The conclusion was based on information that on that same day UB-37 had sunk the SS *Norma* was close to the position in which the fight with *Penshurst* took place. Because no other U-boat was in that immediate area, the victim had to be UB-37. On 28 July 1919 a British prize court awarded *Penshurst* a bounty of £115, based on the rate of £5 per crewman aboard the U-boat.

Sources

Chatterton, *Q-Ships and Their Story,* 117–18.

Records, T-1022, Roll 61, PG61795; T-1022, Roll 71, PG61934, "Londoner Prisenger-ichtsverhandlungen wegen vierzehn deutscher U-Boote."

Spindler, *Der Handelskrieg mit U-Booten,* 3:294–95.

UB-38

Date Lost:	8 February 1918
Commander:	Oberleutnant zur See Günther Bachmann
Location:	Dover Strait
Position:	50°56' N, 1°25' E
Disposition:	Mine

UB-38 departed Zeebrugge on 29 January 1918 at 0200 for operations in the English Channel. On 8 February it was homeward bound west of the Folkestone–Gris Nez deep mine barrage when it exchanged recognition signals with outbound UB-33 at 1230. Ten hours later the drifter *Gowan II* spotted what was probably UB-38 on the surface at the north end of Le Colbart and forced the U-boat to dive. At 2245 there were three powerful explosions, followed by large quantities of oil and debris rising to the surface.

Additional Information

British divers discovered the wreck of UB-38 in position 50°58' N, 1°22' E. The Admiralty awarded the Dover drifters a one-thousand-pound bounty, applied to the Mayor of Dover Fund, for UB-38's destruction.

Sources

Gibson and Prendergast, *The German Submarine War,* 293.
Grant, *U-Boat Intelligence,* 97.
Records, T-1022, Roll 61, PG61796.
Spindler, *Der Handelskrieg mit U-Booten,* 5:117–18.

UB-39

Date Lost:	May 1917
Commander:	Oberleutnant zur See Heinrich Küstner
Location:	English Channel or Dover Strait
Position:	Unknown
Disposition:	Verschollen

UB-39 departed Zeebrugge on 23 April 1917 for operations in the western approaches and the Bay of Biscay. UB-39 did not return.

Additional Information

Two postwar British accounts say that the decoy schooner *Glen* sank UB-39 during a short gun duel thirty-five nautical miles off the Needles on 17 May 1917. According to the more detailed account *Glen* was close hauled on a starboard tack when a round exploded in the water to starboard at 1800. The crew saw a U-boat on the surface about two and a half miles away that quickly closed to eight hundred yards and submerged, but continued to show the upper part of its conning tower.

The partially submerged U-boat came within two hundred yards and held a course parallel to *Glen* while the schooner's panic crew lowered their boat. The U-boat surfaced eighty yards off the schooner's starboard beam, and the decoy opened fire with its 12-pounder. A hit was immediately scored on the conning tower, followed by three more as the U-boat dove. At that point the decoy's 3-pounder went into action and pumped six rounds into the hull before the U-boat went under, "badly holed."

The two accounts do not explain how the decoy's crew identified the U-boat as UB-39, nor is there any confirmation of the sinking. But the time and location make these accounts worthy of consideration.

Another account says that UB-39 hit a mine in the Folkestone–Gris Nez deep mine barrage on the night of 14–15 May. This possibility was based on UB-12's report that lookouts heard a powerful underwater explosion while the U-boat was passing through the Folkestone–Gris Nez barrier. UB-12 was on the surface when the men in the conning tower heard an explosion that they thought was a mine or a torpedo, but they saw nothing. The date is about right for the time that UB-39 should have been returning to Zeebrugge, but beyond that there is no indication that the explosion caused UB-39's destruction.

A postwar German study found that there were no enemy actions that could have involved UB-39 and that UB-12's report offered the best clue to UB-39's fate.

Sources

Chatterton, *Q-Ships and Their Story,* 180–81.
Gibson and Prendergast, *The German Submarine War,* 181.
Records, T-1022, Roll 61, PG61797.
Spindler, *Der Handelskrieg mit U-Booten,* 4:123–24.

UB-40

Date Lost:	1 October 1918
Commander:	Oberleutnant zur See Hans Joachim Emsmann
Location:	Ostend
Position:	51°13.5' N, 2°56' E
Disposition:	Scuttled

On 29 September 1918 the Germans began evacuating Flanders and dismantling their naval facilities at Bruges, Zeebrugge, and Ostend. Boats that could not return to Germany under their own power were blown up. The Germans destroyed UB-40 at Ostend on 1 October.

Additional Information

On 30 July just after dark a British destroyer surprised UB-40 on the surface, forced it to dive, and dropped depth charges. The explosions knocked out the auxiliary systems and shattered the cell walls in the batteries. Auxiliary power failed and water flooded the engine room through several broken valves. Oberleutnant zur See Hans Joachim Emsmann was able to stabilize the situation, and after the destroyer had gone away, he surfaced and returned to Zeebrugge. UB-40's repairs were still not complete when the Germans evacuated Flanders. Emsmann, while commanding UB-116, was lost on 28 October 1918.

Sources

Records, T-1022, Roll 78, PG61739.
Spindler, *Der Handelskrieg mit U-Booten,* 5:120–21, 149.

UB-41

Date Lost:	5 October 1917
Commander:	Oberleutnant zur See Ploen
Location:	Off Scarborough on Britain's east coast
Position:	54°18.5' N, 0°21' W
Disposition:	Mine (German)

UB-41 departed Bremerhaven on 30 September 1917 for operations be-tween Flamborough Head and Whitby. UB-41 did not return.

Additional Information

On the morning of 3 October a U-boat torpedoed the British SS *Clydebrae* (502 tons) five nautical miles north of Scarborough. Two days later a Brit-ish steamer reported a U-boat two nautical miles east of Scarborough. Two hours after the sighting, the Scarborough signal station reported that they had observed an explosion bearing east-northeast in position 54°18.5' N, 0°21' W. A heavy sea was running at the time and the rescue vessels found debris, but no survivors. Since UB-41 was the only U-boat operating in that area at that time, a postwar German study concluded that the U-boat was UB-41. The Germans believe that UB-41 hit a mine that UC-55 had laid in that approximate position on 9 July.

Sources

Records, T-1022, Roll 12, PG61800.
Spindler, *Der Handelskrieg mit U-Booten,* 4:241, 434–35.

UB-44

Date Lost:	August 1916
Commander:	Oberleutnant zur See Wäger
Location:	Eastern Mediterranean
Position:	Unknown
Disposition:	Verschollen

UB-44 departed Cattaro on 8 August 1916 en route to Constantinople (present-day Istanbul) with orders to stop at Hersingstand to take on a pilot for the trip through the Dardanelles. The boat never arrived in Hersingstand.

Additional Information

Two postwar British accounts say that UB-44 fouled the drifter *Quarry Knowe*'s nets in the Otranto Strait on 30 July, and sank. The obvious problem with this claim is that UB-44 did not leave Cattaro until 8 August. The German marine attaché in Athens offered a more likely explanation. He said that the 11 August 1916 Athens newspaper reported that the torpedo boat HMS 368 sank a U-boat six nautical miles off the island Paxoi on 8 August. According to the marine attaché, the weapon used was a *"Handbomb"* (hand bomb), which might have been a lance bomb.

Sources

Lorey, *Der Krieg in den türkischen Gewässern,* 1:269.
Records, T-1022, Roll 40, PG61804.

UB-45

Date Lost:	6 November 1916
Commander:	Kapitänleutnant Karl Palis
Location:	Black Sea
Position:	43°12' N, 28°9' E
Disposition:	Mine

UB-45 departed Varna, Bulgaria, in the Black Sea on 6 November 1916 and hit a Russian mine outside the harbor entrance. Five crewmen survived.

Additional Information

UB-45 departed Varna at 1430 escorted by the Bulgarian destroyer *Stragi* that was equipped to sweep mines. *Stragi* led the way through the north entrance and an hour later UB-45 slid around the destroyer's port side and pulled ahead. Unknown to the Bulgarians or Germans, the Russians had laid a new minefield off Varna during the preceding night. Pulling away from *Stragi,* UB-45 hit a mine that exploded between the control room and the engine room with such force that the boat was torn in two. UB-45 sank so quickly that only the three men on the conning tower and the two on deck survived. All five were wounded, three of them seriously, and one died the following day.

Sources

Records, T-1022, Roll 40, PG61805, "Euere Exelenz, traurige Versammelung."

UB-46

Date Lost:	7 December 1916
Commander:	Oberleutnant zur See Cäsar Bauer
Location:	Black Sea
Position:	41°26' N, 28°35' E
Disposition:	Mine

UB-46 was operating out of Varna in the Black Sea. On 7 December 1917 it was returning to Varna and was three hundred meters from the harbor entrance when it hit a mine. Observers in the observation station at Karaburnu saw the U-boat sink slowly by the stern, and observers saw several swimmers, but high seas prevented rescue boats from reaching them. The Russians regularly laid Hertz horn mines off Varna down to twelve meters. It appears that UB-46 hit a mine in the last row of newly laid mines. Minesweepers had been out on 4 and 5 December, but high seas had prevented them from operating on 6 and 7 December, which meant that UB-46 had approached the harbor without a minesweeper escort.

Sources

Lorey, *Der Krieg in den türkischen Gewässern,* 1:291.
Records, T-1022, Roll 40, PG61806.
Spindler, *Der Handelskrieg mit U-Booten,* 3:178.

UB-48

Date Lost:	28 October 1918
Commander:	Kapitänleutnant Steinbauer
Location:	Pola
Position:	44°52' N, 13°50' E
Disposition:	Scuttled

On 21 October 1918 the Admiralstab ordered all U-boats that were ready for sea to return to Germany, and the Germans began evacuating Pola and Cattaro on 23 October. UB-48 was one of ten boats that either could not make the trip home or was not ready for sea. The Germans destroyed these ten boats during the period 28 October to 1 November 1918 at Cattaro, Fiume, Pola, and Trieste.

Additional Information

UB-48 was the last boat in the type II UB-boat series. It departed Cattaro on 5 October for operations off Crete, and it was at sea on 22 October when Nauen broadcast the Admiralstab's worldwide order to cease attacks on shipping. UB-48 returned to Cattaro on 25 October and was declared unready to make the trip back to Germany. Its crew set explosive charges and scuttled it off Pola on 28 October 1918.

Sources

Records, T-1022, Roll 40, PG61808.
Spindler, *Der Handelskrieg mit U-Booten,* 5:226–27.

UB-52

Date Lost: 24 May 1918
Commander: Oberleutnant zur See Otto Launburg
Location: Otranto Strait
Position: 41°36' N, 18°35' E
Disposition: Torpedo

UB-52 departed Cattaro on 27 April 1918 for operations in the middle and western Mediterranean. On 19 May while heading home, it met outward-bound U-63. U-63's captain, Kapitänleutnant Kurt Hartwig, transferred two civilian prisoners taken from the British SS *Snowden* to UB-52. Whether it was intended to be a practical or a magnanimous act is debatable, but it was fatal for the two prisoners.

UB-52 passed through the Otranto Strait barrier. At 2300 on 23 May Oberleutnant zur See Otto Launburg made radio contact with Cattaro, informing them that he would arrive in Cattaro on the morning of 24 May. Almost immediately after the transmission, Lt. Oliver North, RN, in the British submarine H-4 sighted a surfaced U-boat homeward bound to Cattaro. The target bore 33° off H-4's port bow and was silhouetted by the moon. North made a snap attack, firing two torpedoes at just 250 yards. Both hit and both exploded. The U-boat sank immediately, leaving two swimmers in the water. H-4 surfaced and picked up the captain and the navigator.

Oberleutnant zur See Otto Launburg, UB-52

On 22 May 1918 UB-52 was in the Adriatic forty nautical miles south of Cattaro. At 2320 I saw the wakes of two torpedoes coming at us, and I saw that they had a very narrow spread. I tried to go ahead at full power and turned hard to starboard to avoid them, but both torpedoes struck as the boat was starting to turn and exploded at about the engine room hatch. The UB-52 broke in two and sank in a few minutes. I was swept off the conning tower as the boat went down and when I came to the surface I saw only one other swimmer. There was no sign of the boat. In a short time after the UB-52 sank, the British submarine H-4 surfaced and picked me up. Only the navigator and I survived, and he died in a British prisoner of war camp.

Additional Information

On 14 August 1919 a British prize court awarded the British submarine H-4 a bounty of £170 for sinking UB-52. The bounty was based on the rate of £5 per crewman aboard the U-boat.

Sources

Records, T-1022, Roll 67, PG61812 , "Abschrift aus Fragebogen, Wilhelmshaven, den 27. Oktober 1919, Oberleutnant zur See Otto Launburg."
Wilson and Kemp, *Mediterranean Submarines,* 158.

UB-53

Date Lost:	3 August 1918
Commander:	Oberleutnant zur See Otto Sprenger
Location:	Otranto Strait
Position:	39°58' N, 19°1' E
Disposition:	Explosive Net

UB-53 departed Pola on 1 August 1918 for operations in the eastern Mediterranean. As the boat approached the Otranto Strait in the afternoon of 3 August a line of destroyers barred the way. UB-53 dove, passed under the destroyers, and surfaced on the other side of the line. The boat now faced a second line composed entirely of drifters. Again UB-53 dove and Oberleutnant zur See Otto Sprenger steered toward the middle of the strait. He believed that the newly constructed French-Italian net barrier extended only about one-third of the way from the Italian shore. He was wrong. The French and Italians had been working steadily extending the barrier.

At 1700 UB-53 was at seventy meters when it fouled the Otranto mine-net midway between Cape Santa Maria di Leuca and Fano Island. The crew could hear cables scraping along the hull. While the captain was trying to tear free with full power, two explosions occurred at the stern and the boat dropped to one hundred meters. Both the after ballast tanks were flooded. A torpedo was blown out of the torpedo tube into the after torpedo room, but it did not explode.

The watertight door and the bulkhead between the engine room and the after torpedo room held and remained tight. The after torpedo room quickly flooded and the boat dropped sharply by the stern. The batteries fell over, the electric motors stopped.

Sprenger ordered the tanks blown and brought the boat to the surface. It proved impossible to pump the water from UB-53 and the diesel engines could not be started. Shortly Sprenger saw patrol boats approaching the powerless U-boat. He ordered the sea valves opened and scuttling charges set. By the time the British destroyer HMS *Martin* and the drifter *Whitby Abbey* arrived, UB-53 had sunk and nine men had drowned.

Additional Information

In April 1918 the French and Italians undertook to lay a fixed mine-net south of the established patrol lines from Cape Santa Maria di Leuca to

Fano Island. The top of the net was twenty-four to thirty feet below the surface and the net hung down to 180 to 200 feet. The work moved forward slowly and the net was not completed until the end of September, about six weeks before the war ended.

Sources

Records, T-1022, Roll 67, PG61813, "UB-53, Kiel, den 6. März 1920."
Spindler, *Der Handelskrieg mit U-Booten,* 5:201.

UB-54

Date Lost:	March 1918
Commander:	Oberleutnant zur See Erich Hecht
Location:	North Sea
Position:	Unknown
Disposition:	Verschollen

UB-54 departed Zeebrugge on 1 March 1918 for operations in the English Channel. UB-54 did not return and there were no survivors.

Additional Information

According to the British, the destroyers HMS *Thruster,* HMS *Retriever,* and HMS *Sturgeon* sank UB-54 with depth charges on 12 March 1918 off Britain's east coast between Skegness and Marblethorpe. In that account the three destroyers were screening the 5th Light Cruiser Squadron when a lookout aboard *Sturgeon* spotted a conning tower about a mile distant on the port bow. *Sturgeon* steamed across the U-boat's projected track and dropped two depth charges set for forty feet. Both depth charges exploded and the U-boat's bow and net cutter broke the surface. *Retriever* and *Thruster* crossed the U-boat's projected track based on the place where the bow and net cutter had been seen and dropped more depth charges. The explosions brought oil and wreckage to the surface, but the Admiralty classified the result as probably sunk. The Admiralty denied the destroyers' application for the bounty because the U-boat could not be identified. A postwar German study also rejected the claim because UB-54's operations area was in the English Channel.

Another British source suggested that on 12 March 1918 UB-54 hit a mine in the Folkestone–Gris Nez deep mine barrage. The event is supposed to have occurred near the Varne Bank, and the suggestion was based on idea that UB-54 could have been returning to Zeebrugge at about that time from operations in the English Channel. There is no solid evidence to support the claim, but on 9 August 1918 British divers located two wrecks in position 51°0' N, 1°9' E. One had been there long enough to become barnacle encrusted, while the other wreck was relatively recent. The older wreck may have been UB-54, but it was never identified.

Sources

Chatterton, *Beating the U-Boats,* 130.
Gibson and Prendergast, *The German Submarine War,* 292–93.
Grant, *U-Boat Intelligence,* 97–98.
Records, T-1022, Roll 68, PG61814.
Spindler, *Der Handelskrieg mit U-Booten,* 5:65.

UB-55

Date Lost:	24 April 1918
Commander:	Kapitänleutnant Ralph Wenninger
Location:	Dover Strait
Position:	51°1' N, 1°20' E
Disposition:	Mine

In the early morning of 24 April 1918 UB-55 dove as it approached the Folkestone–Gris Nez deep mine barrage. Twenty-five minutes later UB-55 hit a mine.

Kapitänleutnant Ralph Wenninger, UB-55

About a mile west of the northern edge of the Varne we dove because the entire area was illuminated as bright as day with searchlights and magnesium flares. We were proceeding at periscope depth when we struck a mine that exploded on the starboard side between the engine room and the after torpedo room. Both compartments were instantly flooded and the boat sank in thirty-eight meters.

The bulkhead and watertight door between the engine room and the control room held, but leaked. All the starboard tanks, including the trim tanks, were damaged and taking water. We attempted to blow the tanks with compressed air, but all the starboard tanks were too badly damaged. We lay on the bottom until all measures to surface were exhausted, and then the remaining men were divided into two groups; one at the forward deck hatch and the other below the conning tower hatch. The remaining air pressure from the torpedo flasks was released inside the boat to equalize the pressure inside with the outside pressure. This did not work and we had to wait 1 3/4 hours until the water had risen enough to compress the air inside the hull.

We opened the hatches and went up with the released air. All the men from the conning tower and ten men from the forward hatch reached the surface. Many drowned very quickly because they had inflated their life vests in the boat where the air pressure was 3 kg and the vests burst when they reached the surface. It was dawn when we reached the surface and we were about fifteen hundred meters from the Varne red buoy. After an hour and a half, the British trawler, *Mate,* picked up the chief engineer, and following his directions proceeded to pick up the rest. Römspiess and I were unconscious when we were taken aboard and Römspiess never regained consciousness. The chief engineer died from influenza in the officers camp at Skipton.

Sources

Records, T-1022, Roll 68, PG61815, "Abschrift aus Fragebogen, Wilhelmshaven, den 27. Oktober 1919, Kapitänleutnant R. Wenninger."

UB-56

Date Lost:	19 December 1917
Commander:	Oberleutnant zur See Hans Valentiner
Location:	Dover Strait
Position:	50°57' N, 1°23' E
Disposition:	Mine

UB-56 departed Zeebrugge on 18 December 1917 for operations in the English Channel. On 19 December the destroyer HMS *Gypsy* observed a powerful explosion in the Folkestone–Gris Nez deep mine barrage. *Gypsy* heard shouts coming from the water and saw swimmers. Before *Gypsy*'s boat could reach them all had sunk except for one man who was brought aboard unconscious. He died a short time later, but his clothing identified him as Machinist's Mate Max Bleek, a member of UB-56's crew.

Additional Information

On 12 August 1918 British divers examined UB-56. The stern was badly damaged and there was a considerable amount of sand in the hull. The divers identified the wreck on the basis that it was very close to the scene of the mine explosion.

Sources

Grant, *U-Boat Intelligence,* 98–99.
Records, T-1022, Roll 68, PG61816.
Spindler, *Der Handelskrieg mit U-Booten,* 4:449.

UB-57

Date Lost:	14 August 1918
Commander:	Oberleutnant zur See Lohs
Location:	Off Flanders coast
Position:	51°56' N, 2°2' E (possible)
Disposition:	Mine

On 14 August UB-57 was returning to Zeebrugge. At 2215 Oberleutnant zur See Lohs sent a radio message to Bruges reporting his success and saying that he would use the swept channel from the Sandetti Lightship to Zeebrugge. An hour later Bruges told UB-57 that the escorts had been arranged, but the U-boat did not respond. Eight days later the bodies of Lohs and some of his crew washed ashore at the mouth of the Schelde. The watch officer's body washed up in Zeebrugge the same day and more bodies came ashore on 1 and 2 September at Ostend and the Hague.

Additional Information

A postwar German study concluded that there was little doubt that UB-57 hit a British mine off the Flanders coast on the night of 14 August 1918. Exactly where that happened cannot be determined, but there was a British minefield located in 51°56' N, 2°2' E.

Sources

Records, T-1022, Roll 68, PG61817.
Spindler, *Der Handelskrieg mit U-Booten,* 5:91–92.

UB-58

Date Lost:	10 March 1918
Commander:	Oberleutnant zur See Werner Löwe
Location:	Dover Strait
Position:	50°58' N, 1°14' E
Disposition:	Mine

UB-58 departed Zeebrugge on 9 March 1918 for operations in the western approaches, and it did not return.

Additional Information

According to the French, on 10 March the British P-24 was patrolling south of the Folkestone–Gris Nez deep mine barrage. At 0400 P-24's crew heard three powerful explosions. Two and a half hours later P-24 found oil and wreckage floating on the surface, and the crew fished documents out of the water. Among the documents found were reports detailing UB-58's acceptance trials in October 1917.

The British H2 and H4 mines sank more U-boats between November 1917 and November 1918 than the unreliable Service and Elia mines did from October 1914 to November 1917, and by a wide margin. There were four confirmed losses to mines up to November 1917 and sixteen confirmed losses during the last twelve months of the war.

Sources

Records, T-1022, Roll 68, PG61818.
Spindler, *Der Handelskrieg mit U-Booten,* 5:72.

UB-59

Date Lost:	5 October 1918
Commander:	Kapitänleutnant Fritz Wassner
Location:	Bruges
Disposition:	Mine, Aerial Bomb, Scuttled

UB-59 departed Zeebrugge on 2 May 1918 for operations in the English Channel. On the morning of 4 May it attempted to pass through the Folkestone–Gris Nez deep mine barrage by staying close to the French coast and very close to the bottom. As the boat rose to periscope depth it hit two mines and was violently shaken by two explosions. UB-59 dropped sharply by the bow and rammed its bow into the rocky seabed. What followed was an example of luck and seamanship as Kapitänleutnant Fritz Wassner and his crew fought to keep the boat afloat and avoid the British patrols on the way back to Zeebrugge.

Log Book SMS, UB-59

3 May

0045–0245: Departed Zeebrugge. Dove and proceeded toward our operations area.

0540: Lay on the bottom off Ruytingen Lightship in 39 meters.

2220: Surfaced.

2325: Crossed the antisubmarine net at Buoy No. 4, which was lighted.

2345: Four destroyers in line astern sighted to starboard. They passed across our bow. The destroyers changed course to an intersecting course with UB-59. Passed to port. The destroyers turned toward the boat and we crash dived. Steered a course to take us over the twenty-meter line.

4 May

0045: Surfaced. Diesels all ahead full on course toward Gris Nez. Ahead the light barrier is very bright and there are two very powerful searchlights at Gris Nez.

0125: In order to avoid the searchlights at Gris Nez and to prevent the boat from being silhouetted against the lights of the barrier, we dove. At half speed, course 207° close to the bottom toward the green buoy

SW of Gris Nez. At periscope depth the searchlight was abeam. Took a bearing on the buoy to fix our position.

0115: Went to fifteen meters and passed the green buoy close aboard. Went in as close to Gris Nez as possible where the antisubmarine measures are probably not so strong.

Gave the order to rise to periscope depth to fix our position. At that moment two strong explosions, one after the other, shook the boat. The boat dropped sharply by the bow and hit the bottom at twenty-two meters on rocky ground.

We can hear water flooding in the forward torpedo room. In the conning tower the communications system, depth gauge, lockers and so forth are smashed, or torn loose. The deck plates in the control room are smashed and the people in the forward torpedo room and the conning tower are knocked down.

The main periscope is totally destroyed and the second periscope is seriously damaged. Both are useless.

The forward torpedo room is a shambles. The deck plates, provisions and berths are all jumbled on the deck. All the water level gauges in the boat are destroyed, and the forward diving planes are jammed.

We immediately restarted the motors and proceeded at half speed, course 240° operating the forward diving planes manually. Switched to emergency lighting. We have to move away from the immediate area of Gris Nez.

The after torpedo room and the engine room report all clear and no flooding. The steering rudder is functional. The compass is working. The control room is undamaged.

Both forward torpedo tubes are flooded. Fuel and water are spurting in thick jets from the stand glasses and the water piping to the torpedo tubes is broken. The water is already over the floor plates and rising. We shut off the stand glasses and plugged the broken water lines with wooden plugs despite poor lighting. The bilge pumps are able to handle the water. Relatively little water is entering through popped rivets. Most of the water is entering through the starboard side of the torpedo room, mainly through loosened flanges and pipe fittings. The bilge pumps are running continuously.

The boat cannot be trimmed. The bow dropped down sharply and is again resting on rocky ground. Both motors quit and the lights went out. A quick search revealed that the batteries had failed.

The trimming problem appears to result from the forward fuel tanks taking water. They are leaking and the lost fuel is being replaced with sea water. That increases the weight of the boat forward.

I have decided that in spite of our proximity to surface patrols we must surface. I ordered all tanks blown with compressed air.

0245: Surfaced in the immediate vicinity of the patrols and the search-light at Gris Nez. The boat cannot dive, we have lost a great quantity of fuel, and the sea is mirror flat. The damage to the boat is extensive. A breakthrough to the north is at this time impossible.

We have two more hours of darkness and I have decided to use that time to run on our diesels to the Vergoyer Bank where the enemy anti-submarine measures are less active. And the water is shallower so that we can rest on the bottom.

During the run to Vergoyer Bank the boat was thoroughly examined and work was done in those areas without showing any lights that were accessible. We passed the Vergoyer Bank Buoy at dawn.

0600: Heavy fog. Our Luck! In these conditions we can work on the boat during daylight. Reserve bunkers 5 on both sides and bunker 2 on the starboard side are leaking badly. Ballast tanks 6 and 4, and 3 on the port side, are flooded. Despite repeated blowing with compressed air, the boat remains down by the bow and is listing sharply to port. When we blow the tanks we can hear the air escaping uselessly through the holes in the top of the tanks.

We tried to eliminate the constant oil slick by blowing the oil out of bunker 5. This proved impossible because the air whistled through the holes just as it did with tank 6. We then tried to expel the fuel with the blowers, but they are inoperative. The oil that spurts out through the popped rivets was stopped with wooden plugs.

The forward battery is completely destroyed. The after battery has three damaged cells. We are going to bridge this battery to the forward battery in order to get some electrical power.

We are now able to dive, but we cannot maneuver. If we dive, we must rest on the bottom.

0800: The after battery is sufficient to provide power for lights, the com-pass and the air ventilation system. We can run on the motors at min-imum speed.

Because it was impossible to remain any longer on the surface, we dove. The boat immediately went down by the bow 25° and struck the bottom in thirty-four meters. The bottom was sand. The day was spent repairing the boat. The leaks proved to be manageable. The forward torpedo room was taking about five hundred liters per hour, but the bilge pumps could handle that. To trim the boat we flooded the after tanks and the after torpedo tubes. All moveable weight was shifted aft. We spent the entire day undisturbed.

2225: Rose from the bottom, went ahead at dead slow, and surfaced. The sea was mirror flat. It seemed impossible to break through the Dover Strait because we could already see in the excellent visibility the brightly illuminated Light Barrier.

The after battery is only partially charged, but I have decided to break through the Dover Barrier by passing between the Varne and the Colbart Bank and making for buoy 4. It is an all or nothing proposition. I have chosen that route because the water is shallow enough that if we have to dive, we can lie on the bottom. We will be going against the current for most of the night.

The boat was leaking fuel badly and had a heavy port list. We have to repeatedly blow the forward and port tanks. The low-pressure blowers are not working so that we are using a large amount of compressed air.

2325: Our course was 350° and we were running at full speed and charging the battery. As we approached the Varne Lightship we saw several vessels approaching from dead astern at high speed. We assumed they had picked up our oil trail on the surface and had seen phosphorescence in our wake. Changed course and dove. Several depth charges in the area but none close enough to trouble us.

5 May

0030: Surfaced. Patrol activity along the Light Barrier very active. Course 0° toward the Varne Lightship, which we passed to the north to avoid the Light Barrier. Ahead full on both engines.

0215: Dove to avoid a P-boat that was steaming on a parallel course. Lay on the bottom in thirty meters to conserve the battery. Working against a strong current.

0300: Surfaced. The patrols are as thick as hornets. Ahead full on both engines, course 70°. Red and white rocket signals seen astern. A monitor on converging course sighted to port. She is sweeping the surface with her searchlight in an area that is already lighted bright as day by station ships with magnesium flares. Three trawlers to starboard.

0340: Dove to avoid a searchlight.

0400: Surfaced. The monitor is headed toward Gris Nez. Set course toward buoy 4, ahead full on both engines. Fog developing behind us. Four destroyers in line astern off our starboard beam. They were on a converging course, then changed to a parallel course, and then turned away.

0500: Passed buoy 4 at daybreak. A heavy fog is developing. I have decided to run on the surface for so long as these conditions continue. We will get as far away as possible from the barrier and then rest on the bottom in shallow water until dark.

Because the visibility is getting worse we will continue running on the surface and make for Ostend via the Ruytingen Bank.

2150: Entered Ostend.

Additional Information

UB-59 was towed to Bruges where it went into dry dock for repairs. On 16 May a British airplane dropped a bomb on UB-59 that exploded on the bow torpedo room. The explosion blew a hole in the pressure hull that extended from frame 47 to frame 60, destroyed the starboard ballast tanks, and did extensive interior damage. The Germans estimated that repairs would take at least six months, but UB-59 never went to sea again. On 5 October 1918 a maintenance crew blew it up when the Germans evacuated Flanders.

The day after they had arrived in Ostend, Wassner and his crew left for Wilhelmshaven to take over the newly commissioned UB-117. They made only one war patrol in UB-117, from 5 to 28 September 1918, during which they sank five vessels totaling 9,396 tons. The Germans surrendered UB-117 to the British on 26 November 1918.

Sources

Records, T-1022, Roll 68, PG61819, "Kriegstagebuch *UB-59,* 29. 3. 18 bis 6. 5. 18." and "Stellungnahme der Flotilla."

Spindler, *Der Handelskrieg mit U-Booten,* 5:73–75.

UB-61

Date Lost:	**29 November 1917**
Commander:	**Oberleutnant zur See Theodor Schultz**
Location:	**Off German coast at Weser Mouth**
Position:	**53°20' N, 4°56' E**
Disposition:	**Mine**

UB-61 departed Bremerhaven on 26 November 1917 for operations off Ireland's south coast. High seas and stormy weather forced UB-61 to put in at Ems on 27 November. On the morning of 29 November UB-61, in company with UB-64, UB-75, and UC-49, departed Borkum Roads with two minesweepers as escorts. But gale conditions prevented the minesweepers from deploying their sweeps. At 0900 UB-61, the last boat in line, hit a mine. It went down very fast and the high seas prevented rescuers from saving any of the crew. During the hunt for survivors the minesweeper *Dirk van Minden* also hit a mine and was lost.

Additional Information

The British submarine E-51 laid the mines on 18 November that sank UB-61 and *Dirk van Minden.*

Sources

Records, T-1022, Roll 69, PG61821.
Spindler, *Der Handelskrieg mit U-Booten,* 4:435.

UB-63

Date Lost:	27 January 1918
Commander:	Oberleutnant zur See Gebeschus
Location:	English Channel, Irish Sea, Atlantic Ocean, or North Sea
Position:	Unknown
Disposition:	Verschollen

UB-63 departed Bremerhaven on 14 January 1918 for operations in the English Channel and the Irish Sea. It did not return.

Additional Information

Two British sources report that trawlers engaged a U-boat identified as UB-63 off the Firth of Forth on 28 January. In one account *W. S. Bailey* picked up U-boat noises on its hydrophone and depth charged the area without visible results. Some time later a U-boat surfaced with its periscope bent at a 45° angle. *Fort George* forced the U-boat to dive and then dropped depth charges over the spot.

In the second, more detailed account, the trawlers *Fort George* and *W. S. Bailey* were fourteen miles east of May Island when they picked up sounds on their hydrophones. *W. S. Bailey* listened for an hour and a half until the sounds became very distinct. It dropped a depth charge, listened, and then dropped a second depth charge. Following the second explosion a lookout spotted two periscopes twenty yards away on the starboard quarter, and the trawler dropped two more depth charges that reportedly destroyed UB-63.

The problem with both accounts is that the action took place off the Firth of Forth two weeks after UB-63 should have arrived in the English Channel and the Irish Sea. U-boat captains often left their patrol areas to hunt in more active areas, but none of them ever exceeded their orders to that degree.

A German source credits the drifters *Cormorant II* and *Young Fred* with having destroyed UB-63 with depth charges in position 50°58' N, 1°21' E on 27 January 1918. But the account gives no details to support the claim. If correct, the action took place on the west side of the Folkestone–Gris Nez deep mine barrage. It makes more sense than the first two claims, because that is about the time when UB-63 would have been returning to

186

Bremerhaven from its English Channel operations. Although more likely, the report's reliability suffers from the fact that the Admiralty credited the *Young Fred* with only one action, and that was on 17 April 1918. The cause of UB-63's loss remains unknown.

Sources

Chatterton, *Q-Ships and Their Story,* 239–40.
Gibson and Prendergast, *The German Submarine War,* 287–88.
Herzog, *Deutsche U-Boote,* 94.
Records, T-1022, Roll 57, PG61823.
Spindler, *Der Handelskrieg mit U-Booten,* 5:54.

UB-65

Date Lost:	4 July 1918
Commander:	Oberleutnant zur See Schelle
Location:	Atlantic, off Ireland's south coast
Position:	51°7' N, 9°42' W (possible)
Disposition:	Accident

UB-65 departed Helgoland on 2 July 1918 for operations in the Bristol Channel. On 4 July it reported that it had avoided torpedoes fired at it in the North Sea, the last anyone heard from UB-65.

Additional Information

At 1830 on 10 July 1918 USS L-2 dove after sighting a periscope and heard a tremendous explosion as it dove. Three explanations have been offered for the explosion. One is that a U-boat fired a torpedo that circled and hit the U-boat. A more likely possibility was that the torpedo ran hot in its tube and exploded. The third suggestion, the least likely, is that a second U-boat fired a torpedo at L-2, but the torpedo hit the first U-boat. The boat that blew up was never identified, but the German study concluded that it might have been UB-65 because it should have been in that area at about that time.

Sources

Records, T-1022, Roll 58, PG61825.
Spindler, *Der Handelskrieg mit U-Booten,* 5:297.

UB-66

Date Lost:	18 January 1918
Commander:	Kapitänleutnant Wernicke
Location:	Eastern Mediterranean
Position:	Unknown
Disposition:	Verschollen

UB-66 departed Cattaro on 27 December 1917 for operations from Port Said to Cyprus. On 10 January 1918 it put in at Beirut for fuel and Kapitänleutnant Wernicke said that he planned to be off Alexandria around 15 January. UB-66 torpedoed SS *Windsor Hall* northwest of Alexandria on 17 January, and that was the last anyone heard from UB-66.

Additional Information

The sloop HMS *Campanula* depth charged a U-boat fifteen nautical miles south-southeast of Malta on 18 January 1918. But another account says the action took place over two hundred nautical miles away off Cape Bon on the same date. A postwar German study concluded that it is possible that the *Campanula* sank a U-boat, but it was probably not UB-66. On 17 January UB-66 was about one thousand nautical miles southeast of Cape Bon. To have arrived at Cape Bon the next day would have required a speed of around forty knots, which was considerably faster than UB-66 could make.

Sources

Records, T-1022, Roll 58, PG61826.
Spindler, *Der Handelskrieg mit U-Booten,* 5:231–32.

UB-68

Date Lost:	4 October 1918
Commander:	Oberleutnant zur See Karl Dönitz
Location:	Western Mediterranean, near Malta
Position:	35°56' N, 16°20' E
Disposition:	Technical Problem, Gunfire

On 4 October UB-68 attacked a six-ship convoy 150 nautical miles east of Malta. UB-68 made three night surface attacks. The first attack sank a steamer, but the second and third attacks failed. At dawn UB-68 made a submerged attack. As Oberleutnant zur See Karl Dönitz was making his approach an unexplained technical problem caused UB-68 to suddenly sink by the stern to eighty meters. At that depth the after torpedo tubes' packing glands failed and the boat started taking water. Dönitz tried to trim the boat on an even keel, but now UB-68 assumed a bow-down angle and plunged to 102 meters. Dönitz blew the ballast tanks in a desperate bid to reach the surface. Freed of its ballast, UB-68 rose quickly still down by the bow.

The convoy escorts opened fire on UB-68 when it surfaced, but fortunately for UB-68 their shooting was poor. Dönitz tried to dive but his chief engineer told him they had no more compressed air. Dönitz ordered the boat scuttled. The HMS *Snapdragon* picked up the entire crew except for four men.

Oberleutnant zur See Karl Dönitz, UB-68

We were at 12.5 meters when shortly before the shot the boat dropped 10° by the stern and the net cutter broke the surface. I quickly retracted the periscope. I ordered the boat down to twenty meters and stopped both motors to give the boat a bow down angle. The bow dropped and I ordered the motors ahead half. As the boat passed fifteen meters I ordered her up to periscope depth since I was sure the danger of being rammed had passed and I hoped to get a shot at the wing position steamer. But the diving planes were jammed down and I ordered the bilge pumps turned on. The boat again dropped 10° by the stern and sank quickly. Pumping the trim tanks had no effect. Despite having the diving planes hard up the boat continued to sink stern first, and I ordered both motors ahead full. The boat continued to fall, passed sixty meters and then to eighty meters where it made a brief upward movement. The packing gland around the stern torpedo tube had been forced clear inside the boat.

Tried blowing the tanks with compressed air and went all ahead. The boat rose to forty meters and then thirty meters, still stern down. The boat stopped, hung for about a minute, dropped down by the bow 50°, and dove quickly. I ordered both motors stopped and all tanks blown. The depth gauge showed 102 meters when the chief engineer reported flooding in the after torpedo room. [The bow was at 120 meters and the stern was at 86 meters.] The boat stopped and then rose quickly stern first at a 50° angle to the surface.

As soon as we surfaced rounds began falling close aboard. I opened the hatch and saw that we were in the middle of the convoy behind the first row. A cruiser and two steamers were firing at us. The cruiser and one steamer turned toward us and as the cruiser came within eight hundred meters we took a hit on the starboard after deck. There was no hope of getting away on the surface and I ordered the boat to dive.

I gave the command to dive to fifteen meters and received a report from the chief engineer that we had no more compressed air. I did not fully comprehend the report at first and I was insistent that we dive to escape the shelling. I again ordered the boat to dive. Again came the chief engineer's report that we had no compressed air and we were taking water aft. I finally understood that we could not dive.

I opened the conning tower hatch and as the navigator and I climbed out we took a second hit that entered the conning tower. I then gave the command to scuttle the boat by opening the ballast tank valves and the hatches. I then gave the order to abandon ship, and the UB-68 sank very quickly.

Additional Information

UB-68's captain is the same Karl Dönitz who commanded Germany's U-boat forces at the start of World War II, became the commander-in-chief of the German navy in 1943, and was the last head of the Nazi government in 1945. On 1 October 1946 the Nürnberg Military Tribunal sentenced him to ten years for war crimes and crimes against peace. He was released from Spandau Prison in Berlin in 1956 and died on 24 December 1980.

Sources

Records, T-1022, Roll 58, PG61828, "Bootsverlust *UB-68*."

UB-69

Date Lost:	8 January 1918
Commander:	Oberleutnant zur See Klatt
Location:	Western Mediterranean
Position:	37°30' N, 10°38' E
Disposition:	Paravane

UB-69 departed Kiel on 26 December 1917 en route to Cattaro in the Adriatic, but it never arrived.

Additional Information

According to a report submitted to a British prize court HMS *Cyclamen* was cruising twelve nautical miles northwest off Cape Bon when it received a radio message that a U-boat was operating in the area. *Cyclamen* deployed its explosive paravanes port and starboard and set them for contact explosion. Both paravanes came into contact with a submerged object and exploded, the force being so large that *Cyclamen*'s crew believed they had detonated explosives aboard the U-boat. Thirty seconds later a U-boat's bow rose above the surface at a perpendicular angle and then sank. There were no survivors. The prize court awarded HMS *Cyclamen* a two-hundred-pound bounty for destroying UB-69.

The *Cyclamen*'s explosive paravane report for 8 January 1918 has the "Known Sunk" column checked, and a postwar German report concluded that given the location and date, there is a strong probability that it did in fact sink UB-69.

The explosive paravane was the final development of the towed explosive sweeps the British used during World War I. The explosive paravane was a hydrodynamic device that was fully controllable from the surface and exploded either on contact or was manually fired. The device came in two versions, a high-speed model that destroyers towed and a low-speed model that trawlers towed. Destroyers towed them two at a time, one off each quarter, and trawlers towed only one directly astern. Explosive paravanes were used in an attack fifty-three times from 1916 to 1918, and the attack on UB-69 was the only one that might have been successful.

The same paravane without the explosive charge was called the Otter and was deployed from the bows of warships and freighters to sweep mines. In its Otter form, the paravane was credited with saving hundreds of ships from being sunk by mines.

Sources

Cornford, *The Paravane Adventure,* 278.

Records, T-1022, Roll 11, PG61694, "The Prize Court: Destruction of German Auxiliary Cruiser and Submarines; Bounty; UB-69, U-110, and U-C6"; T-1022, Roll 58, PG61829.

Spindler, *Der Handelskrieg mit U-Booten,* 5:166.

Vickers Ltd., *The Submarine Sweep as Fitted on Trawlers.*

UB-70

Date Lost:	April–May 1918
Commander:	Kapitänleutnant Johannes Remy
Location:	North Sea, Atlantic, or Mediterranean
Position:	Unknown
Disposition:	Verschollen

UB-70 departed Kiel en route to Cattaro on 14 February 1918. It was forced to return to Kiel for repairs because the shafts on the forward diving planes broke in heavy weather. Following the repairs UB-70 again set out for Cattaro on 16 April 1918, but it never arrived. There is no solid clue as to what caused UB-70's loss.

Additional Information

At least two postwar accounts credit the destroyer HMS *Basilisk* and the American armed yacht *Lydonia* with depth charging and sinking UB-70 eighty nautical miles northeast of Algiers on 8 May 1918. But the boat pounded on 8 May was Kapitänleutnant Max Valentiner's U-38, which survived both the depth charging and the war.

Sources

Chatterton, *Beating the U-Boats,* 130.
Gibson and Prendergast, *The German Submarine War,* 269.
Records, T-1022, Roll 17, PG61585 (U-38); T-1022, Roll 58, PG61830 (UB-70).
Spindler, *Der Handelskrieg mit U-Booten,* 5:157, 166.

UB-71

Date Lost:	21 April 1918
Commander:	Kapitänleutnant Schapler
Location:	Strait of Gibraltar
Position:	35°58' N, 15°18' E (probable)
Disposition:	Depth Charge

UB-71 departed Kiel for Cattaro on 4 April 1918. Four days before UB-71 reached Gibraltar, the British had beefed up their surface patrols with motor launches designed specifically for antisubmarine work. Early in the morning on 21 April, motor launch ML-413's hydrophone operator picked up engine noises, and two minutes later a lookout spotted a bow wave approaching. Not knowing the bow wave's source, ML-413 turned on its running lights to avoid a collision. Two minutes later a U-boat crossed its bow just thirty feet away and dove. ML-413 got under way, ran up the U-boat's wake, and dropped four depth charges ahead of the U-boat's estimated position. Following the attack there were no propeller noises, and at dawn ML-413's crew found oil and wreckage on the surface.

The postwar German study determined that ML-413 had probably sunk UB-71.

Sources

Records, T-1022, Roll 58, PG61831.
Spindler, *Der Handelskrieg mit U-Booten,* 5:167.

UB-72

Date Lost:	12 May 1918
Commander:	Oberleutnant zur See Traeger
Location:	English Channel
Position:	50°8' N, 2°41' W
Disposition:	Torpedo

UB-72 departed Kiel on 1 May 1918 for operations in the western approaches to the English Channel. Using the northern route, on 7 May UB-72 met UB-86 fifteen nautical miles west of the Isle of Wight and exchanged lamp signals. On 12 May the British submarine D-4 torpedoed UB-72 twenty-five nautical miles southwest of Portland, in 50°8' N, 2°41' W. There were three survivors, but no survivor reports are available.

Sources

Records, T-1022, Roll 58, PG61832.
Spindler, *Der Handelskrieg mit U-Booten,* 5:26.

UB-74

Date Lost:	26 May 1918
Commander:	Oberleutnant zur See Steindorff
Location:	English Channel
Position:	50°32' N, 2°32' W (possible)
Disposition:	Depth Charge

UB-74 departed Zeebrugge on 11 May 1918 to attack American transports off St. Nazaire. On 25 May UB-74 exchanged information with U-101 west of Quessant. That was the last anyone heard from UB-74.

Additional Information

On 26 May the armed yacht *Lorna* dropped two depth charges on a U-boat in Lyme Bay. The explosions brought large amounts of air, oil, and debris to the surface, and four men. *Lorna* dropped another depth charge that killed three of the swimmers and fatally injured the fourth, but there is no indication that the British identified the man they pulled from the sea. After UB-74 and U-101 exchanged information, UB-74 had time to reach the place where *Lorna* dropped depth charges, making it probable that *Lorna* sank UB-74.

Sources

Grant, *U-Boats Destroyed,* 119.
Records, T-1022, Roll 58, PG61834.
Spindler, *Der Handelskrieg mit U-Booten,* 5:76–77.

UB-75

Date Lost:	December 1917
Commander:	Oberleutnant zur See Franz Walther
Location:	Off Britain's east coast, near Scarborough
Position:	Unknown
Disposition:	Verschollen

On the morning of 29 November 1917 UB-75, in company with UB-61, UB-64, and UC-49, departed Borkum Roads with two minesweepers as escorts. During this first leg of the trip UB-61 hit a mine and sank. UB-75 continued on to its operations area off Britain's east coast between Flamborough Head and Longstone. There was no further word from UB-75 and the cause of its loss is unknown.

Additional Information

On 4 December the British laid an explosive net barrage off Scarborough and on that same day they laid a deep minefield off Flamborough Head. It is possible that UB-75 either fouled the explosive net or struck a deep mine in one of those two locations.

Sources

Grant, *U-Boats Destroyed,* 57.
Records, T-1022, Roll 80, PG61835.
Spindler, *Der Handelskrieg mit U-Booten,* 4:438.

UB-78

Date Lost:	9 May 1918
Commander:	Oberleutnant zur See Stosberg
Location:	English Channel
Position:	49°50' N, 1°40' W
Disposition:	Ramming

UB-78 departed Zeebrugge on 18 April 1918 for operations in the English Channel and the western approaches. UB-78 did not return.

Additional Information

On 9 May a lookout aboard the cross-channel steamer, SS *Queen Alexandria,* spotted a U-boat just as the boat was going under. *Queen Alexandria* turned and rammed the U-boat at twenty knots just as its conning tower rim was awash. *Queen Alexandria's* escort, P-35, heard the collision and dropped a depth charge and a marker buoy. Later that morning P-35 returned to the area and found a seven-mile stretch of oil and debris. A dry dock examination of *Queen Alexandria* showed that its stem, rudder, and screws were badly damaged in the collision. A German postwar study concluded that, based on time and location, *Queen Alexandria* probably rammed UB-78.

Sources

Records, T-1022, Roll 80, PG61838.
Spindler, *Der Handelskrieg mit U-Booten,* 5:77–78.

UB-81

Date Lost:	2 December 1917
Commander:	Oberleutnant zur See Reinhold Saltzwedel
Location:	English Channel, off Isle of Wight
Position:	50°27' N, 0°53' W
Disposition:	Mine

UB-81 departed Zeebrugge on 28 November 1917 for operations in the English Channel. At 0545 on 2 December it was running at twenty meters when it hit a mine two nautical miles south of Owers Lightship and sank. The mine destroyed the after part of the boat and flooded it to the control room. Unable to surface, Oberleutnant zur See Reinhold Saltzwedel blew the forward tanks and lifted the bow above the surface so that the crew could escape through one of the forward torpedo tubes. Seven men managed to go out through the torpedo tube, but when British patrol boats arrived, heavy seas forced one of the patrol boats against UB-81's bow, driving it under. Water poured through the open torpedo tube, and Saltzwedel and most of his crew died inside UB-81.

Marine Ingenieur Hans Denker, UB-81

Lieutenant Freudendal was OOD [officer of the deck] and was on the periscope. The captain and I were drinking coffee when Freudendal reported a steamer on a converging course. I took over in the control room and the captain and the navigator went into the conning tower. A torpedo shot missed probably due to heavy seas. The time was 1620.

Suddenly the order "Go to twenty meters!" Shortly after that there was a heavy explosion aft, and all the lights went out. Reports from the individual compartments indicated that we were tight forward, but the after torpedo room was flooding through the torpedo tube. The after torpedo room was abandoned and the watertight door was closed.

The boat sank quickly to the bottom in thirty-five meters. The radioman reported propeller sounds over the boat moving from left to right. I went to the engine room. The watertight door to the torpedo room was leaking badly and the engine room was flooding. The watertight door to the after torpedo room could not be sealed. I reported to the captain that the boat must surface before she became too heavy. The captain ordered all tanks blown, but air would not go to tank 1. The steering rudder and after dive planes were jammed. The emergency valve on tank 1 was not accessible. Tank 2 was filled with diesel oil and I had that tank blown. The boat did not rise, but the stern down angle went to 20°. The time was 1700.

The propeller noises were still heard overhead. The water was rising quickly in the engine room but the electric motors were still clear. Another attempt was made to rise using the electric motors, but the boat did not move. The main fuses blew with a bright flash. The water continued to rise. The bilge pumps did not work because the down angle was too great and the suction lines were out of the water.

More fuses were blowing in the engine room and the water would soon reach the electric motors. I ordered everyone in the engine room forward. Maschinistenmaat Redlin remained in the engine room to pull the electric motor fuses. I pulled all the control room fuses except those for the emergency lighting system. The watertight door to the engine room was closed, and the entire crew, except for the radioman, gathered in the forward torpedo room. The time was 1730.

The up angle had increased to the point that the captain thought that the forward deck hatch must be above the water. I went forward and tried to open the hatch, but was unable to do so. It was then decided to escape through one of the forward torpedo tubes. With the present angle, given the water depth of thirty-five meters and the length of the boat, fifty-five meters, the torpedo tube outer doors must be above the surface. Luckily it was low water and we still had two compressed air cylinders with 50-kg pressure.

The trim tanks and all ballast tanks were blown or pumped clear. One of the four torpedoes had to be removed. The job required enormous effort and was very difficult. It took the combined efforts of the entire crew two hours to haul the torpedo inboard and secure it. The last of the compressed air was used to blow the forward tanks one more time.

All extra weight in the bow was moved aft. The forward depth gauge was working and showed nine meters. Then the interior air pressure was slowly bled off through the torpedo tube outer door. The interior pressure had become almost unbearable.

Bootsmannsmaat Wagner took signal flares and was shoved up the tube. Behind him went Heizer Köhler, Matrose Sell, and Heizer Schröder. Wagner took a strap so that we could rig a tackle to haul out the remaining crewmen. The job of getting people outside took longer than expected. Finally Wager was out and reported that the opening was one meter above the surface and in the lee. There was a heavy sea running. The time was 2100.

Most of the men inside the boat had donned life jackets. Unfortunately, the strain had taken a toll on many of the men. Someone had broken open the provisions and many men sat around eating and taking no part in the continuing rescue operation.

After the first four men were out, Leutnant zur See Freudendal, Steuermann Bäthge, Matrose Sell, Kirschbaum, Blunk and Heizer Meyer went through the tube. The flares were being fired and the watch officer called down that everyone should remain below because it was too cold outside. Shortly, Wagner came back inside to obtain more flares, but they were all in the flooded after torpedo room. Shortly after that Schröder and Sell came back inside. Both were half frozen and kept saying that they would rather drown than freeze to death. Right behind them were Köhler and Meyer. There were now four people outside.

A short discussion was held between the captain and I. We decided that everyone should go outside because there was a strong possibility that chlorine gas would soon develop. There was also the possibility that the heavy seas would pour enough water down the open tube to sink the boat. That possibility increased as the tide rose and the boat turned, bringing the open tube to the windward side.

The captain ordered me to lead the way out. I took the portable searchlight with me and behind me came Maschinistenmaat Redlin. The order was passed below for everyone to come out. It was terribly cold and the waves were now breaking over the bow. The time was 2200.

Maschinistenmaat Bories was in the opening at the outer end of the torpedo tube when a destroyer was sighted. He was the last man out of the boat. The destroyer approached cautiously to windward, but was unable to lower a boat due to the high seas. Instead the crew threw life rings and lines over the side. The destroyer came so close to our bow that Matrose Kirschbaum was able to leap aboard. Moments later the destroyer rammed the UB-81, sinking it instantly.

Of the seven men who were outside when the UB-81 sank, six were picked up. The seventh and last man out, Bories, died before he could be rescued. The British destroyers remained in the area for an hour but there were no more men to pick up.

Maschinistenmaat Paul Redlin, UB-81

At about 1745 we struck a mine that destroyed and flooded the after torpedo room. There was also damage done to the electric motors and the diesel engines. There were no injuries as a result of the explosion, but the boat sank in forty meters.

One torpedo was removed from a forward torpedo tube and made safe. A man was shoved through the tube and he made a line fast to the outboard door. Six men used the line to pull themselves through the tube to the outside. The net cutter was above the water and a man climbed on it to act as a lookout and to signal for help.

Sometime after 2200 a British patrol boat came near, but changed course and went away. Just before midnight two destroyers came along and illuminated us with searchlights. A half an hour later another destroyer, number P-28 arrived, came along the starboard side and rammed us. The blow drove the bow under and our boat disappeared with the torpedo door open. At the time of the ramming there were six men on the net cutter as lookouts, but one of them managed to jump from the U-boat to the deck of the P-boat. The seventh man who came out through the torpedo tube died of heart attack shortly after he emerged. The destroyers picked up the five swimmers and the body.

Leutnant zur See Hermann Freudendal, UB-81

We were running submerged at twenty meters when a sharp explosion was felt near the stern. There was a small amount of flooding in the after torpedo room, but we assumed the explosion had been a depth charge, so we did not surface. The after bulkheads were holding, the motors were operating, but the main lighting, compass and some instruments were inoperable. We blew tanks 3 and 4 and brought the bow up. The forward depth gauge showed that the forward diving planes were still 9.5 meters below the surface. Both electric motors failed due to continued flooding in the engine room. At 2115 we blew tank 1 to lift the bow higher.

The bow rose above the surface and we withdrew one torpedo from its tube. The outer door was opened and four people were shoved through the tube. The outer opening was 20 centimeters above the water. First a line was rigged and then tackle was rigged to the outer door. Signal lights and flares were sent up. At the captain's command we fired red flares and attracted the attention of four patrol boats. P-32 came alongside to take us off and in maneuvering she rammed the ballast tank. The boat sank instantly.

Matrose Karl Blunk, UB-81

There was a powerful explosion that shook the boat. In fact, it seemed to me there were two explosions, a sort of rum-bum. The captain ordered the tanks blown, but we fell to the bottom. The lights flickered and we went to emergency lighting. The capstan motor was damaged, but other than that there was no damage in the forward torpedo room. Those of us who were forward remained optimistic and were certain that we would come out of this OK. We made jokes about the British and finished our evening meal. We all thought the explosion had been a depth charge.

Shortly came the word that the after torpedo room was flooded. Attempts were made to surface. The tanks were blown, but the boat did not respond and the opinion was that the after ballast tanks had been destroyed. Tank 2 was filled with fuel and an attempt was made to pump it out, but that too failed. They next tried to pump out all our drinking water since we would not need it and it was just extra weight. But that failed too and it seemed that the lines must be broken. Word came forward that emergency plugs were needed aft and at that point those of us in the forward torpedo room knew the boat was lost.

The captain now decided to try raising the bow to the surface and raise the forward deck hatch above the surface. Slowly the bow rose until the forward depth gauge showed eight meters at the forward diving planes. So the forward hatch was still under water.

Then came the command for two seamen to lay aft to the engine room. I went aft and found Redlin and Meyer. They were trying to plug the leaks, but it was an impossible task. Water was spurting through popped rivets in finger-thick jets. There were dozens of holes in the starboard overhead and along the side. And there must have been more that we did not see because you could hear the water pouring in. The water had already risen to the lower lip of the engine room door, and would soon flow over into the engine room.

Everyone except Redlin was ordered to abandon the engine room and go forward. Redlin remained to pull the fuses and then close off the engine room. We went forward and they sealed the petty officers room behind us. It was very difficult to move forward due to the steep up angle. As I passed through the command central I saw the captain, the chief engineer and the navigator sitting on the floor discussing our situation. We all gathered in the forward three compartments.

We now had to remove a torpedo and open the outer door. Removing the torpedo was a hard and nerve-racking job. We rigged a tackle to the after end of the torpedo and lowered it from the tube and attached it to the overhead track. Everyone had to lend a hand. The track gear kept jamming because of the uneven load imposed by the up angle. Torpedoheizersmaat

Tiedt used a hammer to free the jams. The hard work quickly used up the air and we were all breathing very hard.

With the torpedo removed, the captain used up our remaining compressed air to blow the forward ballast tanks again. We still did not know if the outer door was above the water or not. The outer door was opened slowly and there was a rush as the air pressure inside the boat rushed out. We again had fresh air, and no water came down the tube. It seemed our way out was clear.

The captain called for volunteers to go through the tube and Wagner stepped forward. We shoved him up the tube, but he said that he could not reach the outer lip because the angle was too steep. Köhler went into the tube so that Wagner was standing on his shoulders and we shoved them both up the tube. When that did not work, Schröder went in and we shoved all three up the tube. Wagner still could not reach the top, so we placed a block between Schröder's legs and used a gun staff to push them higher. Finally Wagner said that he was outside and the opening was a half meter above the water, and only just the bow was above the surface. The other two went out and rigged a tackle so that we could hoist the rest of the men up the tube. Water came down the tube from time to time and anyone below the tube was wringing wet.

The captain sent the watch officer up next with orders to set a lookout. The navigator followed him and then Matrose Otto. By now the sea was coming down the tube in larger amounts. Shortly Wagner, Köhler and a couple of others came back inside and said they would rather die below than freeze outside.

In the meantime I had shed my oil skins, taken a Morse lantern and several flares, and climbed into the sling. My comrades hauled me up and I never saw them again. Outside it was pitch black and the light at Beachy Head was only faintly visible. The bow stuck up out of the water like a lone rock pinnacle. The watch officer and the navigator were sitting on it, but I did not see anyone else. The sea was breaking over the bow. I found a spot on the net cutter and sat down to wait. It was terribly cold and I was soon sorry that I had shed my oil skins. In a short time my feet were numb.

Shortly the chief engineer came out and brought with him more flares. He asked me if I wanted to go back inside and I said no. While we were sending SOS against the clouds, more men came up. I do not know in what order they arrived, but they were Kirschbaum, Redlin, and Bories.

After a long while a ship appeared headed toward us. We soon recognized it as a British patrol boat, and we did not know if we were all going to be shot or rescued. A second boat appeared and one moved in close, in fact so close that Redlin was able to jump aboard. The seas were so heavy that one minute the deck was above us and the next it was below us.

Then there was a crash as the patrol boat rammed the UB-81. I tried to jump but found myself under water. When I regained the surface our boat was gone. All of us were picked up, but Bories was dead by the time the British fished him out of the water.

Sources

Records, T-1022, Roll 81, PG61841, "Abschrift vom Fragebogen, Emden den 4. November 1919, Marine Ingenieur Johann Denker"; "Auszug aus dem Kriegstagebuch des Marine Ing. d.R. Hans Denker"; "Abschrift aus Fragebogen, Cuxhaven den 9. Oktober 1919, Masch. Maat Paul Redlin"; "Abschrift vom Fragebogen, 26. Oktober 1919, Leutnant zur See d.R. Hermann Freudendal"; and "Erlebnisse auf *UB-81* von Karl Blunk, 15 May 1934."

Spindler, *Der Handelskrieg mit U-Booten,* 4:452–53.

UB-82

Date Lost:	17 April 1918
Commander:	Kapitänleutnant Walter Gustav Becker
Location:	North Channel of Irish Sea
Position:	55°13' N, 5°55' W
Disposition:	Depth Charge, Gunfire

UB-82 departed Helgoland on 7 April 1918 and on 15 April met U-19 in the North Channel west of Rathlin Island. There was no further word from UB-82 and there were no survivors.

Additional Information

Late in the afternoon on 17 April the drifters *Pilot Me* and *Young Fred* were patrolling off Torr Head. A crewman aboard *Pilot Me* spotted a periscope fifty yards off the starboard quarter at 1730. *Pilot Me* dropped four depth charges across the U-boat's track, and fifteen minutes later a U-boat surfaced between *Pilot Me* and *Young Fred.* Both drifters opened fire with their 6-pounder (57-mm) guns, scoring several hits. The U-boat dove and *Young Fred* dropped two depth charges on the spot. A powerful explosion raised a mast-high water column and brought oil and debris to the surface. The drifters picked up two caps that identified the boat as UB-82.

Sources

Records, T-1022, Roll 81, PG61842.
Spindler, *Der Handelskrieg mit U-Booten,* 5:59–60.

UB-83

Date Lost:	10 September 1918
Commander:	Oberleutnant zur See Buntebardt
Location:	North Sea, near Orkney Islands
Position:	58°28' N, 1°50' W (possible)
Disposition:	Depth Charge

UB-83 departed Helgoland on 7 September 1918 for operations off Britain's west coast. UB-83 did not return.

Additional Information

At 0624 on 10 September the destroyer HMS *Ophelia*'s kite balloon observer sighted UB-83 on the surface southwest of the Orkneys. The U-boat dove, *Ophelia* dropped three depth charges set at two hundred feet, and the explosions brought oil to the surface. Later that day *Ophelia* found more oil in a position fifteen miles from the first position, and dropped four more depth charges.

It is impossible to say with certainty that *Ophelia* sank UB-83. Given UB-83's destination and its probable route, the postwar German study concluded that it is possible that *Ophelia* sank it on 10 September.

Sources

Grant, *U-Boats Destroyed*, 103–4.
Records, T-1022, Roll 81, PG61843.
Spindler, *Der Handelskrieg mit U-Booten*, 5:312.

UB-85

Date Lost:	30 April 1918
Commander:	Kapitänleutnant Günther Krech
Location:	North Channel of Irish Sea
Position:	54°47' N, 5°27' W
Disposition:	Accident, Gunfire

UB-85 departed Helgoland on 16 April 1918 for operations in the Irish Sea. At 0400 on 30 April UB-85 was running on the surface when the drifter *Coreopsis* sighted it at a range of about a quarter of a mile. The drifter opened fire and the U-boat dove. As it went under the conning tower hatch was not properly closed and dogged down. As the boat reached twenty meters, massive flooding in the conning tower and the control room shorted the batteries, shut down the electric motors and pumps, and created chlorine gas. Kapitänleutnant Günther Krech blew the tanks with compressed air and surfaced. The patrol boats opened fire on UB-85. The captain and chief engineer scuttled the boat and the British patrol boats took off the entire crew.

Kapitänleutnant Günther Krech, UB-85

At 0400 on 30 April 1918 there was a full moon and the visibility was excellent and there was a low, moderate swell. We could see many patrol boats in the area and as one of them came to a crossing situation, we crash dived. The navigator reported the conning tower hatch closed, but as we went under heavy flooding occurred through the hatch. The water flow was so powerful that it was impossible to close the conning tower hatch or the lower hatch into the control room. There was a strong build up of chlorine gas and the bilge pumps failed. We blew the tanks and surfaced, down sharply by the bow. Enemy patrol boats fired on us, but we could not return fire because our ammunition was under water and the water was rising in the boat. The crew was taken off in rowboats. The UB-85 along with all secret documents and codebooks sank in 80 meters.

Oberheizer Julius Gottschämmer, UB-85

On 30 April 1918 at 0400 we were ordered to crash dive to avoid an oncoming patrol boat. During the diving maneuver the conning tower hatch was not properly closed and it opened as we passed twelve meters and water poured in. It must be noted here that extra cables had been run in. One of the new cables went from the conning tower to the compass repeater in the control room. The other passed through the watertight door from the control room to the officers' compartment to supply power for a heater in that compartment. Kapitänleutnant Krech had ordered those new cables installed, but they were unnecessary because there were already existing cables in place for those things. The result was that the new cables allowed water to flow unhindered from the conning tower, into the control room and then into the officers' compartment. When the water reached the officers' compartment it shorted the batteries that were below that deck.

We were seventeen men in the engine room, and as the boat dropped by the stern, I tried to speak to the control room through the speaking tube. When I opened the flap, water shot out of the speaking tube with such force that I thought the control room must be completely under water. We opened the watertight door into the control room and managed to make our way against the in-rushing water into the control room and exit the boat through the conning tower.

We signaled a British patrol boat that continued to fire at us, and we waited an hour and a half until they took us off.

Steuermannsmaat Franz Bucholz, UB-85

On 30 April 1918 after British patrols had forced us repeatedly to crash dive, we were again surprised on the surface. We dove and conning tower hatch lugs failed so that we dove to twenty meters with an open hatch. We blew the tanks and surfaced, but it was touch and go, and the only way we could stay on the surface was by going ahead full speed. Finally, after we had risen completely, the boat remained afloat.

We signaled a British patrol boat that immediately opened fire on us and scored a hit below the waterline. Pretty soon five drifters arrived and took off the entire crew. The captain and the navigator scuttled the boat.

Oberheizer Probst, UB-85

On 30 April 1918 British destroyers surprised us and we had to crash dive. At sixty meters the conning tower hatch failed and water poured into the boat. The electric motors stopped, the pumps failed and we had to blow the tanks to surface. The captain and the chief engineer scuttled the boat while the British destroyers and fishing boats took us aboard.

Sources

Grant, *U-Boats Destroyed,* 113.

Records, T-1022, Roll 81, PG61845, "Bericht des Kommandanten von *UB-85*"; "Auszugsweise Abschrift von Fragebogen, Oberheizer Julius Gottschämmer, Wilhelmshaven, den 29. September 1919"; "Abschrift aus Fragebogen, Steuermanns-
maat Franz Bucholz, Wilhelmshaven, den 23. November 1919"; and "Abschrift
aus Fragebogen, Oberheizer Probst, Bremen, den 14. November 1919."

Spindler, *Der Handelskrieg mit U-Booten,* 5:61.

UB-89

Date Lost:	21 October 1918
Commander:	Kapitänleutnant Gude
Location:	Atlantic, off Ireland's west coast
Position:	54°21' N, 10°10' W
Disposition:	Accident

UB-89 was a hard luck boat. It made only two patrols, one to the Shetlands and the second to the south coast of Ireland. During the second patrol heavy seas washed a sailor overboard, and the navigator dove over the side to save him. While the crew fired pistols to drive off the sharks around the two swimmers, the navigator brought the sailor back to the boat and the crew hauled him aboard. As the unconscious sailor lay on the deck, another wave swept over the boat and carried him away again. This time the watch officer went after him, but the sailor was dead by the time the crew got him back aboard.

On 21 October 1918 UB-89 was entering the Kaiser Wilhelm Canal at the Kiel end when the light cruiser SMS *Frankfurt* rammed and sank it. Two petty officers and four seamen were killed in the accident. UB-89 saw no more war service. It was raised and towed to Britain on 7 March 1919. The British scrapped it in 1920.

Sources

Records, T-1022, Roll 41, PG61849.
Spindler, *Der Handelskrieg mit U-Booten,* 5:297–98.

UB-90

Date Lost:	16 October 1918
Commander:	Oberleutnant zur See von Mayer
Location:	North Sea
Position:	57°55' N, 10°27' E
Disposition:	Torpedo

UB-90 departed Kiel on 23 September 1918 for operations in the Bristol Channel. On 13 October Oberleutnant zur See von Mayer reported that he was forty-five nautical miles north of the Shetlands and that he was having propulsion and diving control problems. He added that he was making for the Faeroes where he would make repairs. In three days he expected to be operating off Peterhead. On 15 October von Mayer sent another radio message saying he was seventy nautical miles west of Stavanger, Norway, and he wanted an escort to meet him on 18 October at the entrance to Store Belt. He did not make it. The next day the British submarine L-12 torpedoed UB-90 at the point where the Skagerrak becomes the Kattegat and sank it with all hands.

Sources

Records, T-1022, Roll 41, PG61849; T-1022, Roll 71, PG61934, "Londoner Prisenger-ichtsverhandlungen wegen vierzehn deutscher U-Boote."

Spindler, *Der Handelskrieg mit U-Booten,* 5:298.

UB-103

Date Lost:	16 September 1918
Commander:	Kapitänleutnant Paul Hundius
Location:	Dover Strait
Position:	50°52' N, 1°27' E
Disposition:	Depth Charge or Mine

UB-103 departed Zeebrugge on 14 August 1918 for operations off the west coast of France. UB-103 did not return and there were no survivors.

Additional Information

According to the British, on 16 September the airship SS-Z1 spotted and reported an oil track on the surface seven nautical miles off Gris Nez. Six drifters joined the hunt, and dropped depth charges that caused two heavy explosions. Because UB-103 was in the Folkestone–Gris Nez deep mine barrage area and there was a thirty minute spread between the depth charging and the last explosion, it seems probable that UB-103 hit a mine. If so, it was the last U-boat destroyed in the barrier during World War I. British divers visited the wreck of UB-103 and made a positive identification.

Sources

Chatterton, *Beating the U-Boats,* 150–51.
Grant, *U-Boats Destroyed,* 92–93.
Records, T-1022, Roll 42, PG61865.
Spindler, *Der Handelskrieg mit U-Booten,* 5:96–97.

UB-104

Date Lost:	September 1918
Commander:	Oberleutnant zur See Bieber
Location:	English Channel, Irish Sea, or North Sea
Position:	Unknown
Disposition:	Verschollen

UB-104 departed Zeebrugge on 6 September 1918 for operations in the English Channel. Oberleutnant zur See Bieber took the northern route around Scotland, and on 11 September UB-104 and U-57 exchanged recognition signals at the entrance to the North Channel in the Irish Sea. That was the last anyone heard from UB-104.

Additional Information

One source says that UB-104 went down near Fair Island, and another says that it hit a mine in the Northern Mine Barrage on 19 September 1918. Both suggestions offer reasonable explanations for the boat's loss, but no one knows exactly how UB-104 was destroyed.

Sources

Gibson and Prendergast, *The German Submarine War,* 320.
Grant, *U-Boats Destroyed,* 104.
Records, T-1022, Roll 41, PG61859.
Spindler, *Der Handelskrieg mit U-Booten,* 5:122–23.

UB-106

Date Lost:	15 March 1918
Commander:	Oberleutnant zur See Thielmann
Location:	Baltic Sea
Position:	54°42' N, 10°9' E
Disposition:	Accident

UB-106 was commissioned on 7 February 1918 and sank during a trial dive in the Baltic on 15 March 1918. All thirty-five crewmen died. The salvage vessel *Vulkan* raised UB-106 on 18 March, but the boat was not returned to service. It was delivered to the British on 26 November 1918 and they scrapped it in 1921. Oberleutnant zur See Thielmann is the same officer who was commanding UC-69 on the night of 6 December 1917 when U-96 rammed UC-69.

Sources

Records, T-1022, Roll 41, PG61861.
Spindler, *Der Handelskrieg mit U-Booten,* 5:103.

UB-107

Date Lost: 27 July 1918
Commander: Kapitänleutnant von Prittwitz und Gaffron
Location: North Sea, off Britain's east coast
Position: Unknown
Disposition: Verschollen

UB-107 departed Zeebrugge just after midnight on 26 July 1918 for operations in the Hoofden and off the east coast of Britain. UB-107 did not return and there were no survivors.

Additional Information

The British say that on 27 July at 2100 the trawler *Calvia* was southeast of Whitby in position 54°23' N, 0°24' W when a U-boat broached close by. The trawler and the destroyer depth charged the U-boat and *Calvia* stopped after the first barrage to listen on its hydrophones. The operator heard propeller noises and the HMS *Vanessa* dropped another string of depth charges. The pounding continued for two hours after which oil and air rose to the surface. The group dropped more depth charges. The next morning a headless body was seen floating in the area.

On that same day at 2325 a U-boat attacked a convoy in position 53°52' N, 0°10' W, and torpedoed two ships—the Swedish SS *John Retting* (1,999 tons) and the British SS *Chloris* (984 tons). However, the attack on the convoy occurred two hours after and thirty-two nautical miles from the scene of the depth charge attack.

A postwar German study concluded that UB-107 could have been in either place, but not in both places. According to the Germans, if UB-107 was the U-boat involved in the depth charge attack it could not have attacked the convoy because the depth charging lasted until about 2300. For UB-107 to have survived the depth charge attack and have also attacked the convoy thirty-two miles distant at 2325 would have required a surface speed of over sixty-four knots. UB-107 could make only thirteen knots at best. Vice versa, if UB-107 did actually attack the convoy, it could not have been sunk during the depth charge attack. The German study assumed that the times given in both accounts, as well as the positions, were correct.

217

Sources

Grant, *U-Boats Destroyed,* 128.
Records, T-1022, Roll 41, PG61862.
Spindler, *Der Handelskrieg mit U-Booten,* 5:126–27.

UB-108

Date Lost:	July 1918
Commander:	Kapitänleutnant Wilhelm Amberger
Location:	Dover Strait
Position:	51°0' N, 1°9' E (Probable)
Disposition:	Mine

UB-108 departed Ostend on 2 July 1918 for operations in the western section of the English Channel. UB-108 did not return.

Additional Information

On 14 July British patrols saw a powerful explosion accompanied by oil and bubbles in the Folkestone–Gris Nez barrage. The Germans believed that the explosion destroyed either UB-108 or UC-77. On 8 and 11 August, British divers found two wrecks in the barrage. One wreck could not be identified at all. The divers reported that on the other wreck the forward section from the bow back to the gun appeared to have been blown off by an internal explosion. This might lead one to believe the wreck was a UC-boat because only minelayers would exhibit such damage. But on 12 August divers recovered a 105-mm gun, thus eliminating UC-77 because it carried an 88-mm gun. UB-108 carried a 105-mm gun, but it was not a minelayer.

Sources

Grant, *U-Boat Intelligence,* 97–98.
Records, T-1022, Roll 41, PG61863.
Spindler, *Der Handelskrieg mit U-Booten,* 5:97.

UB-109

Date Lost:	**29 August 1918**
Commander:	**Oberleutnant zur See Ramien**
Location:	**Dover Strait**
Position:	**51°4' N, 1°14' E**
Disposition:	**Mine**

UB-109 departed Zeebrugge on 27 July 1918 to conduct operations off the Azores. On 16 August it started its homeward trip and arrived off Dungeness at 0200 on 29 August. Oberleutnant zur See Ramien intended to go through the Folkestone–Gris Nez barrage by passing through the Folkestone gate. Instead he went outside the steamer channel and entered a controlled minefield. A mine exploded, blowing off the stern and sinking UB-109 in one hundred feet of water.

Oberleutnant zur See Ramien, UB-109

I heard loud shouting in the boat and then everything was still. The explosion had thrown me against the periscope and it took a while for me to regain my senses. I had fallen into the periscope well, and I crawled back into the conning tower where I found the navigator and the helmsman. I tried to talk to them but the noise of released compressed air drowned out our voices. Even shouting was impossible.

The boat was flooded up to the conning tower. I climbed up the ladder to the hatch and the navigator stood on the rungs right below me. When I tried to open the hatch it blew open and the navigator and I were blown into the opening where we became wedged together. It took thirty seconds of hard struggle to free ourselves, but the navigator was able to pull himself back inside the conning tower. That freed me and I rose to the surface.

I rose quickly and at no time did I have any feeling that I was running out of air. The compressed air in my lungs flowed out naturally and in large amounts. I reached the surface and right behind me came the helmsman, the navigator and the radioman who was unable to explain how he had managed to reach the conning tower.

I was astounded to find five other men on the surface. The torpedomen had opened the forward hatch immediately following the explosion and these five men were by chance blown through the hatch. Included in those five men was a machinist who had been carried through all the compartments on the crest of the rising water and shoved out the forward hatch.

I shed my heavy leather coat and boots. We were swimming for about three quarters of an hour before a British patrol boat that had been attracted by the explosion arrived and picked us up.

Additional Information

At each end of the barrier, between the gates and the shore, the British laid controlled minefields in which operators ashore could selectively detonate the mines. The heart of the system was a device called the Bragg Loop that was an electrical cable laid in loops on the seabed that sent a signal to a galvanometer every time a steel hull vessel entered the minefield. An operator ashore read the galvanometer, determined where the ship was in the minefield, and detonated the mine or mines nearest the indicating loop.

On 29 August 1918 a Folkestone hydrophone operator reported fast running propellers proceeding to the eastward. About fifteen minutes later the minefield operator saw the needle of his galvanometer swing, and he pressed the button. The results were dramatic and instantaneous. An enormous explosion accompanied by a powerful rumbling noise lifted the sea surface and produced a tall water column. Several minutes later nine men came to the surface and forty-five minutes later a trawler picked up eight of them. They were the very lucky survivors of UB-109.

Sources

Cowie, *Mines, Minelayers and Minelaying,* 76.
Spindler, *Der Handelskrieg mit U-Booten,* 5:97–98.

UB-110

Date Lost:	19 July 1918
Commander:	Kapitänleutnant Werner Fürbringer
Location:	North Sea, near Dogger Bank
Position:	54°39' N, 0°55' W
Disposition:	Depth Charge, Ramming

UB-110 departed Zeebrugge on 4 July 1918 for operations in the Hoofden and off Britain's east coast. On 19 July it attacked a convoy three nautical miles south of Hartlepool, and motor launch ML-263 depth charged UB-110. The explosions jammed the forward diving planes and caused the U-boat to broach. While it was on the surface the destroyer HMS *Garry* rammed it and UB-110 sank. Kapitänleutnant Werner Fürbringer managed to bring UB-110 back to the surface by blowing the tanks, but *Garry* rammed it again; this time UB-110 went down for good.

Kapitänleutnant Werner Fürbringer, UB-110

During an attack on a British convoy three nautical miles south of Hartlepool a British patrol boat dropped a depth charge that seriously damaged the UB-110 and blew her to the surface. It was impossible to dive because the forward diving planes were jammed hard up and flooding the trim tanks did not work. A destroyer rammed us and we sank. I blew the tanks and regained the surface. While the crew was abandoning the UB-110, another destroyer rammed us at the conning tower and the boat sank.

After the boat sank there was plenty of time for the men in the water to be shot, and they were even hit with heavy lumps of coal. It was not until the Neutrals arrived that the firing stopped. From thirty-two swimmers, only thirteen lived. The largest number floated dead in their life vests.

Additional Information

On 14 July 1919 a British prize court awarded HMS *Garry* a bounty of £180 for the destruction of UB-110. The prize court based the award on the belief that there had been thirty-six crewmen aboard UB-110, and the court set a head price of £5 per man. Actually, there were thirty-four men and officers aboard UB-110, so the prize court had overpaid the bounty.

Sources

Gibson and Prendergast, *The German Submarine War,* 313–14.

Records, T-1022, Roll 42, PG61865, "Abschrift aus Fragebogen, Wilhelmshaven, den 27. Oktober 1919, Kapitänleutnant Werner Fürbringer"; T-1022, Roll 71, PG61934, "Londoner Prisengerichtsverhandlungen wegen vierzehn deutscher U-Boote."

Spindler, *Der Handelskrieg mit U-Booten,* 5:127.

UB-113

Date Lost:	September 1918
Commander:	Oberleutnant zur See Pilzecker
Location:	North Sea
Position:	Unknown
Disposition:	Verschollen

UB-113, in company with UB-111, departed Zeebrugge on 19 September 1918 for operations in the English Channel. UB-113 did not return and there were no survivors. The British were not able to offer any firm suggestions about what happened to UB-113. It is possible that the boat hit a mine in the Northern Mine Barrage while outbound.

Sources

Records, T-1022, Roll 42, PG61868.
Spindler, *Der Handelskrieg mit U-Booten,* 5:131–32.

UB-114

Date Lost:	13 May 1918
Commander:	Oberleutnant zur See Berlin
Location:	Kiel Harbor
Disposition:	Accident

Commissioned on 13 May 1918, UB-114 was conducting diving tests in Kiel harbor when it suffered a diving accident and sank. Seven crewmen were killed. The salvage vessel *Vulkan* raised UB-114, but it was not returned to service. It was surrendered to the French on 26 November 1918 and they used it as an antisubmarine weapons target. The French scrapped UB-114 at Toulon in 1921.

Sources

Records, T-1022, Roll 42, PG61869.
Spindler, *Der Handelskrieg mit U-Booten,* 5:103.

UB-115

Date Lost:	29 September 1918
Commander:	Oberleutnant zur See Reinhold Thomsen
Location:	North Sea
Position:	Unknown
Disposition:	Verschollen

UB-115 departed Zeebrugge on 18 September 1918 for operations off Britain's east coast. UB-115 did not return.

Additional Information

According to the British, on 29 September at 1330 the British airship R-29 spotted an oil slick north of Sunderland in position 55°14' N, 1°22' W. R-29 summoned the destroyers HMS *Ouse* and HMS *Star* and six trawlers to the spot and they pounded the area with depth charges for several hours. Later the British dragged the area and found an obstruction that they concluded was a wrecked U-boat. A postwar German study concluded that it was possible that UB-115 was off Sunderland on that date, but the British account was too vague to form a definite conclusion that UB-115 was actually sunk there.

Sources

Gibson and Prendergast, *The German Submarine War,* 321.
Grant, *U-Boats Destroyed,* 129.
Records, T-1022, Roll 42, PG61870.
Spindler, *Der Handelskrieg mit U-Booten,* 5:99.

UB-116

Date Lost: 28 October 1918
Commander: Oberleutnant zur See Hans Joachim Emsmann
Location: Orkney Islands, entering Scapa Flow
Position: 58°50' N, 3°4' W
Disposition: Controlled Minefield

UB-116 was the last U-boat destroyed during World War I. On 21 October 1918 the Admiralstab sent a worldwide radio order to all U-boat commands and U-boats directing them to cease anti-shipping attacks and to return home to Germany. At the time the German civilian government under Theobald von Bethmann-Hollweg had opened negotiations with the Entente to end the war and the German military was preparing for the stand down. But the German navy intended to go out with a last hurrah, and was planning a major fleet engagement that employed all the battle units of the Kaiserliche Marine in an attack on the Grand Fleet. The final act was not carried out because of widespread mutiny in the German navy at the close of the war. However, UB-116 did make its final effort as planned.

UB-116 departed Helgoland on the evening of 25 October 1918 with orders to attack the Grand Fleet in Scapa Flow in an attempt to "weaken the enemy as much as possible before the decisive battle." It was to enter the fleet anchorage via Hoxa Sound, essentially the same route that U-18 had used in 1914, because the Germans believed that the Hoxa Sound entrance was not mined. They were wrong.

The British had laid a controlled minefield that included shore-based hydrophones, which provided early warning of an approaching U-boat. The Hoxa Sound hydrophones picked up UB-116 at 2121 on 28 October and alerted the minefield control operator. All other movement in the area was stopped so that there would be no outside interference with the hydrophones that were tracking UB-116's progress.

At 2332 the galvanometer indicated that a U-boat was in the minefield, and the operator flipped the switch. A row of mines exploded and UB-116's motor noises ceased. The next morning the surface was covered with oil and air bubbles were rising steadily. Patrol boats dropped depth charges that brought debris to the surface, including a jacket. British divers visited the wreck on 29 October and on 4 November they returned and recovered UB-116's logbook.

Sources

Grant, *U-Boat Intelligence,* 60.
Grant, *U-Boats Destroyed,* 138–39.
Records, T-1022, Roll 42, PG61871.
Spindler, *Der Handelskrieg mit U-Booten,* 5:338–40.

UB-119

Date Lost:	April 1918
Commander:	Oberleutnant zur See Walter Kolbe
Location:	North Sea
Position:	Unknown
Disposition:	Verschollen

UB-119 was commissioned on 9 February 1918. After its workup, UB-119 departed Helgoland on 27 April 1918 for operations in the North Sea, off Britain's west coast, and in the Irish Sea. On 30 April it reported being ninety-five nautical miles west-southwest of Lindesnes, Norway. That was the last thing anyone heard from UB-119. It did not return and there were no survivors. The Northern Mine Barrage was not yet in place when UB-119 disappeared and its last reported position was well outside the British minefields off Helgoland. UB-119 was a new boat with a new crew and it was Oberleutnant zur See Walter Kolbe's first command. It is possible that inexperience or technical problems resulted in a diving accident from which Kolbe and his crew could not recover.

Sources

Records, T-1022, Roll 42, PG61874.
Spindler, *Der Handelskrieg mit U-Booten,* 5:38.

UB-123

Date Lost:	October 1918
Commander:	Oberleutnant zur See Ramm
Location:	North Sea
Position:	Unknown
Disposition:	Verschollen

UB-123 departed Helgoland on 26 September 1918 for operations in the Irish Sea. UB-123 did not return and there were no survivors.

Additional Information

On 18 October at 0910 outbound UB-125 copied a radio message from homeward-bound UB-123 asking for the best route to use when passing through the Northern Mine Barrage. UB-125 provided the information and the acknowledgment was the last anyone heard from UB-123. The Americans reported that UB-123 hit a mine in the Northern Mine Barrage on 18 October and the British reported that UB-123 hit a mine in the Northern Mine Barrage on 19 October off the Orkneys. There is no way to determine which of the two reports is correct, but it is very probable that UB-123 was the last U-boat destroyed in the Northern Mine Barrage.

Sources

Records, T-1022, Roll 42, PG61878.
Spindler, *Der Handelskrieg mit U-Booten,* 5:320.

UB-124

Date Lost:	20 July 1918
Commander:	Oberleutnant zur See Wutsdorff
Location:	Atlantic, at North Channel entrance
Position:	55°43' N, 7°51' W
Disposition:	Technical Problem

UB-124 was commissioned on 22 April 1918 and completed its sea trials on 1 July. On 6 July UB-124 departed Helgoland and took the northern route to its operations area in the Irish Sea. On 20 July just before 0900 UB-124 sighted SS *Justicia* under tow, and between 1100 and 1130 it fired two torpedoes at a range of eight hundred meters. When the torpedoes left the tubes, UB-124 broached, exposing the conning tower. The torpedoes struck the steamer and exploded. At that moment a through-hull fitting in the engine room failed and flooding caused the boat to sink to the bottom in ninety meters of water. As UB-124 lay on the bottom the destroyer escorts for SS *Justicia* dropped sixty-five depth charges; none caused any damage.

During the time on the bottom the water rose in the bilge until it was over the floor plates. At 1800 Oberleutnant zur See Wutsdorff made the decision to surface, but he wanted to first rise to periscope depth to be sure the destroyers were gone. When he tried to lift the boat off the bottom he found that UB-124 had taken so much water that he had considerable difficulty getting it off the bottom. Wutsdorff decided to blow the tanks and take his chances with whatever he might find on the surface, but as the boat rose the stern dropped sharply, causing the water in the bilge to inundate the electric motors and stop them. When UB-124 came to the surface, Wutsdorff's worst fears were realized because the boat surfaced close to three British destroyers that were lying dead in the water. They immediately got under way and opened fire.

Unable to dive and outgunned, Oberleutnant zur See Wutsdorff decided to scuttle the boat. The chief engineer and the watch officer remained below to carry out that assignment while the crew went over the side. The chief engineer and the watch officer were not seen again. UB-124 sank in position 55°43' N, 7°51' W.

Additional Information

SS *Justicia* sank on 20 July 1918 at 1240 in position 55°38' N, 7°39' W.

Source

Spindler, *Der Handelskrieg mit U-Booten,* 5:321–22.

UB-127

Date Lost:	September 1918
Commander:	Oberleutnant zur See Scheffler
Location:	North Sea
Position:	Unknown
Disposition:	Verschollen

UB-127 was commissioned on 1 June 1918. After its workup, it departed Brunsbüttel on 4 September for operations off Britain's west coast. On 9 September UB-127 reported being in the North Sea south of Fair Island, and that was the last anyone heard from it. UB-127 was a new boat with an inexperienced crew, and it is possible that it suffered a diving accident. It is also possible that it hit a mine in the Northern Mine Barrage on its return trip, but there is no evidence to support either possibility.

Sources

Records, T-1022, Roll 43, PG61822.
Spindler, *Der Handelskrieg mit U-Booten,* 5:280.

UB-129

Date Lost:	28 October 1918
Commander:	Kapitänleutnant Karl Neumann
Location:	Fiume
Position:	45°19' N, 14°26' E
Disposition:	Scuttled

UB-129 departed Kiel on 4 September 1918 en route to Cattaro. During the long trip the starboard diesel engine broke down, which greatly reduced surface speed. Despite having only one diesel, Kapitänleutnant Karl Neumann attacked a convoy on 16 September, and made four stop-and-visit searches under the Prize Regulations on 19 September. On 1 October just after passing through the Otranto Strait an enemy submarine fired two torpedoes at UB-129. But the U-boat managed to avoid both. It arrived in Cattaro on 2 October 1918.

On 21 October 1918 the Admiralstab ordered all U-boats that were ready for sea to return to Germany, and on 23 October the Germans began evacuating Pola and Cattaro. UB-129's diesel engine repairs were not complete so the crew blew it up at Fiume on 30 October 1918.

Sources

Records, T-1022, Roll 40, PG61808.
Spindler, *Der Handelskrieg mit U-Booten,* 5:205–6, 227.

An unidentified type I UB-boat. The presence of an early type of net cutter indicates that the picture was probably taken in the winter of 1915. The type I UB-boats—UB-1 to UB-15—were the smallest U-boats built during World War I. Also note the absence of any identifying number. Not all U-boats displayed a number and those that did had it either on the conning tower or on the bow.

A type I UB-boat outboard and a type I UC-boat inboard. The squares on a UC-boat's forward deck are the loading hatches for the mines. Neither of these boats is displaying an identifying number, making it impossible to identify them positively. The absence of identifying numbers is one reason that the fate of many boats remains uncertain.

Two type II UB-boats. Note, again, that there are no identifying numbers. The different conning tower designs are a result of builder preference.

UC-5 interior. The interior arrangement in UC-5 explains why so many UC-boats blew up on their own mines. As the UC-boat passed over the dropped mine, the depth setting and release mechanism sometimes failed and the mine would rise quickly enough to hit the UC-boat near the stern.

UC-5 was stranded and captured on 27 April 1916. The British salvaged UC-5 and put it on display.

utſches U-Boot ſtellt ein
remder Flagge faḥrendes,
liſches Handelsſchiff.

This staged German propaganda photo was intended to illustrate the so-called illegal use of neutral flags. The supposedly stopped British freighter is flying the U.S. flag. But what the photo really shows is how dangerous it was for a U-boat to surface near its victim. If that freighter were in fact a decoy vessel, the unidentified U-boat would have been sunk moments after this picture was taken.

Eight U-boats, on the eve of World War I. *Front row, left to right:* U-13 verschollen in August 1914, U-5 verschollen in December 1914, U-11 verschollen in December 1914, U-3 scrapped after the war, and U-16 scuttled in the North Sea on 8 February 1919. *Back row, left to right:* U-9 scrapped in 1919, U-12 sunk by an explosive sweep on 10 March 1915, and U-6 sunk on 15 September 1915 when E-16 torpedoed it.

U-33 meets UB-7 in the Mediterranean sometime between 4 and 12 December 1915. UB-7 was lost somewhere in the Black Sea in October 1916. U-33 was surrendered to the British in January 1919.

UC-39 is shown sinking after HMS *Thrasher* depth charged it on 8 February 1917 and drove it to the surface. Many crewmen, including the captain, were killed when *Thrasher* shelled UC-33 after it surfaced. *Thrasher* is in the background.

UC-44 is salvaged and beached after hitting a mine off Waterford on 5 August 1917. The British used radio intelligence to lure UC-44 onto a mine that UC-42 had laid in June 1917. British divers recovered many valuable documents and codebooks from the wreck.

U-28 was the victim of a bizarre twist of fate. On 2 September 1917 U-28 fired an 88-mm round into the ammunition-laden SS *Olive Branch,* causing the cargo to explode. The resulting blast obliterated *Olive Branch* and sank the surfaced U-boat. No one from U-28 survived.

U-58 is shown sinking after USS *Fanning* and USS *Nicholson* depth charged it and drove it to the surface on 17 November 1917. The Germans surrendered and the American destroyers picked them up.

UB-22, a type II UB-boat, headed out to sea from Helgoland. UB-22 hit a British mine on 19 January 1918 and went down with all hands.

A typical *Deutschland*-class U-cruiser. The class was originally designed to be submarine freighters that would break the blockade and reestablish trade with the United States. Instead, six of them were completed as war boats, and *Deutschland* was converted to become U-155. E-35 torpedoed U-154 in the Atlantic on 11 May 1918. There were no survivors. U-156 vanished without a trace in September 1918 and may have been a victim of the Northern Mine Barrage.

PART 3

UC-Boats UC-1 to UC-91

UC-1

Date Lost:	July 1917
Commander:	Oberleutnant zur See Mildenstein
Location:	Dover Strait or English Channel
Position:	Unknown
Disposition:	Verschollen

UC-1 departed Zeebrugge on 18 July 1917 to lay mines off Calais. UC-1 did not return and the cause of its loss is unknown. There are no close, or even possible, matches to be made with British and French antisubmarine actions during this period. The most likely explanation is that UC-1 blew up on one of its own mines during the laying process. It is also possible that the boat hit a British or French mine. UC-1 had been in service since 7 May 1915 and its mines had accounted for 59,088 tons of shipping. Oberleutnant zur See Mildenstein had been in command since early June 1917, and his crew was experienced.

Sources

Records, T-1022, Roll 81, PG61885.
Spindler, *Der Handelskrieg mit U-Booten*, 4:307.

UC-2

Date Lost:	2 July 1915
Commander:	Oberleutnant zur See Mey
Location:	Hoofden, off Britain's east coast at Lowestoft
Position:	52°28' N, 1°48' E
Disposition:	Ramming, Own Mine

UC-2 departed Zeebrugge on 29 June 1915 to lay mines off Lowestoft. On 2 July SS *Cottingham* accidentally rammed UC-2 off Lowestoft, slashing a three-foot opening in the pressure hull just forward of the conning tower. UC-2 sank. Capt. Colin Mitchell reported the incident and minesweepers dragged the area. They fouled an obstruction and a powerful underwater explosion occurred. On 3 July a diver found UC-2 in eight fathoms lying on the bottom with a 45° list. He saw the damage caused by *Cottingham,* and he found that one of UC-2's mines had exploded, doing extensive damage aft of the conning tower. Apparently the mine had been discharged from its chute, which was forward of the conning tower, and ended up near or under UC-2's stern. When the minesweepers fouled the wreck, they shifted it so that it made contact with the mine.

Sources

Grant, *U-Boat Intelligence,* 13.
Records, T-1022, Roll 82, PG61887.
Spindler, *Der Handelskrieg mit U-Booten,* 2:229.

UC-3

Date Lost:	26 May 1916
Commander:	Oberleutnant zur See Kreysern
Location:	Off Zeebrugge
Position:	51°35' N, 3°8' E (approximate)
Disposition:	Mine

UC-3 departed Zeebrugge on 25 May 1916 to lay mines off the south Aldborough Nappes buoy. During the early morning hours of 26 May UC-1, UC-3, and UC-6 were often in sight of each other; at 1100 UC-3 and UC-6 exchanged light signals. That afternoon UC-1 was on the edge of a newly laid British minefield off Zeebrugge when it saw a UC-boat surface nearby and then immediately dive. UC-1 reported the boat as UC-3.

Both UC-1 and UC-6 returned safely to Zeebrugge, having passed through the minefield, but UC-3 did not and there were no survivors. Because the three boats were in repeated contact with each other throughout 26 May and all three were accounted for as they arrived at the edge of the British minefield, it is safe to assume that UC-3 hit a mine and went down with all hands.

Sources

Records, T-1022, Roll 82, PG61892.
Spindler, *Der Handelskrieg mit U-Booten,* 3:189–90.

UC-4

Date Lost:	**2 October 1918**
Commander:	**Oberleutnant zur See E. Schmidt**
Location:	**Zeebrugge**
Position:	**51°21' N, 3°12' E**
Disposition:	**Scuttled**

On 29 September 1918 the Germans began evacuating Flanders and dismantling their naval facilities at Bruges, Zeebrugge, and Ostend. Boats that could not be made ready for return to Germany under their own power were destroyed with explosives. On 5 October the Germans scuttled UC-4 off the Zeebrugge mole.

Additional Information

By 1918 UC-4 was an old boat of very limited capability, and war demands had kept it on operations long past the time for a major overhaul. It carried out its last minelaying operation on 16 July 1918 north of Shipwash, and then returned to Bruges for a major engine overhaul. The work was not completed when the order came to evacuate the base.

Sources

Records, T-1022, Roll 78, PG61739.
Spindler, *Der Handelskrieg mit U-Booten,* 5:149.

UC-5

Date Lost:	27 April 1916
Commander:	Oberleutnant zur See Mohrbutter
Location:	Britain's east coast, near Harwich
Position:	51°59' N, 1°38' E
Disposition:	Stranded, Scuttled

UC-5 departed Zeebrugge on 24 April 1916 to lay its twelve mines one nautical mile east of the Shipwash Lightship. As it approached North Hinder Lightship, Oberleutnant zur See Mohrbutter encountered increasingly strong British patrols that included entire destroyer groups. The surface activity forced him to return to Zeebrugge until things cooled down.

That evening he again put to sea, but turned back because sea phosphorescence was so bright that the glow from the bow wave blinded the lookouts. He had concluded that his bow wave and wake were so luminous that it would be impossible to pass unseen through the British patrols.

UC-5 made its third departure on the morning of 25 April, and things started badly. A British destroyer forced it to dive at 1000 and remain down for four hours. UC-5 surfaced at 1400 and found itself almost on top of an explosive net. Mohrbutter tried to blow a hole in the net with scuttling charges. While his crew was doing that a French seaplane surprised and attacked them. UC-5 dove. Thirty minutes later it surfaced and proceeded along the net looking for the end so that it could go around it. By 1600 Mohrbutter had still not found the end of the net and he now concluded that he had lost so much time that his mission was now pointless. He returned to Zeebrugge at 1900.

On 26 April UC-5 started its fourth attempt to lay mines off the Shipwash Lightship. A thick fog reduced visibility to nearly zero and Mohrbutter never did see the Thornton Bank buoy or the North Hinder Lightship. Unable to find his navigational references, he tried to find the Galloper Lightship, but instead found a lightship he could not identify.

At 2330 on 26 April UC-5 was pushing through the fog on the surface when it ran hard aground. Mohrbutter estimated that he was east of Shipwash when the boat grounded. As the tide continued to fall, the U-boat was left high and dry on the sand; only the fog prevented British patrols from seeing it. While they waited for the flood tide, the crew threw as much weight over the side as possible, and at 0600 on 27 April, Mohrbutter used all his engines' power to back the boat into deep water.

UC-5 lay on the bottom and waited for slack water. Mohrbutter rose once to periscope depth in an attempt to fix his position and did see a lightship through his periscope, but he was unable to identify it. His rest on the bottom was disturbed by numerous patrols that plowed around on the surface trailing explosive sweeps, which makes one think that the British knew he was in the area.

At 0915 Mohrbutter rose to periscope depth and steered toward the lightship to identify it, but his passage was hampered by strong surface patrols that included several destroyers. When he got close enough to the lightship to make out more detail, he was still unable to identify it. He gave up and shaped a course toward deeper water.

At 1015 his hunt for deeper water ended abruptly when UC-5's bow rammed into a sandbar with such force that the bow rose above the surface. Mohrbutter backed off and ran aground again. Now he surfaced to see where he was and immediately grounded again; this time he stayed grounded. The strong current pushed UC-5 farther onto the sandbar until it rolled over on its port chine.

Despite the thick fog, and having been unable to find or identify his navigational aids, Mohrbutter had arrived in his operations area. UC-5 was firmly aground on Shipwash Sands. It was obvious that they were not going to get the boat off, so Mohrbutter set his crew to placing scuttling charges. But even that did not go according to plan. The charges failed to destroy the hull and the British were able to tow the wreck to Harwich. Mohrbutter and his entire crew became prisoners of war.

Sources

Records, T-1022, Roll 84, PG61899.
Spindler, *Der Handelskrieg mit U-Booten,* 3:57–59.

UC-6

Date Lost:	September 1917
Commander:	Oberleutnant zur See Reichenbach
Location:	Hoofden
Position:	Unknown
Disposition:	Verschollen

UC-6 departed Zeebrugge on 27 September 1917 to lay mines off Kentish Knock. It did not return.

Additional Information

The British laid explosive nets off Kentish Knock on 27 September, the same day that UC-6 departed Zeebrugge. Patrols reported strong explosions in the nets the same day. The position in which the explosions occurred was 51°30' N, 1°34' E. Two other British sources attribute the boat's destruction to British seaplane 8676 on 28 September 1917 at the southwest corner of Thornton Ridge. The Germans feel that the mine net explosions near the Kentish Knock Lightship offered the most likely possibility.

Sources

Chatterton, *Beating the U-Boats,* 94.
Gibson and Prendergast, *The German Submarine War,* 214.
Grant, *U-Boats Destroyed,* 57.
Records, T-1022, Roll 62, PG61903.
Spindler, *Der Handelskrieg mit U-Booten,* 4:309.

UC-7

Date Lost:	5 July 1916
Commander:	Oberleutnant zur See Haag
Location:	Hoofden, off Flanders coast
Position:	Unknown
Disposition:	Verschollen

UC-7 departed Zeebrugge on 3 March 1916 to lay mines off Elbow Buoy at the north entrance to the Downs, and did not return.

Additional Information

On 5 July UB-12 was west of Bligh Bank when a lookout saw a surfaced U-boat coming from the direction of North Hinder and steering east. UB-12 assumed the boat was UC-7 and noted that its course would carry it toward a minefield. The time and place are correct if UC-7 was returning from its minelaying mission. The bodies of two UC-7 crewmen washed ashore on the Flanders coast on 19 July, adding evidence that it hit a mine off the coast. The German study doubted a claim that HMS *Salmon* had depth charged and sunk UC-7 on 7 July off Southwold because the position was too far west of UC-7's operations area.

Sources

Chatterton, *Beating the U-Boats,* 190.
Records, T-1022, Roll 63, PG61905.
Spindler, *Der Handelskrieg mit U-Booten,* 3:185–86.

UC-8

Date Lost:	**4 November 1915**
Commander:	**Oberleutnant zur See Walter Schmidt**
Location:	**Dutch coast, near Harlingen**
Position:	**53°23' N, 5°5' E**
Disposition:	**Stranded, Interned**

UC-8 departed Emden on 3 November 1915 en route to Zeebrugge to join the Flanders Flotilla (Marinekorps). On the morning of 4 November UC-8 ran aground in Dutch territorial waters near the Terschelling Lightship. Oberleutnant zur See Walter Schmidt was unable to free the boat under its own power. A Dutch tug pulled it off the sand. Because UC-8 was a fully equipped war boat and had not suffered mechanical breakdown or storm damage that caused it to enter Dutch territorial waters, the Dutch government interned it and the crew for the remainder of the war.

Sources

Records, T-1022, Roll 63, PG61908.
Spindler, *Der Handelskrieg mit U-Booten,* 3:54.

UC-9

Date Lost:	October 1915
Commander:	Oberleutnant zur See Schürmann
Location:	Hoofden, near Harwich
Position:	Unknown
Disposition:	Verschollen

UC-9 departed Zeebrugge on its first and last minelaying operation on 20 October 1915 to lay mines off Long Sand. It did not return and there were no survivors. There are no clues as to what happened to UC-9, but it is possible that it either hit a British mine or that one of its own mines exploded while being laid. It is also possible that UC-9 suffered a diving accident.

Additional Information

On 12 November 1915 the body of chief engineer Hans Neuhaus washed ashore on a British beach near Long Sand. Given that his duty station was in the engine room, it would appear that he attempted to reach the surface from the sunken wreck. The only other answer would be that an explosion tore open the hull and his body washed out through the hole.

Sources

Records, T-1022, Roll 63, PG61909.
Spindler, *Der Handelskrieg mit U-Booten,* 3:50.

UC-10

Date Lost:	21 August 1916
Commander:	Oberleutnant zur See Werner Albrecht
Location:	Off Dutch coast
Position:	52°2' N, 3°54' E
Disposition:	Torpedo

UC-10 departed Zeebrugge on the evening of 17 August 1916 to lay mines off the Humber. On the morning of 21 August UC-10 exchanged information with UB-10 off the North Hinder Lightship. The two boats parted and UC-10 continued its trip home, passing from UB-10's view at 1330. At 1630 UC-10 reached the Schouwen Bank, and at 1635 the British submarine E-54 fired two torpedoes at four hundred yards. One torpedo passed astern but the second hit UC-10 at the base of the conning tower, sinking it with all hands.

Additional Information

The German study concluded that E-54 sank UC-10. Their belief is based on previously known positions and the known track home.

Sources

Chatterton, *Fighting the U-Boats,* 192–93.
Gibson and Prendergast, *The German Submarine War,* 117.
Grant, *U-Boats Destroyed,* 37.
Records, T-1022, Roll 63, PG61910; T-1022, Roll 108, PG61911.
Spindler, *Der Handelskrieg mit U-Booten,* 3:193.

UC-11

Date Lost:	**26 June 1918**
Commander:	**Oberleutnant zur See Kurt Utke**
Location:	**Off Britain's east coast, near Harwich**
Position:	**51°55' N, 1°41' E**
Disposition:	**Mine**

On 24 June 1918 UC-11 hit a mine. Only its captain survived.

Oberleutnant zur See Kurt Utke, UC-11

We were two or three nautical miles east of the Sunk Lightship and were rising to periscope depth when at fifteen meters the stern struck a mine that exploded and blew a hole in the hull. The lights went out, the electric motors stopped and water poured into the pressure hull. In just minutes the boat was entirely flooded and she fell to the bottom in twenty-five meters of water. My command to blow the tanks could not be carried out because my entire crew was already dead. In about three to five minutes the water reached my chest and I opened the conning tower hatch. I was blown through the opening and quickly and without difficulty to the surface where a half-hour later a lifeboat from the Sunk Lightship picked me up.

Source

Records, T-1022, Roll 44, PG61914, "Abschrift aus Fragebogen."

UC-12

Date Lost:	16 March 1916
Commander:	Oberleutnant zur See N. Fröhner
Location:	Gulf of Taranto
Position:	40°27' N, 17°11' E
Disposition:	Own Mine

UC-12 departed Cattaro on 12 March 1916 to lay mines off the Italian harbor of Taranto. While laying the mines the tenth mine exploded in the chute, sinking UC-12 in thirty-one meters of water. There were no survivors. Divers who visited the wreck found that the explosion had destroyed the boat's interior, but had left the exterior virtually undamaged. The Italians decide to salvage the boat. After several weeks they succeeded in bringing UC-12 to the surface in two parts, which they took to Taranto. There they reassembled the halves, repaired UC-12, and in 1917 they commissioned it in the Italian navy as the X-1. X-1 served until the Italians scrapped it in 1919.

Sources

Herzog, *Deutsche U-Boote,* 97.

Records, T-1022, Roll 44, PG61915, "Abschrift von Z-42/22, Anl. 10 bis 17, Niederschrift der begutachtenden Beschreibung der Leichen" and "Unterseeverlust. Deutschland."

Spindler, *Der Handelskrieg mit U-Booten,* 3:46–47.

UC-13

Date Lost:	29 November 1915
Commander:	Oberleutnant zur See Johannes Kirchner
Location:	Black Sea
Position:	41°9' N, 30°30' E
Disposition:	Compass Failure, Stranded, Scuttled

UC-13 departed Constantinople (present-day Istanbul) on 12 November for operations in the Black Sea. Although it was having some minor success under the Prize Regulations, stormy weather and technical problems that included a malfunctioning compass plagued UC-13's patrol. On 29 No-vember the storm was so bad that it was impossible to maintain a watch on the conning tower. With the seas sweeping over the conning tower, and visibility zero, Oberleutnant zur See Johannes Kirchner ordered the watch below and closed the conning tower hatch. He was navigating entirely on dead reckoning.

It was under those conditions that UC-13 ran hard aground fifty-five miles east of the Bosporus near the mouth of the Melen River. The crew stripped the U-boat of all salvageable equipment and set explosive charges in the hull. Turkish vessels picked up the entire crew and the salvaged equipment, and took them to Constantinople.

Oberleutnant zur See Johannes Kirchner, UC-13

At 1500 I left the bridge and spent an hour talking to the chief engineer about our troubles. I wanted to know how long our batteries would last if we had to dive. At 1600 the watch changed and five minutes later we hit something and the bow rose. I knew we were grounding and immediately ordered the engines full astern, but before that order could be carried out, the boat grounded again. I ordered the tanks blown just as she struck a third time, heeled over 60° to starboard, and turned diagonally to the seas. I dogged down the conning tower hatch because it appeared that the boat was going to roll over. The seas raised the stern and shoved her onto her starboard side, and it was obvious that we were not going to get off.

In order to at least save the crew, I ordered hard starboard rudder and ahead full on both diesel engines to drive us through the surf and onto the beach. At the same time I ordered the tanks blown and succeeded in laying the boat square on the bank. The seas that were now coming directly over the stern drove us farther onto the bank.

We fired flares and I saw that the surf was too high to safely get the crew ashore, so we buttoned down for the night and waited for dawn. At first light we saw that the boat lay about fifty meters from the beach and the seas were still breaking over the boat, but we knew that we were saved. While we remained in the boat waiting for the storm to subside, the boat remained tight.

At 0810 the surf had subsided and I was able to send the first men ashore. I sent Oberleutnant zur See Kümpel, the navigator and our Turkish radioman with instructions to locate the nearest telegraph and get help. Throughout the day I continued to send men ashore where they set up camp. I left the boat at 1500 to direct the salvage operations.

Additional Information

The Germans made every effort to pull UC-13 off the sand with tugs, but it was too firmly grounded. Kirchner blamed the grounding on a failed compass that, combined with the powerful storm and wind, caused UC-13 to steer a course other than what Kirchner thought he was steering. He said that he and his navigator checked the three compasses regularly to ensure that they were all working and were in agreement with each other. He did not know when the main compass failed, but he assumed it was when the boat was taking a terrible beating from the storm. Certainly, steering a course according to dead reckoning in a storm was difficult enough, but with a failed compass it was an impossible task.

Sources

Records, T-1022, Roll 44, PG61916, "Bericht über die Strandung UC-13, Konstantinopel den 27. Dezember 1915" and "Bericht über die Bergungsarbeiten UC-13, Konstantinopel, den 19. Dezember 1915."
Spindler, *Der Handelskrieg mit U-Booten,* 3:178.

UC-14

Date Lost:	3 October 1917
Commander:	Oberleutnant zur See Feddersen
Location:	Off Flanders coast, at Zeebrugge
Position:	51°19' N, 2°43' E (approximate)
Disposition:	Mine

UC-14 departed Zeebrugge on 1 October 1917 to lay mines in Stanford Channel. UC-14 did not return and there were no survivors.

Additional Information

At 2215 on 3 October lookouts on Zeebrugge mole and the signal stations at Zeebrugge and Knock reported a brilliant flash followed by a powerful explosion to the north of the Zeebrugge mole. The Germans later learned that five British motor launches had laid five mines two nautical miles north of the Zeebrugge mole on 24 September 1917. The Germans believe that UC-14 hit one of those mines on 3 October at 2215.

Sources

Records, T-1022, Roll 45, PG61918.
Spindler, *Der Handelskrieg mit U-Booten,* 4:454.

UC-15

Date Lost:	November 1916
Commander:	Oberleutnant zur See Heller
Location:	Black Sea
Position:	Unknown
Disposition:	Verschollen

UC-15 departed Constantinople on 13 November 1916 to lay mines off the mouth of the Sulina River, which is on the Romanian coast in the Black Sea. The boat did not return. There is no clue as to what happened to UC-15, but it is possible that it either hit a Russian mine or one of its own mines. It is known that UC-15 reached its assigned area and laid its mines because Austrian minesweepers swept up two German mines off the Sulina mouth on 4 May 1918. No other German boats had been sent there to lay mines, so UC-15 had to have laid the mines that the Austrians found.

Sources

Lorey, *Der Krieg in den türkischen Gewässern,* 1:291.
Records, T-1022, Roll 45, PG61919.
Spindler, *Der Handelskrieg mit U-Booten,* 3:178.

UC-16

Date Lost:	October 1917
Commander:	Oberleutnant zur See Reimarus
Location:	Off Flanders coast, near Zeebrugge
Position:	Unknown
Disposition:	Verschollen

UC-16 departed Zeebrugge on 2 October 1917 to lay mines off Boulogne and to attack shipping in the western part of the English Channel. The boat did not return and there were no survivors.

Additional Information

The body of the watch officer, Leutnant zur See Becswarzowski, washed ashore at Norwik, Holland, on 26 October 1917. Based on this evidence, the Germans concluded that UC-16 probably hit a mine off the Flanders coast while it was on the surface, either going to its operations area or returning to Zeebrugge.

Sources

Gröner, *Die deutschen Kriegsschiffe,* 1:370–71.
Herzog, *Deutsche U-Boote,* 40–41.
Records, T-1022, Roll 45, PG61920.
Rössler, *The U-Boat,* 40–44.
Spindler, *Der Handelskrieg mit U-Booten,* 4:454.

UC-18

Date Lost:	19 February 1917
Commander:	Oberleutnant zur See Kiel
Location:	English Channel, south of Jersey
Position:	49°15' N, 2°34' W
Disposition:	Gunfire

UC-18 departed Zeebrugge on 16 February 1917 to lay mines from Boulogne to Le Havre and to attack shipping in the English Channel. On 19 February UC-18 attacked the British decoy *Lady Olive* (Q-18) in the English Channel. According to the British, UC-18 opened fire at a range of three nautical miles, and *Lady Olive* stopped. While the panic party went over the side the U-boat drew nearer, firing steadily into the hull and doing serious damage. The ship was in a sinking condition when the U-boat hauled up close under its stern at a range of just one hundred yards. The decoy's gunners opened fire, scoring several hits that sank the U-boat with all hands. The *Lady Olive* also sank at 0930, but the French destroyer *Dunois* rescued its crew on 20 February.

Sources

Chatterton, *Q-Ships and Their Story,* 104–7.
Grant, *U-Boats Destroyed,* 64.
Records, T-1022, Roll 46, PG61923.
Spindler, *Der Handelskrieg mit U-Booten,* 4:128–29.

UC-19

Date Lost:	December 1916
Commander:	Oberleutnant zur See Nitzsche
Location:	English Channel or western approaches
Position:	Unknown
Disposition:	Verschollen

UC-19 departed Zeebrugge in company with UB-29 on 27 November 1916 to lay mines from Boulogne to Le Havre, and to attack shipping in the English Channel. Both boats failed to return and claims about their destruction are often applied to both boats.

Additional Information

According to one account, the destroyer HMS *Lewellen* sighted UC-19 awash at three hundred yards on 4 December 1916 off Calais. The destroyer tried to ram the U-boat but failed and then dropped a depth charge. The following morning *Lewellen* found a large oil slick on the surface; oil was still rising to the surface four days later. The problem with this claim is that the position given is too far east of UC-19's operations area. All the confirmed position reports put UC-19 west of Land's End.

In a postwar study, the Germans noted that on 6 December 1916 the armed steamer SS *John Sanderson* engaged in a gun battle with a large U-boat in position 49°13' N, 6°40' W. The Germans said that the U-boat could have been UC-19 because the battle occurred in the area that UC-19 was known to have been operating. The Germans introduced a third possibility when they reasoned that if UC-19 shot it out with *John Sanderson,* then it is possible that HMS *Ariel* sank UC-19 in the afternoon on 6 December. According to the British on that date *Ariel* spotted a U-boat a mile and a half away that was just starting to dive. *Ariel* deployed both its explosive paravanes at thirty feet. The paravanes crossed the U-boat's estimated track and the starboard paravane exploded. The explosion brought large amounts of heavy oil and debris to the surface. UC-19 was unaccounted for after 5 December and did not return from its patrol.

There is another important piece of information that is not included in the postwar German study. The explosive paravane was newly issued in 1916 and each use had to be reported. The paravane report form had four result options to check: Possibly Slightly Damaged, Probably Seriously Damaged, Probably Sunk, or Known Sunk. *Ariel*'s paravane report shows no results checked for the 6 December 1916 attack, thus implying that *Ariel*'s crew did not think that their attack had been successful.

Sources

Chatterton, *Fighting the U-Boats,* 206.
Cornford, *The Paravane Adventure,* 277.
Records, T-1022, Roll 46, PG61924.
Spindler, *Der Handelskrieg mit U-Booten,* 3:292–93, 316–18.

UC-21

Date Lost:	September or October 1917
Commander:	Oberleutnant zur See Zerboni di Sposetti
Location:	English Channel
Position:	Unknown
Disposition:	Verschollen

UC-21 departed Zeebrugge on the morning of 13 September 1917 to lay mines off the west coast of France. The boat did not return and there were no survivors. There are no clues as to what happened to UC-21, but it is possible that it hit either a French or a British mine, or that one of its own mines exploded while it was being laid.

Sources

Records, T-1022, Roll 69, PG61927.
Spindler, *Der Handelskrieg mit U-Booten,* 4:314–15.

UC-24

Date Lost:	24 May 1917
Commander:	Kapitänleutnant Willich
Location:	Adriatic approach to Otranto Strait
Position:	42°6' N, 18°19' E
Disposition:	Torpedo

UC-24 departed Cattaro on 25 May 1917 in company with UC-74 for operations in the Mediterranean. Austro-Hungarian destroyers and a seaplane escorted the U-boats to the two thousand meter line and then turned back toward Cattaro. Shortly after 1145 the French submarine *Circe* torpedoed UC-24, sinking the U-boat almost instantly. Only watch officer Oberleutnant zur See Horst Wulle and Obermatrose Scharschmidt survived.

Oberleutnant zur See Horst Wulle, UC-24

On the morning of 24 May 1917 UC-24 departed Cattaro in company with UC-74, Kapitänleutnant Marschal, and escorted by the Austrian destroyer *F 90*. At 0930 we had the minefield behind us, and the *F 90* turned back. Because the UC-74 was a newer boat she was faster than we were and she steadily pulled away. At two thousand meters we exchanged separation signals and at 1000 the navigator came onto the bridge to tell me that we had reached our turning point and handed me our new course 168°. I could still see the UC-74 through my binoculars.

There were five of us on the conning tower. Kapitänleutnant Willich was leaning against the starboard net cutter support, and I was also on the starboard side, slightly back of him so that I could see over the conning tower rim. The navigator was standing in the conning tower hatch with both feet on the top rung of the ladder. Obermatrose Diedrich was the port lookout and on the perch above the telephone buoy. Obermatrose Scharschmidt was the after lookout. I raised my binoculars to take another look at the UC-74 and I saw something pass right across the lens, and at the same moment the captain shouted, "Oh my God! My God! What is that?"

I dropped my binoculars and looked forward as a torpedo wake crossed our bow from starboard. I shouted down the hatch to turn hard to port but I had not even finished giving the order when I saw the wake of a second torpedo that led directly to our mine chutes. At first I thought the torpedo had passed below us, but there was suddenly a horrific explosion. I

259

suddenly found myself under water and tried to reach the surface, but my right arm was caught in something. I felt around with my left hand and felt a wire wrapped around my wrist. The wire had to be the antenna wire. I was wearing gauntlet gloves and I was able to free my hand. When I reached the surface I found myself right alongside the sinking UC-24. Her stern was out of the water, exposing the propellers and propeller guards. I tried to push off with my left foot, but something grabbed me and I was pulled under again. I again freed myself and reached the surface.

It was totally dark and the sun was just a red ball in the sky. I swam a bit and realized that the smoke cloud from the detonation was hanging overhead. I looked around, saw Obermatrose Scharschmidt, and called to him, asking if he had seen anyone else. He said no. I saw UC-74 in the distance, but she quickly disappeared. Since we had no lifeboat, we started swimming in the direction of land. After a while my feet grew heavy and I shed my sea boots. That made things easier and I benefited from air trapped inside my leather jacket. Finally I saw a spot in the sky that I knew was an airplane and beyond that a smoke column. The airplane landed and the pilot told us that two destroyers were coming to pick us up. He offered to fly us to the destroyers, but I declined. In the meantime the *F 90* arrived and took us aboard.

Additional Information

According to Kapitänleutnant Marschal, UC-74's commander, as soon as UC-24 was torpedoed, the torpedo boats and the airplane headed in that direction. In his estimation, the two survivors could not have been in the water longer than fifteen minutes, essentially the time it took the airplane to reach the spot and land. He adds that *Circe* was torpedoed under similar circumstances, and it also had only two survivors.

Sources

Records, T-1022, Roll 71, PG61930, "Aus dem Schreiben des Oberleutnants zur See Horst Wulle vom 31. März 1929" and "Aus dem Schreiben des Kapitänleutnants Marschal vom 5. April 1929."

UC-25

Date Lost:	29 October 1918
Commander:	Oberleutnant zur See Lippold
Location:	Pola
Position:	44°52' N, 13°50' E
Disposition:	Scuttled

On 21 October 1918 the Admiralstab ordered all U-boats that were ready for sea to return to Germany, and on 23 October the Germans began evacuating Pola and Cattaro. UC-25 was one of ten boats that either could not make the trip home or was not ready for sea. The Germans destroyed these ten boats during the period 28 October to 1 November 1918 at Cattaro, Fiume, Pola, and Trieste.

Additional Information

UC-25 departed Cattaro on 23 July 1918 to lay mines off Korfu and to attack shipping. It returned to Cattaro on 7 August without any reported damage or mechanical problems. Shifted to Pola, UC-25 was undergoing overhaul and refitting when the order came to evacuate the port. Because the work was not yet complete, it was unable to make the return trip to Germany; a maintenance crew blew up UC-25 in Pola on 29 October 1918.

Sources

Records, T-1022, Roll 71, PG61932.
Spindler, *Der Handelskrieg mit U-Booten,* 5:217–18, 226–27.

UC-26

Date Lost:	9 May 1917
Commander:	Kapitänleutnant Graf von Schmettow
Location:	Dover Strait
Position:	51°3' N, 1°40' E
Disposition:	Ramming, Depth Charge

UC-26 departed Zeebrugge on the evening of 30 April 1917 to lay mines off Le Havre and to conduct anti-shipping operations in the English Channel. On 9 May a British destroyer rammed it as it was diving. UC-26 sank immediately in forty meters and came to rest on its port side. Flooding was so extensive that there was no hope of blowing it to the surface with compressed air. Eight men managed to exit the boat through the engine room hatch and the conning tower hatch, but only two men survived. HMS *Milne* picked up Leutnant zur See Heinrich Petersen and Maschinistenmaat Acksel.

Leutnant zur See Heinrich Petersen, UC-26

At 0100 on 9 May we were on the surface eight miles northeast of Calais when we saw three destroyers. Before we could dive, we were rammed in the conning tower and UC-26 sank very quickly, landing hard on the bottom. There was no panic even when a depth charge exploded near us and put out the lights. The batteries were flooded and it was impossible to surface. The men trapped in the after section never lost their courage. An attempt to expel water from the after section with compressed air failed and the water continued to rise slowly, forcing the men to take refuge in the overhead. Some of the men climbed up above the engines near the deck hatch.

The captain, Graf von Schmettow, said that we should prepare for our deaths for the Kaiser, and led us in three cheers. In the meantime the Boatswain had another idea. He opened the compressed air bottles in the after torpedo room and all eyes turned toward the water level that stopped rising. We were saved. All we had to do now was wait until the air pressure inside the hull equaled the water pressure outside. Then it would be possible to open the engine room hatch. That happened quickly. But we had waited too long and when the hatch was opened the blast of escaping air killed the men who were near the hatch. Then things equalized and I left the boat. It took a long time to reach the surface. I suffered no injury other than discomfort and general pain from the excessive pressure.

Maschinistenmaat Acksel had a life vest on when he exited through the engine room hatch. But he too said that it seemed a long time before he reached the surface.

British Report

On the night of 9 May 1917 we were patrolling with two other destroyers in the Pas de Calais when we spotted a U-boat on the surface and very near. We knew that there were no Allied submarines in the area, and this one had to be German. We were so close to her that our stem almost immediately struck the forward part of her superstructure and she sank immediately. But to be sure we also dropped a depth charge. We passed over the spot several times but the depth, twenty-three fathoms, made the likelihood that there would be any survivors very small. Imagine, then, our surprise when we heard shouts for help. We saw two men in the water, one wearing a life vest and the other dressed in oil skins. Both were swimming with great effort. We brought them aboard.

Sources

Records, T-1022, Roll 71, PG61934, "Das Ende von *U26,* Nach englischen noch nicht veröffentlichen Quellen" and "Leutnant zur See Heinrich Petersen"; T-1022, Roll 71, PG61934, "Londoner Prisengerichtsverhandlungen wegen vierzehn deutscher U-Boote."
Spindler, *Der Handelskrieg mit U-Booten,* 4:134–35.

UC-29

Date Lost:	7 June 1917
Commander:	Oberleutnant zur See Rosenow
Location:	Atlantic, off Southern Ireland
Position:	51°50' N, 11°50' W
Disposition:	Gunfire

UC-29 departed Helgoland on 29 May 1917 to lay mines off the Dingle Bight. On 7 June it torpedoed the Q-ship *Pargust,* blowing a hole in the side that caused massive flooding in the engine room, boiler room, and hold number 5 and destroying one lifeboat. *Pargust* stopped and set out its panic party in the remaining lifeboat. Thirty minutes later UC-29 surfaced. When it came up, the U-boat exposed only the conning tower and kept the decks awash. Oberleutnant zur See Rosenow called to the boat to come closer, but the boat rowed back toward *Pargust.* The U-boat moved closer in an apparent attempt to overtake the boat. When UC-29 was fifty yards off *Pargust*'s starboard side, the decoy opened fire. UC-29 attempted to get away, but it continued taking hits and sank three hundred yards from the *Pargust.* Only the watch officer and a seaman survived.

Sources

Chatterton, *Q-Ships and Their Story,* 200–203.
Records, T-1022, Roll 84, PG61940.
Spindler, *Der Handelskrieg mit U-Booten,* 4:230–31.

UC-30

Date Lost:	19–20 April 1917
Commander:	Kapitänleutnant Stenzler
Location:	North Sea
Position:	Unknown
Disposition:	Mine (possible)

UC-30 departed Helgoland on 30 March 1917 to lay mines off the south coast of Ireland and to attack shipping in that area. On 4 April it reported being twenty-five nautical miles south of the Scillies. Experiencing engine problems, it was necessary for it to return to Helgoland. On 13 April UC-30 met U-50 at sea and exchanged information, and on 19 April UC-30 radioed that it was seventy-five nautical miles west-southwest of Lindesnes. UC-30 was not seen or heard again and there were no survivors.

Additional Information

The British had laid a new minefield off Horn's Reef during 18–20 April, and the Germans believe UC-30 may have hit one of those mines. On 4 June 1917 the body of a UC-30 crewman washed ashore north of Esbjerg on the Danish coast and a second body came ashore at Sundvik, Denmark, on 25 June.

Sources

Records, T-1022, Roll 84, PG61941.
Spindler, *Der Handelskrieg mit U-Booten,* 4:46–47.

UC-32

Date Lost:	23 February 1917
Commander:	Oberleutnant zur See Breyer
Location:	Off Britain's east coast, near Newcastle
Position:	54°55.25' N, 1°20' W
Disposition:	Own Mine

UC-32 departed Helgoland on 17 February 1917 to lay mines off the mouth of the Tyne. At 1830 on 21 February it was trimmed down and preparing to lay mines east of the Roker Pier Lighthouse off Sunderland. Just as UC-32 started its minelaying run, the first mine dropped exploded. Because the boat was trimmed down so that just the conning tower was above the surface, it sank very quickly and only the three men who were atop the conning tower survived. British divers visited the wreck three days later.

Sources

Records, T-1022, Roll 85, PG61944.
Spindler, *Der Handelskrieg mit U-Booten,* 4:48–49.

UC-33

Date Lost:	26 September 1917
Commander:	Oberleutnant zur See Alfred Arnold
Location:	St. George's Channel in Irish Sea
Position:	51°55' N, 6°14' W
Disposition:	Ramming

UC-33 departed Helgoland on 16 September 1917 to lay mines off Waterford in the Irish Sea and to attack shipping in that area. After laying three minefields UC-33 fouled a net off Waterford at twenty meters. Oberleutnant zur See Alfred Arnold tore through the net by flooding and allowing the boat to fall. When he restarted the motors the net fouled the starboard propeller. That night he surfaced and cleared away the net, but he was unable to clear the fouled propeller. Reasoning that U-boats were often operated on one engine to save fuel, Arnold did not feel the loss of one propeller was a serious hindrance, so he continued his patrol.

On the morning of 26 September UC-33 carried out a submerged torpedo attack on the British steamer SS *San Zeferino* (6,430 tons) in St. George's Channel. Arnold fired one torpedo that struck the freighter amidships and exploded, but the ship did not sink. Visibility on the surface was poor due to heavy fog when UC-33 surfaced to complete the job with gunfire. Because of the fog, Arnold had not seen the freighter's escort, and before his gun crew could man the weapon, P-boat P-61 suddenly appeared. Arnold now paid the price for having only one propeller. UC-33 tried to dive but at the critical moment the coupling on the port electric motor failed, leaving UC-33 dead in the water and trimmed down. P-61 rammed UC-33 just aft of the conning tower and rolled the U-boat on its beam ends. Water poured through the hole in the side, sinking UC-33 almost immediately. Only the captain survived.

Oberleutnant zur See Alfred Arnold, UC-33

The enemy was coming closer and we had to get under. The chief engineer reported that he would have the motor clutched any moment, but we waited, measuring the time in seconds. Finally he said that the coupling was frozen solid. But he would have it free shortly. The boat was trimmed down ready to dive, all we needed was power. I could see the patrol boat clearly through the conning tower port, and he was very near. Then he rammed us.

The UC-33 rolled onto her beam ends and water poured in through the gash in the pressure hull. I ordered the tanks blown but the boat was already too heavy and falling fast. The engine room and the command central were already fully flooded. The batteries shorted, the lights went out and chlorine gas started contaminating the small amount of air in the boat.

There were two of us in the conning tower and a stoker was standing on the ladder below the hatch that opened into control room. The water was rising very quickly and we tried to help the stoker through the hatch into the conning tower. But the surge swept him off the ladder. We slammed shut the lower hatch, but the water continued to rise in the conning tower. It was entering through the speaking tubes and around the cabling that connected the conning tower to the other compartments.

When the water reached our thighs I told the navigator to try opening the hatch, but the outer pressure was still too great. I knew that we were in two hundred meters of water and the boat was falling fast. We had passed the twenty-meter mark when the lights failed, so we did not have much time left. I told him to try one more time, and by now the water was chest deep. The hatch popped open and we were blown through the opening. I had no difficulty reaching the surface. The P-61 picked us up, but the navigator died shortly after he was brought aboard.

Sources

Records, T-1022, Roll 85, PG61945, "Abschrift vom Fragebogen, Oberleutnant zur See Arnold."

UC-34

Date Lost:	30 October 1918
Commander:	Oberleutnant zur See Hans Schüler
Location:	Pola
Position:	44°52' N, 13°50' E
Disposition:	Scuttled

On 21 October 1918 the Admiralstab ordered all U-boats that were ready for sea to return to Germany. The Germans began the evacuation of Pola and Cattaro on 23 October. UC-34 was one of ten boats that either could not make the trip home or was not ready for sea. The Germans destroyed these ten boats during the period 28 October to 1 November 1918 at Cattaro, Fiume, Pola, and Trieste.

Additional Information

UC-34 laid mines off Port Said on 9 August and returned to Cattaro on 19 August 1918 for a scheduled major overhaul, but shifted to Pola to have the work done. When the order came to evacuate the base UC-34's overhaul was not complete and its crew scuttled it off Pola on 30 October 1918.

Sources

Records, T-1022, Roll 85, PG61946.
Spindler, *Der Handelskrieg mit U-Booten,* 5:226–27.

UC-35

Date Lost:	16 May 1918
Commander:	Oberleutnant zur See Korsch
Location:	Western Mediterranean, near Sardinia
Position:	39°48' N, 7°42' E
Disposition:	Gunfire

UC-35 departed Cattaro on 28 April 1918 for operations in the western Mediterranean. On 16 May, while returning to Cattaro, it made a surface attack on a group of fishing boats. The gunfire attracted the French destroyer *Ailly* that opened fire at long range as it approached the scene. Whether it was a matter of superb marksmanship or pure luck is debatable, but one round scored a direct hit on UC-35's conning tower, destroying the conning tower and the hatch. A second round, also fired at long range, destroyed the forward ballast tanks, the compressed air piping, and exploded the ready ammunition on deck. The deck explosion blew a hole in the pressure hull and the boat either sank or Oberleutnant zur See Korsch attempted to dive despite the heavy damage to his boat. Five crewmen and a Spanish prisoner escaped from the U-boat as it went down.

Honoratus Glas, UC-35

On 16 May 1918 at 0730 we sighted two sail and an armed drifter on a course toward Marseilles. At the time we were about sixty nautical miles off the west coast of Sardinia. At 0830 we opened fire on the sail, firing six or seven rounds before turning our fire on the armed escort.

The escort returned our fire and after several rounds scored a hit on the ready ammunition stored on deck. The explosion blew a hole in the conning tower and destroyed all the forward compressed air piping. Oberleutnant zur See Korsch attempted to dive and the UC-35 sank. Five crewmen and a Spanish prisoner escaped from the boat and a drifter picked us up. We were landed in Toulon. The wounded survivor, Maschinist Suker, died in the hospital at Marseilles.

Sources

Records, T-1022, Roll 85, PG61947, "Abschrift aus Fragebogen, Munsterlager, den 15. February 1920, Honoratus Glas."

Spindler, *Der Handelskrieg mit U-Booten,* 5:185.

UC-36

Date Lost:	May 1917
Commander:	Kapitänleutnant Buch
Location:	Hoofden, off Dutch coast
Position:	Unknown
Disposition:	Verschollen

UC-36 departed Zeebrugge on 16 May 1917 to lay mines off the Rab Lightship. The boat did not return and there were no survivors.

Additional Information

On 14 August 1919 a British prize court awarded the British seaplane No. 8663 a bounty £125 for sinking UC-36 on 20 May 1917 twenty nautical miles east-northeast of the North Hinder Lightship. Reportedly the airplane dropped two bombs on UC-36, which sank stern first. There were no survivors. The bounty was based on the rate of £5 per crewman aboard the U-boat. Actually, UC-36 had a twenty-six-man crew, so the prize court underpaid the bounty. There is no explanation in the prize court award for how the British identified the boat as UC-36, but a postwar German study concluded that time and place made it possible that the seaplane did sink it on 20 May.

Sources

Records, T-1022, Roll 85, PG61948; T-1022, Roll 71, PG61934, "Londoner Prisenger-ichtsverhandlungen wegen vierzehn deutscher U-Boote."
Spindler, *Der Handelskrieg mit U-Booten,* 4:136.

UC-38

Date Lost:	14 December 1917
Commander:	Oberleutnant zur See Hans Wendlandt
Location:	Eastern Mediterranean
Position:	38°15' N, 22°22' E
Disposition:	Depth Charge, Gunfire

On 1 December 1917 UC-38 departed Cattaro for operations in the Gulf of Patras. On 14 December it torpedoed the French cruiser *Chateaurenault*, which was carrying troops. The escorting destroyers depth charged UC-38, drove it to the surface, and sank it with gunfire.

While he was a prisoner of war, Oberleutnant zur See Hans Wendlandt put his firsthand account into code and gave it to Oberleutnant Baue of the 84th Uhlans Regiment while they were both in the Sisteron Prison in France. The French exchanged Oberleutnant Baue in 1918 and sent him to Engelberg where he passed on the information Wendlandt had given him. But by the time Baue returned to Germany he was no longer able to decode Wendlandt's first-person report. Instead, Baue provided the Germans with a paraphrased report based on several conversations he had with Wendlandt in prison.

Oberleutnant Baue, 84th Uhlans Regiment

Wendlandt said that after the UC-38 torpedoed the *Chateaurenault*, her escorts depth charged the UC-38 with man-size depth charges. The UC-38 was at twenty meters and when the depth charges exploded the explosions sprung the torpedo loading hatches fore and aft. Wendlandt said that in his opinion the torpedo loading hatches were too large so that when even partially sprung, the rubber seals failed completely. He also said that the access hatches in the deck were also sprung, but their rubber seals held.

The water was pouring in through the torpedo loading hatches and Wendlandt resorted to blowing the inner spaces with compressed air to expel the water. Within an hour the compressed air supply was exhausted, and Wendlandt surfaced to allow his crew to escape.

When the UC-38 came up, the French destroyers immediately took her under fire, doing severe damage and killing several of the crewmen as they abandoned the sinking U-boat. The UC-38 sank in 250 meters. The French destroyers picked up eighteen survivors.

Additional Information

The French held Wendlandt until 7 November 1920, on war crimes charges, but they never prosecuted him.

Sources

Records, T-1022, Roll 86, PG61950, "Untergang des U-Bootes des Oberleutnant zur See Wendlandt am 14. Dezember 1917."

Spindler, *Der Handelskrieg mit U-Booten,* 4:485.

UC-39

Date Lost:	8 February 1917
Commander:	Kapitänleutnant Ehrentraut
Location:	Off Britain's east coast, at Flamborough Head
Position:	53°56' N, 0°6' E
Disposition:	Depth Charge, Gunfire

UC-39 departed Zeebrugge on 7 February 1917 to lay mines off Flamborough Head. On 8 February, while in the process of sinking SS *Hornsey* with gunfire, UC-39's firing attracted the attention of the destroyer HMS *Thrasher*. The destroyer sped toward the sounds and at 0122 saw a surfaced U-boat to port three thousand yards distant. *Thrasher* opened fire and the U-boat dove. *Thrasher* crossed the spot and dropped one depth charge that exploded so close to UC-39 that serious flooding occurred almost immediately. Kapitänleutnant Ehrentraut blew the tanks with compressed air and brought UC-39 to the surface. The destroyer immediately opened fire.

The first round exploded in the conning tower, killing Ehrentraut. More rounds hit the hull, killing six more men and reducing UC-39 to a sinking wreck. The watch officer, Leutnant zur See Lauterbach, ordered the crew to abandon ship.

London Times report

The UC-39 was on her first war cruise. She sank the Norwegian steamer SS *Hans Kinck,* and on the following day she sank the British steamer SS *Hanna Larsen* with scuttling charges according to the Prize Regulations. The captain and chief machinist were taken aboard the UC-39 as prisoners. The next day she sank the Norwegian steamer SS *Ida* and then attacked two fishing vessels. At about 1300 that afternoon she surfaced and opened fire on a steamer. A British destroyer returned the fire. The UC-39 tried to dive, but it was too late. A round struck the conning tower, blowing a hole in the pressure hull and flooding the control room. Ehrentraut and six men were killed. The destroyer picked up seventeen survivors.

Steuermann Max Eschenbach, UC-39

On 8 February we tried to attack a small British cruiser seven nautical miles east of Flamborough Head. We were unable to carry out the attack. That afternoon the fog developed and I knew that we were near our northern operations boundary. Before the fog became too thick I took a sun shot to establish our exact position. I was below plotting the position and laying a new course when I heard the command to man the deck gun and bring up ammunition. I next heard several rounds fired from our gun and then the alarm command to crash dive. We reached seventeen meters very quickly.

Shortly after reaching that depth we felt a heavy explosion to starboard and aft that violently shook the boat. The force of the explosion was so powerful that the entire hatch lid on the engine room hatch fell to the floor in the engine room. Water entered through that large hold in an uncontrollable torrent. Almost immediately we felt two smaller explosions. The captain ordered all tanks blown with compressed air and we surfaced with a 20° starboard list. The British immediately opened fire on us, but ceased fire when they saw we had two British prisoners aboard. The boat rolled steadily to starboard and water poured through the open hatches. The UC-39 sank very quickly.

Maschinist Paul Preuss, UC-39

UC-39 was in the Humber Mouth when the British destroyer B-94 sank her with depth charges. The explosions loosened rivets and the engine room hatch, causing flooding in the engine room, control room and the forward torpedo room. The boat could not remain submerged. When we surfaced the British destroyer shelled us, hitting the conning tower and killing the captain as he opened the hatch. The boat was destroyed by artillery and brought to a sinking condition. The British destroyer picked up the survivors.

Bootsmann Carl Stolte, UC-39

On 8 February the UC-39 was in the Humber Mouth attacking a steamer with gunfire. Suddenly a destroyer appeared out of the fog and we crash dived to fifteen meters. The destroyer dropped two depth charges that started flooding and we were forced to surface. The UC-39 was sunk by gunfire.

FT-Obergast Richard Lässig, UC-39

On 8 February 1917 in the afternoon we were on line with Hull off the British coast. We were shelling a steamer when a destroyer came up from astern and surprised us. We crash dived to twenty meters and the destroyer dropped the first depth charge. The explosion was directly above the boat and so close that it tore open both the engine room hatch and the forward hatch. We were, however, able to secure them and stop the flooding. It was clear to all of us that we had to lie on the bottom to avoid further depth charging. Despite our expectations the tanks were blown and the boat shot to the surface where the destroyer destroyed us.

We have ascertained that the captain did not give the order to blow the tanks. It appears the lieutenant who was in the command central gave the order or it was the chief engineer, Arthur Gerlach. That possibility is strengthened by what we saw on deck. I was apparently the last man to come out of the boat and as I came on deck I saw the lieutenant and Arthur Gerlach standing in the conning tower. They were already stripped to the waist whereas we were all still wearing our oil skins. The lieutenant and Gerlach dove overboard leaving the rest of the crew to their fate. Eight lost their lives.

U-Heizer August Sauer, UC-39

The UC-39 left Zeebrugge on 5 November 1917 en route the Humber. Along the way we sank two ships under the Prize Regulations and took two British seamen prisoner; a fireman and a navigator. We were to rendezvous with UC-48 on 8 November, but before we kept the rendezvous we stopped a steamer and were approaching her when a British destroyer came up from astern.

The destroyer turned toward us and opened fire, several rounds falling close aboard. We crash dived and had just reached sixteen meters when a depth charge exploded directly overhead. The blast blew out a port in the conning tower, causing serious flooding in the command central. The same blast blew open the forward and after deck hatches causing major flooding. The depth gauge and most of the other gauges were destroyed. The tanks were blown with compressed air and the boat surfaced.

As the captain, Oberleutnant zur See Ehrentraut climbed onto the conning tower and a round stuck the conning tower, killing him. The destroyer lay 150 meters away and continued firing. The watch officer, the chief engineer aspirant, the entire crew and the two prisoners were on the deck. The destroyer ordered the UC-39, which was still under way with the electric motors to stop. The rudder was hard over and the boat was running in a circle. The motors were shut down and the destroyer ceased firing. The British sent a boat across.

In the meantime the UC-39 was down by the bow, but the after deck was dry. Someone closed the forward hatch so that the flooding forward was greatly reduced. The British boat came alongside and the watch officer, Leutnant zur See Luchterhand and the chief engineer aspirant Arthur Gerlach boarded the boat with two badly wounded men. They were taken to the destroyer. The boat returned and removed the rest of the crew in several trips. The captain's body was also removed and is now buried in Hull. A British officer came aboard and took a set of binoculars from the conning tower.

Additional Information

Because no one thought to scuttle it, UC-39 remained afloat and HMS *Itchen* took it in tow, hoping to get it in to port. But *Thrasher*'s gunfire had done so much damage that UC-39 sank at 1420 three nautical miles south of Flamborough Head in position 53°56' N, 0°6' E.

The failure to scuttle the boat prompted the German postwar interrogators to look closely at what happened when UC-39 was abandoned. The following are comments written by the German naval officer who interrogated the survivors after the war.

Sauer swore that neither Leutnant zur See Lauterbach nor the chief engineer aspirant Arthur Gerlach gave an order to sink or scuttle the UC-39 with explosives. After Sauer and Gerlach had left the boat in the British boat none of the remaining noncommissioned officers aboard the UC-39 gave such an order. The result was that when the last man was taken off, the UC-39 was still afloat. Furthermore, the men were angry that the watch officer and the chief engineer aspirant had left the UC-39 first.

Sauer swore under questioning that when the last man was taken off the UC-39, she was still afloat. Her forward deck was under water back to the conning tower, but the after deck was dry and her screws were out of the water. Other destroyers had arrived and appeared to be making an effort to salvage the UC-39 and tow her in to port. Sauer did not know if that attempt succeeded or not, but he and the crew believe the boat sank.

I have given Sauer a direct order to discuss this with no one under any circumstances. The only exception to that order is in the event that a naval officer, acting officially, questions him again.

Sources

Records, T-1022, Roll 86, PG61951, "Abschrift Z14119/19, 19 October 1919, Steuermann Max Eschenbach"; "Maschinist Paul Preuss, Abschrift aus Fragebogen, Emden, den 5. November 1919"; "Bootsmann Carl Stolte, Abschrift aus Fragebogen, Bremerhaven, den 13. November 1919"; "FT-Obergast Richard Lässig, Abschrift aus Fragebogen, Emden, den 13. November 1919"; "Bericht über die Letzte Fahrt S. M. U-Boot *UC-39* nach Abgaben des U-Heizers August Sauer [Zentralheizer], undated"; and "*London Times.*"

Spindler, *Der Handelskrieg mit U-Booten,* 4:137–38.

UC-41

Date Lost:	**21 August 1917**
Commander:	**Oberleutnant zur See Hans Förste**
Location:	**Off Britain's east coast, near Firth of Forth**
Position:	**56°25' N, 2°35' W**
Disposition:	**Own Mine**

UC-41 departed Zeebrugge on 18 August 1917 to lay mines in the Tay Estuary. On 21 August, while submerged and laying mines, it apparently maneuvered to avoid two minesweeping trawlers, *Jacinth* and *Thomas Young,* and struck one of its own mines. The explosion attracted the trawlers and they each dropped a depth charge near the spot. A short while later another trawler, *Chikara,* arrived and dropped another depth charge. British divers visited the wreck a month later and provided the explanation of what happened to UC-41.

Sources

Gibson and Prendergast, *The German Submarine War,* 200.
Grant, *U-Boats Destroyed,* 70–71.
Records, T-1022, Roll 47, PG61954.
Spindler, *Der Handelskrieg mit U-Booten,* 4:235.

UC-42

Date Lost:	September 1917
Commander:	Oberleutnant zur See Hans Albrecht Müller
Location:	St. George's Channel, off Cork, Ireland
Position:	51°41' N, 8°14' W
Disposition:	Own Mine

UC-42 departed Helgoland on 1 September 1917 to lay mines off Cork on the south coast of Ireland. On 5 September it sank two British sailing vessels under the Prize Regulations in the English Channel. After that nothing more was heard from UC-42.

Additional Information

On 10 September UC-42 was laying mines off Cork, two and a half nautical miles south of Point Roche, when a mine exploded under the stern. The explosion tore open the pressure hull aft to the screws, and the boat sank in fourteen fathoms. The British did not discover the wreck until 31 October when trawlers noticed oil on the surface and dropped depth charges. Divers went down to the wreck on 3 November and found the conning tower hatch and forward torpedo room hatch open, indicating that some of the crew had escaped from the wreck.

Sources

Grant, *U-Boats Destroyed,* 71.
Records, T-1022, Roll 47, PG61955.
Spindler, *Der Handelskrieg mit U-Booten,* 4:236.

UC-43

Date Lost:	10 March 1917
Commander:	Kapitänleutnant Sebelin
Location:	Atlantic, north of Shetlands
Position:	60°57' N, 1°11' W
Disposition:	Torpedo

UC-43 departed Helgoland on 25 February 1917 to lay mines off the southern coast of Ireland and to attack shipping in the area. UC-43 was active in the anti-shipping role from 27 February until 9 March. Between 2 and 5 March it laid mines off Cape Clear east of Fastnet and off the southern coast of Ireland near Seven Heads. UC-43 then headed home by the northern route.

On 10 March 1917 the British submarine G-13 was on antisubmarine patrol twelve miles north of Muckle Flugga Lighthouse. The weather was terrible and very cold. There was a gale blowing, the seas were heaped up, and snow squalls intermittently reduced visibility to zero. Between the snow squalls visibility was momentarily good, and it was at such a moment at 1600 that G-13 sighted UC-43 on the surface.

G-13 dove and had a hard time holding at periscope depth because of the high seas. At one point it broached. At 1640 a snow squall cut visibility to zero and when the squall cleared, UC-43 had changed course. Unable to close the range, Lieutenant Commander Bradshaw fired two torpedoes at three thousand yards.

Two and a half minutes later Bradshaw saw "a great black pencil shoot four hundred feet into the air directly forward of the enemy's conning tower." As he watched, UC-43 jackknifed in the middle and sank. There were no survivors. UC-76 was in the area and witnessed the explosion, which made it possible for the Germans to identify UC-43 as the victim.

Additional Information

On 14 August 1919 a British prize court awarded the British submarine G-13 a bounty of £145 for sinking UC-43 on 10 March 1917. The bounty was based on the rate of £5 per crewman aboard the U-boat. Actually, UC-43 had a twenty-six-man crew, so the prize court overpaid the bounty.

Sources

Edwards, *We Dive at Dawn,* 302–4.

Records, T-1022, Roll 47, PG61956; T-1022, Roll 71, PG61934, "Londoner Prisenger-
ichtsverhandlungen wegen vierzehn deutscher U-Boote."

Spindler, *Der Handelskrieg mit U-Booten,* 4:53–54.

UC-44

Date Lost:	5 August 1917
Commander:	Kapitänleutnant Kurt Tebbenjohanns
Location:	St. George's Channel, off Waterford
Position:	52°7' N, 6°59' W
Disposition:	Radio Intelligence, Mine (German)

UC-44 departed Helgoland on 31 July 1917 to lay mines off Waterford and arrived there on the evening of 4 August. It laid a four-mine group in ten meters of water at the entrance to Waterford just before midnight. At 0030 UC-44 had just dropped the fifth mine in a five-mine group when a powerful explosion occurred at the stern of the boat. UC-44 sank instantly in twenty-five meters.

Kapitänleutnant Kurt Tebbenjohanns, UC-44

On the evening of 4 August we arrived off Waterford. Because it would be several hours before the tide was favorable for minelaying, I laid the boat on the bottom. Shortly after midnight we surfaced. It was a crystal clear, moonlit night with a mirror flat sea and no wind. The Waterford light was working and I had an exact position fix. We dove to lay the nines in two groups, one of four and one of five.

During the minelaying, I personally plotted the course and recorded the mines' positions. I had just given the order to drop the ninth mine, and had received the reply, "mine dropped," when the boat was shaken by a powerful explosion. The lights went out and there was a strong odor of sulfur.

The explosion threw me against the bulkhead, cut my eyelid and momentarily stunned me. I never lost consciousness. Two enlisted men took refuge with me in the conning tower, and from beneath us in the command central I could hear water rushing in and I could feel the boat sinking. It hit bottom hard, but there was no sound from the crew. Not a sound. I closed the hatch into the control room.

It was absolutely black in the conning tower, but I tried to contact the crew through the speaking tube. I knew that the boat was lost and the entire crew, except for we three, were dead. We were jammed tightly in the cramped confines of the conning tower with the water rising slowly. We could not see it, but we could feel it rising around our feet.

It was a terrifying and hopeless situation, but the will to live was strong.

It was so dark that we could not see each other, which is probably good because that meant that we could not see the fear on our faces. I knew our exact position, and I knew that the chances of us swimming to shore were very small. In any event, I was not sure that we could survive the escape from the boat. I have a strong fear of drowning, but as we stood there in total darkness I had the urge to at least try. There was, after all, nothing to lose.

We took our positions on the ladder leading to the conning tower hatch. The explosion had ripped open the stern and the entire boat was flooded except for our portion of the conning tower. That worked in our favor because the steadily rising water was compressing the air inside the conning tower and soon it would equal the outside water pressure.

I loosened the upper hatch and it sprang open. We were blown through the opening and I tried to control my ascent so that I would not rise too quickly. Despite the endless time it took for me to reach the surface, I never had a problem with running out of breath. My lungs automatically adjusted to the diminishing water pressure as I rose, and a constant stream of air issued from my mouth. What we all did wrong was that none of us had shed our clothes before we opened the hatch.

We all three men surfaced in a tight group, and I pointed toward the light tower at the Waterford entrance and told them that was their goal. But the current was setting us away from the lighthouse, and after several minutes of fruitless swimming, I told them to swim with the current toward the shore. That was the last I saw of them. For a while I heard one of them calling for help and then the calling ceased. I was having my own problems.

I was developing cramps and my clothing was dragging me down. I was a good swimmer but my clothes were getting too heavy. I now realized what fools we had been to have not shed our clothes while we were still inside the U-boat. It would have been so easy. But now I had to struggle out of my sea boots, my heavy watch coat and my sweater. Finally I was down to my undershirt, trousers and socks. I remembered to unhook my Iron Cross First Class from my coat and shoved it into my trousers pocket.

After an hour and a half two men in a rowboat pulled me out of the water and took me to Waterford. At the time they believed I was a neutral seaman or an Auxiliary Patrol member whose ship had hit a mine. They had rowed out looking for survivors after hearing the explosion just after midnight. If I had any thoughts of escaping disguised as a neutral seaman those hopes were dashed in the morning. I was lying in bed when a man entered the room with two constables. The man had my iron cross in his hand.

"Are you a German?" he asked.

I nodded yes.

"Then you are a prisoner of war."

Additional Information

Room 40, the British radio intelligence service responsible for reading German radio messages, knew that the Germans were monitoring British minesweeping operations. After the UC-boats would lay mines, the British would sweep them up and report the cleared areas by radio. The Germans copied that information and then sent another UC-boat to lay new mines in the swept area.

The British decided to make a false report that recently laid mines off Waterford had been swept up. The Germans copied the report and dispatched Tebbenjohanns in UC-44 to lay new mines. While he was laying his mines, he may have struck a mine that UC-42 had laid on 14 June 1917. It is also possible that UC-44's ninth mine may have exploded as it dropped from the chute and the boat passed over it. All that is certain is that the British engineered the trap and a mine destroyed UC-44.

Sources

Grant, *U-Boats Destroyed,* 56.

Hashagen, *U-Boote Westwärts!,* Kurt Tebbenjohanns's account, 114–21.

Records, T-1022, Roll 47, PG61957.

Spindler, *Der Handelskrieg mit U-Booten,* 4:237–38.

UC-46

Date Lost:	8 February 1917
Commander:	Oberleutnant zur See Fritz Moecke
Location:	Hoofden, at entrance to Dover Strait
Position:	51°7.6' N, 1°38.5' E
Disposition:	Ramming

On the night of 7–8 February 1917 UC-46 was returning to Zeebrugge from laying mines in the English Channel. Oberleutnant zur See Fritz Moecke went through the Dover-Dunkirk barrage submerged, and surfaced in bright moonlight off the Goodwin Sands at 0354, just three hundred yards from the destroyer HMS *Liberty*. When UC-46 came up it lay at almost a right angle to *Liberty* and slightly off its starboard bow. *Liberty* fired one round that missed and rammed the U-boat at twenty-four knots, its stem cutting four feet into the pressure hull. The blow brought the destroyer to a shuddering halt and rolled the U-boat on its beam ends. As *Liberty* backed away, UC-46 sank with all hands. *Liberty* was badly damaged and taking water, although it was in no immediate danger of sinking. The destroyer returned to Harwich and then went into dry dock for repairs.

Sources

Grant, *U-Boats Destroyed,* 44.
Records, T-1022, Roll 48, PG61959.
Spindler, *Der Handelskrieg mit U-Booten,* 4:138–39.

UC-47

Date Lost:	18 November 1917
Commander:	Oberleutnant zur See Wigankow
Location:	Off Britain's east coast, near Flamborough Head
Position:	54°3' N, 0°22.5' E
Disposition:	Ramming, Depth Charge

UC-47 departed Zeebrugge on 17 November 1917 to lay mines off Flamborough Head. On 18 November at 0623 HMS P-57 spotted UC-47 with its decks awash east-southeast of Flamborough Head and rammed the U-boat just forward of the conning tower. As P-57 passed over the sinking U-boat it dropped a depth charge, then doubled back and dropped another one. Oil and debris rose to the surface, but there were no survivors. British divers recovered UC-47's log and charts.

Sources

Grant, *U-Boats Destroyed,* 63.
Records, T-1022, Roll 48, PG611960.
Spindler, *Der Handelskrieg mit U-Booten,* 4:456–57.

UC-48

Date Lost:	**24 March 1918**
Commander:	**Oberleutnant zur See Helmut Lorenz**
Location:	**El Ferrol, Spain**
Position:	**43°31' N, 8°25' W**
Disposition:	**Depth Charge, Interned, Scuttled**

UC-48 departed Zeebrugge on 17 March 1918 to lay mines off Cherbourg and Point de Barfleur. On 20 March a British destroyer surprised it on the surface off the Isle of Wight, forced the U-boat to crash dive, and depth charged it. Three depth charges damaged UC-48 so badly that it had to surface and was unable to dive again. Its fuel tanks were ruptured and it had lost so much fuel that it was not able to return to Zeebrugge. Oberleutnant zur See Helmut Lorenz concluded that his only choice was to enter El Ferrol, which he did on 23 March.

Additional Information

The Spanish government interned the boat and the crew for the remainder of the war, taking the precaution of removing UC-48's propellers. The Spanish authorities took the precaution because UB-49 had escaped from interment in Cadiz on 6 October 1917. On 15 March 1919 UC-48's crew scuttled it rather than turn it over to the British.

Sources

Records, T-1022, Roll 48, PG61961.
Spindler, *Der Handelskrieg mit U-Booten,* 5:134–35.

UC-49

Date Lost:	8 August 1918
Commander:	Oberleutnant zur See Kükenthal
Location:	English Channel, off Start Point
Position:	50°20' N, 3°26' W (possible)
Disposition:	Depth Charge

UC-49 departed Zeebrugge on 1 August 1918 to lay mines off Plymouth and to attack shipping in the English Channel. On 5 August it torpedoed SS *Tuscan Prince* (5,275 tons). The British reacted by deploying a special hydrophone-equipped hunting patrol composed of the destroyer HMS *Opossum* and six motor launches (MLs) to track UC-49 down. On 8 August the hunting patrol found the U-boat.

At 1505 a lookout aboard the motor launch ML-191 spotted an oil slick on the water and the ML dropped a depth charge. Fifteen minutes later, *Opossum*'s hydrophone officer picked up engine sounds on his Mark II hydrophone and confirmed his bearing with a cross bearing from one of the MLs. The point on the chart was designated position one.

The destroyer detailed three MLs to remain on position one and sent the other three to a remote position three nautical miles away. Then *Opossum* depth charged position one, bringing up oil that formed a slick on the surface.

Opossum moved to a point one and three-quarter miles away and again stopped and listened. At 1800 the hydrophone officer heard UC-49. The destroyer signaled the three MLs stationed over position one to leave the area and shut down two miles away in order to fool UC-49 into believing the group had gone away.

Seventeen minutes later UC-49 surfaced seven hundred yards from *Opossum* and two hundred yards from ML-135. The ML got off two rounds that missed before the U-boat dropped beneath the surface. The group knew where UC-49 was and launched their second attack. The three MLs dropped five depth charges along the suspected track. The first one exploded "just astern of the submarine's wash," and the next four exploded at thirty-yard intervals in front of UC-49. After the MLs had made their runs, *Opossum* dropped its pattern around UC-49's suspected location, which brought a considerable amount of brown oil and air bubbles to the surface. The destroyer dropped a buoy to mark the spot and stopped to listen.

At 1917 ML-465 dropped one depth charge and forty-five minutes later *Opossum* dropped eight more. More brown oil and air bubbles came to the surface and the entire group settled down for the night, all engines stopped, listening.

At noon on 9 August minesweepers arrived and dragged the area looking for a wreck. They found nothing and *Opossum* dropped thirty-six more depth charges. At 2120 there was a sudden burst of oil and air on the surface, but the hydrophone officers heard nothing. Again the groups settled in for the night.

Oil and air were still rising on the morning of 10 August when one of the sweeps fouled an obstruction. *Opossum* passed across the position and dropped four depth charges, bringing up a stronger rush of air and oil. The last attack also produced a light bulb that popped up on the surface; it was retrieved by a minesweeper. The bulb bore the mark of an Austrian firm. Satisfied that they had sunk a U-boat, the group buoyed the position and returned to Dartmouth.

Additional Information

A postwar German study concluded that though the circumstantial evidence supported the hunting group's claim to having destroyed a U-boat, it was uncertain exactly which U-boat they sank. Time and place made it possible that the group did sink UC-48.

Sources

Admiralty Technical History Section, *Technical History and Index,* 22–24.
Records, T-1022, Roll 48, PG61962.
Spindler, *Der Handelskrieg mit U-Booten,* 5:136.

UC-50

Date Lost:	4 February 1918
Commander:	Kapitänleutnant Seuffer
Location:	Dover Strait, off Dungeness
Position:	50°49' N, 0°59' E
Disposition:	Depth Charge

UC-50 departed Zeebrugge on 7 January 1918 to lay mines off the Loire and the Gironde, and to attack shipping in the Bay of Biscay. On 4 February the destroyer HMS *Zubian* sighted UC-50 four hundred yards off its port bow. UC-50 was on the surface with its tall radio masts up and rigged when the destroyer turned toward it to ram. The Germans got the masts down in record time and UC-50 dove, but *Zubian* passed over the spot and dropped depth charges that brought large quantities of oil and debris to the surface. *Zubian* marked the spot with a buoy and an hour later HMS P-12 arrived and dropped six more depth charges. Trawlers dragged the area and found an obstruction that British divers later identified as UC-50.

Sources

Chatterton, *Beating the U-Boats,* 127–28.
Grant, *U-Boats Destroyed,* 81.
Records, T-1022, Roll 49, PG61964.
Spindler, *Der Handelskrieg mit U-Booten,* 5:85.

UC-51

Date Lost:	17 November 1917
Commander:	Oberleutnant zur See Hans Galster
Location:	English Channel, off Plymouth
Position:	50°8' N, 3°42' W
Disposition:	Mine

UC-51 departed Zeebrugge on 15 November 1917 to lay mines off Plymouth and to attack shipping in the Bristol Channel and off the southern Irish coast. Unknown to Oberleutnant zur See Hans Galster the British had laid 680 deep mines south of Start Point on 5 and 11 November. At 0910 on 17 November UC-51 either tried to surface or broached south of Start Point and the drifter *Lois* spotted its conning tower. As *Lois* headed toward the conning tower, the U-boat went under and a violent explosion occurred immediately. In fact, the explosion was so violent that it also damaged *Lois*. The U-boat partially rose to the surface, exposing its conning tower and part of the deck, and sank. Oil and debris came to the surface, including a German U-boat mine and a rubber boot with the name Ewald Metzger written inside. The boot belonged to a UC-51 crewman.

Sources

Records, T-1022, Roll 73, PG61965.
Spindler, *Der Handelskrieg mit U-Booten,* 4:458.

UC-53

Date Lost:	29 October 1918
Commander:	Kapitänleutnant Erich Gerth
Location:	Pola
Position:	44°52' N, 13°50' E
Disposition:	Scuttled

On 21 October 1918 the Admiralstab ordered all U-boats that were ready for sea to return to Germany, and on 23 October the Germans began evacuating Pola and Cattaro. UC-53 was one of ten boats that either could not make the trip home or was not ready for sea. The Germans destroyed these ten boats during the period 28 October to 1 November 1918 at Cattaro, Fiume, Pola, and Trieste.

Additional Information

UC-53 departed Cattaro on 19 September 1918 to lay mines off Messina and to attack shipping in the Tyrrhenian Sea. Destroyers depth charged it severely as it passed through the Otranto Strait, and engine problems hampered its patrol. Returning to Cattaro on 13 October, UC-53 was sent to Pola for engine repairs. The engine repairs were not complete when the order to evacuate came, and UC-53's crew blew it up in Pola on 29 October 1918.

Sources

Records, T-1022, Roll 73, PG61967.
Spindler, *Der Handelskrieg mit U-Booten,* 5:226–27.

UC-54

Date Lost:	29 October 1918
Commander:	Oberleutnant zur See Loycke
Location:	Trieste
Position:	45°39' N, 13°45' E
Disposition:	Scuttled

On 21 October 1918 the Admiralstab ordered all U-boats that were ready for sea to return to Germany, and on 23 October the Germans began evacuating Pola and Cattaro. UC-54 was one of ten boats that either could not make the trip home or was not ready for sea. The Germans destroyed these boats during the period 28 October to 1 November 1918 at Cattaro, Fiume, Pola, and Trieste.

Additional Information

Convoy escorts severely depth charged UC-54 off Sardinia on 23 September. UC-54 returned to Cattaro on 27 September. The chief engineer reported that the engines were worn out and that UC-54 had been through five patrols since its last major engine service. Sent to Trieste for a major overhaul, it was not ready for sea when the order came to evacuate the base. UC-54's crew scuttled it off Trieste on 29 October 1918.

Sources

Records, T-1022, Roll 73, PG61968.
Spindler, *Der Handelskrieg mit U-Booten,* 5:226–27.

UC-55

Date Lost:	29 September 1917
Commander:	Oberleutnant zur See Rühle von Lilienstern
Location:	Off Shetlands, near Lerwick
Position:	60°2' N, 1°2' W
Disposition:	Technical Problem, Gunfire, Scuttled

UC-55 departed Helgoland on 25 September 1917 to lay mines off Lerwick. On 29 September, just as it started dropping its mines, the U-boat suddenly became uncontrollable and sank past its maximum rated depth. Water flooded the forward part of the boat, reached the battery compartment and created chlorine gas. Oberleutnant zur See Rühle von Lilienstern ordered the tanks blown, and destroyers and patrol boats opened fire the moment UC-55 broke surface. The crew set explosive charges and opened all the hatches to sink the boat. Twelve men, including Lilienstern, went down with UC-55. The British picked up the rest of the crew.

Leutnant zur See Herbert Sauer, UC-55

We entered the harbor entrance at twenty meters and were about to start laying mines when the boat dropped by the bow 35° and the boat sank to sixty-eight meters. Water entered from somewhere forward. We pumped the regulator tank and blew tank 1. The bow rose but the boat now dropped 25° by the stern. We flooded tank 1 and blew tank 4 but the boat dropped 40° by the bow. We blew tanks 1, 2 and 3 and surfaced, but the moment the boat broke the surface the captain ordered her to dive. The boat assumed a sharp bow-down angle and water flooded the forward compartments. A fire broke out in the electric motor room, the cable to the main switchboard burned through and chlorine gas began developing. We were unable to find the source of the flooding. There were only 65 kg compressed air left and the captain ordered all the tanks blown.

The boat surfaced and came to an even keel. The diesel engines were started and we attempted to get away at full speed, but we were surrounded by destroyers and trawlers that were about a thousand meters away. The captain ordered the men to don their life vests and go on deck. Ten minutes later the destroyers opened fire and the blast from a near miss blew me overboard. Moments later a round hit the conning tower, throwing bodies everywhere. The boat was sinking by the stern when a round hit her squarely in the after torpedo room that caused a tremendous explosion. The boat sank instantly and a short while later there were two more strong underwater explosions.

The destroyers moved in closer, put out boats and picked up the survivors.

Obermaschinistenmaat Kegelmann, UC-55

At 1415 were ready to lay our mines in the harbor entrance. The watch officer, the leading seaman and a torpedo mate were forward in the mine room. The captain called from the conning tower, "Clear the mines for laying." And the watch officer answered, "Clear." Suddenly the boat dropped down by the bow and everything that was not fastened down, tumbled forward. Everybody grabbed on to something to keep from being thrown forward.

The chief engineer, who was in charge of the boat's steering and trim, blew the forward tanks, but the stern dropped, and he blew the after tanks. The boat went through a repetition of dropping by the bow and then by the stern and all the time we were sinking until we reached ninety-five meters. There was still no seabed and then the shout from forward, "Flooding," to which the captain respond by ordering all the tanks blown. The boat rose stern first, but the moment she came to the surface the captain shouted "Dive," and the boat went down with a sharp bow-down angle.

The chief engineer could not get the boat on an even keel and we again went through the repetitions of being down by the bow one moment and then quickly down by the bow the next. The commands were continuous, blow forward, blow aft, pump the forward bilge, pump the after bilge. The forward compartments flooded, the batteries failed and chlorine gas developed. The compressed air was nearly exhausted when the captain ordered the tanks blown so that we could surface.

As soon as the boat surfaced the watch officer, chief engineer and navigator went out on the conning tower with the captain. The order came down to start the diesel engines and I went back to the control room. Just as I arrived in the control room the helmsman shouted, "The rudder is not answering the helm." The batteries had failed and there was no power for the rudder motor. The rudder was over 10° and the boat was running in a circle. While we were coupling the rudder to the manual controls the order came down to destroy the secret papers, codebooks and log. Another order directed us to set explosive charges in the mine room and in the engine room.

While we were placing the charges a round exploded against the conning tower, killing six men including the chief engineer. We finished setting the charges and activated the time fuses, and went out on deck. Maschinistenmaat Hansen and I went through the conning tower hatch and as we came out the captain said to Hansen, "Mate Hansen, the boat is not sinking quickly enough. Please go below and open the flooding valves on all the tanks." Hansen went below, did that and returned to the captain. By the time he got there the boat was already down by the stern. We went over the side and swam away. We had not gone far when a violent explosion tore the UC-55 apart and she vanished. A little while later there were two more explosions.

There were destroyers and fishing boats all around us and after about a half an hour they picked us up.

Source

Records, T-1022, Roll 74, PG61969, "Bericht des Ob.Masch.Mts. Kagelmann übermittelt von Mar. Ing. Appl. Tönningsen"; "Angaben des Lt. z. S. Herbert Sauer von UC-55"; and "Auszug aus einer Niederschrift des Obermaschinistenmaat Kagelmann."

UC-56

Date Lost:	24 May 1918
Commander:	Kapitänleutnant Wilhelm Kiesewetter
Location:	Santander, Spain
Position:	43°28' N, 3°48' W
Disposition:	Technical Problem, Interned

On 13 May 1918 UC-56 departed Zeebrugge to lay mines off the Loire and to attack shipping in the Bay of Biscay. UC-56 started having problems with it starboard propeller shaft shortly after it cleared the Dover Strait, and at almost the same time its starboard electric motor failed. Nevertheless, Kapitänleutnant Wilhelm Kiesewetter carried on until his port electric motor quit. His engine room crew cannibalized the starboard electric motor for parts and got the port motor working again. With one diesel engine and one electric motor working, he continued his minelaying mission. But things became critical when the port electric motor's armature burned out; without electric propulsion, UC-56 could not dive. Because he could only operate on the surface, Kiesewetter knew that a return passage through the Dover Strait was impossible. He decided to have the boat interned at Santander, Spain, arriving there on 24 May. The Spanish government interned his boat and crew for the remainder of the war.

Source

Spindler, *Der Handelskrieg mit U-Booten,* 5:86.

UC-57

Date Lost: November 1917
Commander: Kapitänleutnant Friedrich Hans Bernhard
                    Wissmann
Location: Eastern Baltic or Gulf of Finland
Position: Unknown
Disposition: Verschollen

UC-57 departed Danzig on 12 November 1917 under the direction of the Army General Staff on Special Operation Latvia. Aboard were six agents of the Finnish Jägerbatallion 27 as well as small arms, ammunition, and explosives that UC-57 was to land near Helsingfors. The agents, weapons, ammunition, and explosives were destined for Gen. Gustav Mannerheim's White Army.

En route to the landing UC-57 passed submerged through several Russian minefields; the crew repeatedly heard mine anchor cables scraping along the hull. Despite the obstacles, Kapitänleutnant Friedrich Hans Bernhard Wissmann delivered the agents and the cargo on 17 November. UC-57 started its return trip on 18 November, and the Kurland flotilla command expected its arrival in Danzig on 24 November. Radio calls to UC-57 on 23 and 24 November went unanswered, and the U-boat was never seen again. UC-57 probably hit a Russian mine on the way home.

Sources

Records, T-1022, Roll 74, PG61972.
Spindler, *Der Handelskrieg mit U-Booten,* 4:490–91.

UC-61

Date Lost:	26 July 1917
Commander:	Kapitänleutnant Georg Gerth
Location:	Off French coast, between Calais and Cape Gris Nez
Position:	50°53' N, 1°37' E
Disposition:	Stranded, Scuttled

UC-61 departed Zeebrugge on 25 July 1917 to lay mines off Boulogne and Le Havre. Passing through the Dover Strait on the French side on the morning of 26 July the U-boat was close to the French coast in heavy fog. Kapitänleutnant Georg Gerth had recently been promoted and this was his first trip with his new rank, and for that reason his navigational error was particularly embarrassing. Unable to fix his position, with visibility nearly zero and a strong ebb tide, Gerth ran hard aground on a falling tide near the village of Wissant. He radioed Bruges for help, but before help could arrive Gerth saw a destroyer standing in and he knew that he had to destroy his boat. The crew set explosive charges and rigged torpedo warheads. Shortly after they had blown up UC-61 a French cavalry patrol arrived and captured the entire crew.

Additional Information

The destruction of UC-61 was not as complete as the Germans preferred. French experts examined the hulk and reported that although the boat was beyond salvage, the explosions and fire had left the forward section largely undamaged. They recovered UC-61's eighteen mines and its hydrophone. The French interrogation officer reported that Gerth spoke excellent French. The captain would not discuss military matters, but freely explained how UC-61 went aground. Gerth told the French officer that he had laid a course that kept him well off shore, but thick fog prevented him from taking accurate bearings and the current set him in toward the beach. UC-61 went aground twice. On the first instance, Gerth was able to get it off after considerable effort. What he did not know was that while the boat was aground the ebb had uncovered a sand bar behind him. When he backed off the first shoal, he ran hard aground on the second. The crew tried to lighten the boat by removing all torpedoes and ammunition, but by the time that work was completed the fog had lifted. As soon as the visibility improved people ashore spotted the boat and alerted the

French military. Knowing that they would soon be captured, Gerth ordered the crew to blow up the boat.

Sources

Records, T-1022, Roll 108, PG61982, "Kriegstagebuch S. M. Ubt. UC-61 für die Zeit vom 8.7.17 bis zur Strandung"; "Unterseeboot Verlust, Deutschland, 30 July 1917"; and "Abschrift, Johannes Giese, Ingenieur, Bremen 9. February 1920."
Spindler, *Der Handelskrieg mit U-Booten,* 4:320.

UC-62

Date Lost:	October 1917
Commander:	Oberleutnant zur See Max Schmitz
Location:	English Channel
Position:	Unknown
Disposition:	Verschollen

UC-62 departed Zeebrugge on 11 October 1917 to lay mines off St. Albans Head and Portland. The boat did not return.

Additional Information

UC-62 did lay nine mines off St. Albans Head and the British swept them on 18 October, but the Germans think the U-boat hit a mine off Plymouth before it laid mines there. The British credit their submarine E-54 with sinking UC-62 on 19 October 1917. A note in UC-62's file says that Royal Navy vessels reported a U-boat destroyed on 19 October 1917 that could only have been UC-62. However, E-54 is not credited with sinking a U-boat in the official postwar list, and the fact is that no one knows what happened to UC-62.

Sources

Chatterton, *Beating the U-Boats,* 96.
Gibson and Prendergast, *The German Submarine War,* 220.
Records, T-1022, Roll 108, PG61983, "Abschrift zu Z-13911/20, Berlin, den 15.9.1920."
Spindler, *Der Handelskrieg mit U-Booten,* 4:458–59.

UC-63

Date Lost:	1 November 1917
Commander:	Oberleutnant zur See Uwe Karsten von Heydebreck
Location:	Dover Strait
Position:	51°23' N, 2°0' E
Disposition:	Torpedo

UC-63 departed Zeebrugge on 11 October 1917 to lay mines off the Owers Lightship and to attack shipping off the French coast. At 0100 on 1 November it reported its position and gave an estimated time of arrival in Zeebrugge. Fourteen minutes later the British submarine E-52 torpedoed UC-63. One crewman, Fritz Marsal, survived.

U-Bootsmannsmaat Fritz Marsal, UC-63

During the night of 31 October to 1 November we passed across the Dover-Calais net on the surface, and established our exact position with radio bearings at eighteen nautical miles off Dover. I was on watch in the conning tower and none of us saw the torpedo. The boat sank very quickly and only the conning tower watch, the chief engineer and the control room stoker got off the boat. The E-52 surfaced almost immediately after the UC-63 went down, but I was they only one that they picked up. I do not know what happened to the others.

Source

Records, T-1022, Roll 108, PG61984, "Bericht des U-Bootsmannsmaat Fritz Marsal."

UC-64

Date Lost:	20 June 1918
Commander:	Oberleutnant zur See Schwartz
Location:	Dover Strait
Position:	50°58' N, 1°23' W
Disposition:	Mine

UC-64 departed Zeebrugge on 18 June 1918 to lay mines off Brest and the Gironde, after which it was to attack shipping in the English Channel and the Bay of Biscay. UC-64 did not return.

Additional Information

According to the British, UC-64 was approaching the Folkestone–Gris Nez deep mine barrage on the surface during the early morning of 20 June when patrol boats forced it to dive. The result was exactly what the British had intended when they designed the barrage, and UC-64 dove into a mine. It was lost with all hands. British divers found the wreck two months later and identified it as UC-64.

Sources

Grant, *U-Boats Destroyed,* 89.
Records, T-1022, Roll 108, PG61985.
Spindler, *Der Handelskrieg mit U-Booten,* 5:139.

UC-65

Date Lost:	3 November 1917
Commander:	Kapitänleutnant Lafrenz
Location:	English Channel, off Beachy Head
Position:	50°31' N, 0°27' E
Disposition:	Torpedo

On 3 November C-15 torpedoed UC-65 off Beachy Head. Four men survived.

Kapitänleutnant Lafrenz, UC-65

UC-65 was surfaced fifteen nautical miles south of Beachy Head. I was on the conning tower with the lookouts. I spotted a periscope slightly forward of the beam on the starboard side, and gave the order to turn hard to port. The submarine fired a double shot at four hundred meters. The first torpedo struck us amidships but did not explode, but the second torpedo blew off the stern. The boat sank instantly.

Log Book, C-15

1443: Enemy SM 5 points off the bow. Flooded both tubes.
1515: Fired double shot at four hundred yards. One torpedo hit, slight explosion noise, SM sank immediately.

Sources

Edwards, *We Dive at Dawn*, 298–99.
Records, T-1022, Roll 109, PG61986.

UC-66

Date Lost:	12 June 1917
Commander:	Oberleutnant zur See Pustkuchen
Location:	Western approaches to English Channel
Position:	49°56' N, 5°10' W (probable)
Disposition:	Depth Charge

UC-66 departed Zeebrugge on 22 May 1917 to lay mines in the Bristol Channel and off Swansea and Milford, and to attack shipping along the southern coast of Ireland. UC-66 did not return.

Additional Information

The trawler *Sea King* was off the Lizard on 12 June when a lookout spotted a U-boat that was surfacing four hundred yards off the trawler's port bow. Cdr. Godfrey Herbert, former captain of the decoy vessel *Carrigan Head,* ordered *Sea King* to head toward the U-boat. UC-66 dove. As the trawler passed over the spot it dropped a depth charge that caused six secondary explosions. A large amount of oil rose immediately to the surface and covered a wide area. Despite the fact that the U-boat could not be positively identified, the Germans concluded in a postwar study that given the time and place, the U-boat was probably UC-66.

Sources

Grant, *U-Boats Destroyed,* 62.
Records, T-1022, Roll 109, PG61987.
Spindler, *Der Handelskrieg mit U-Booten,* 4:327–28.

UC-68

Date Lost:	13 March 1917
Commander:	Oberleutnant zur See Degatau
Location:	English Channel
Position:	50°17' N, 3°31.5' W (possible)
Disposition:	Own Mine

UC-68 departed Zeebrugge on 10 March 1917 to lay mines off Dartmouth and Plymouth, and to attack shipping in the English Channel. UC-68 did not return.

Additional Information

British patrols observed a powerful underwater explosion six nautical miles off Start Point on 13 March. Minesweepers later swept up four German mines in that area, leading the Germans to believe that UC-68 probably blew up on one of its own mines. The Germans doubted an account that the British submarine C-7 torpedoed UC-68 on 5 April 1917 because UC-boats rarely remained out for over three weeks. C-7 is not officially credited with sinking a U-boat.

Sources

Chatterton, *Beating the U-Boats,* 56.
Gibson and Prendergast, *The German Submarine War,* 167.
Grant, *U-Boats Destroyed,* 69.
Records, T-1022, Roll 109, PG61989.
Spindler, *Der Handelskrieg mit U-Booten,* 4:151.

UC-69

Date Lost:	6 December 1917
Commander:	Oberleutnant zur See Thielmann
Location:	English Channel
Position:	49°57' N, 1°10' W
Disposition:	Accident, Ramming

UC-69 departed Zeebrugge on 4 December 1917 to lay mines off Cherbourg and to attack shipping in the English Channel. At 2000 on 6 December it was eight and a half nautical miles north of Cape Barfleur and on a collision course with homeward-bound U-96. The night was very dark and U-96 did not see UC-69 until it was too late to avoid a collision. U-96's stem slammed into the starboard side of UC-69 midway between the conning tower and the stern.

UC-69 immediately sank by the stern, but its net cutter fouled U-96's bow; for a short time the two boats were locked together. That turned out to be a blessing, because most of UC-69s crew made their way aboard U-96 by going over the bows. Finally the bows separated. When UC-69's stern hit the seabed, the after torpedo exploded, killing ten men who were in the water.

Kriegstagebuch, 6.XII.17, UC-69

2002: Completely dark night, visibility 50–100 meters: To starboard, three to four points off the bow I suddenly see a dark shadow that is closing on me. It is too late to turn away so I order hard starboard rudder and all ahead full in an attempt to ram. Neither command was executed because a collision aft occurred immediately; UC-69 was rammed starboard side aft. Only now was it possible to recognize that the other vessel was a U-boat. The distance at which I first saw the other U-boat was at the most thirty to fifty meters.

I shouted the captain of the U-96 to remain alongside until I had determined what our condition was. The chief engineer told me that we were taking some water on the starboard side aft, but that the boat would remain afloat. I went below to see for myself what the situation was. The chief engineer now told me that the flooding had become serious and he was having difficulty keeping the boat afloat.

The water in the engine room was already over the deck plates and a stream of water 30- to 40-cm thick was entering through the hole in the hull. It would be impossible to plug a leak of that size. As we stood there the boat settled by the stern so that the hole in the side went deeper. I ordered all the men to go on deck and directed the torpedomen to rig demolition charges.

I hurried back to the conning tower and gave the order to abandon ship. The men were able to step directly from the UC-69 onto the bow of the U-96. The boat was starting to settle quickly by the stern and I ordered the men to leave the UC-69 quickly. I went down to the deck to open the after hatch so that the men could use it to go out on deck, but the hatch was already under water. I returned to the conning tower to be sure that the men were getting off as quickly as possible. When I climbed up the conning tower I grabbed onto the anti-mine wire that was now bar taut from the strain of being fouled in the U-96's net cutter. The wire parted under the strain and I was hurled overboard. There were four or five other men from the conning tower in the water with me.

The U-96 threw me a line and hauled me onto the saddle tank. The parting of the anti-mine wire freed the U-96 from the UC-69, which now sank very quickly. The UC-69 had just disappeared underwater when a powerful explosion occurred. Apparently when the stern hit the bottom the torpedo in the after tube was thrown against the door and exploded. The explosion killed two men who were still in the water. A head count showed that we were missing eleven men.

Sources

Records, T-1022, Roll 109, PG61990 (UC-69), "Kriegstagebuch S. M. U-Boot UC-69, Anfangen am 7. November 1917, Abgeschlossen am 8. Dezember 1917" and "Vorläufige Bemerkungen zu Kriegstagebücher, s. Eingang, Berlin den 5. Januar 1918"; T-1022, Roll 39, PG61679 (U-96).

Spindler, *Der Handelskrieg mit U-Booten,* 4:429–30, 462.

UC-70

Date Lost:	28 August 1918
Commander:	Oberleutnant zur See Dobberstein
Location:	Off Britain's east coast, near Whitby
Position:	54°32' N, 0°40' W
Disposition:	Depth Charge

UC-70 departed Zeebrugge on 21 August 1918 to lay mines in the Hoofden and then to attack shipping along Britain's east coast. UC-70 did not return.

Additional Information

According to the British, on 28 August a British seaplane spotted an oil slick on the surface. It dropped a 520-pound bomb that exploded and brought more oil and air bubbles to the surface. The airplane summoned the destroyer HMS *Ouse,* and the destroyer dropped ten depth charges set for fifty feet.

The British believe the U-boat was lying on the bottom and may have been leaking oil as the result of earlier damage. On 14 September 1918 British divers visited the wreck and identified it as UC-70.

Sources

Grant, *U-Boats Destroyed,* 128–29.
Records, T-1022, Roll 109, PG61991.
Spindler, *Der Handelskrieg mit U-Booten,* 5:140–41.

UC-72

Date Lost:	20 August 1917
Commander:	Oberleutnant zur See Ernst Voigt
Location:	Bay of Biscay
Position:	46°0' N, 4°48' W (probable)
Disposition:	Gunfire

UC-72 departed Zeebrugge on 12 August 1917 to lay mines off the west coast of France between Les Barges and Chassiron, and to attack shipping in the Bay of Biscay. On 20 August UC-72 attacked the British decoy vessel *Acton* with gunfire at a range of three thousand yards. *Acton* stopped, blew off steam, and its panic party abandoned ship. *Acton*'s crew started controlled fires in the well deck, and Oberleutnant zur See Ernst Voigt dove and moved in close to examine *Acton* through his periscope. Satisfied that it was a harmless tramp, he surfaced close aboard, and *Acton*'s gunners opened fire at point-blank range. UC-72 received several hits and sank stern first.

Additional Information

Acton's crew did not claim a victory, instead they described the action as inconclusive. A postwar German study concluded that *Acton* probably sank UC-72 on 20 August 1917.

Sources

Records, T-1022, Roll 86, PG61994.
Spindler, *Der Handelskrieg mit U-Booten,* 4:335–36.

310

UC-75

Date Lost:	**31 May 1918**
Commander:	**Oberleutnant zur See Walter Schmitz**
Location:	**Off Britain's east coast, near Flamborough Head**
Position:	**53°57' N, 0°9' W**
Disposition:	**Ramming**

On 31 May 1918 UC-75 was making a submerged attack on a convoy off Flamborough Head when HMS *Fairy* rammed it. The captain ordered the tanks blown and the crew abandoned UC-75. While the crew was abandoning the boat, *Fairy* rammed it again, sinking UC-75. *Fairy* also sank as a result of the damage caused by the ramming. There were fourteen survivors from UC-75.

Oberleutnant zur See Walter Schmitz, UC-75

At 0300 on 31 May 1918 the UC-75 made a submerged attack on a strongly defended convoy south of Flamborough Head. During the approach a steamer rammed us and serious flooding occurred through the conning tower hatch. We surfaced and a destroyer tried to ram us, but we succeeded in ramming her. Her second attempt to ram us resulted in minor damage to the UC-75. The destroyer then opened fire.

We were unable to dive. I ordered all the men on deck and opened the vents and the deck hatches. As the boat went down the crew went into the water and swam toward the destroyer. Men were hanging on the destroyer's side when she got under way, which resulted in many men being killed. Some time later a drifter picked up the chief engineer, the watch officer and me. Fifteen minutes after we were aboard the drifter the destroyer sank and the men who had already gone aboard her were back in the water. Not all of them were rescued.

Obersteuermannsmaat Hermann Stengel, UC-75

The UC-75 sank in the North Sea, eight to ten nautical miles south of Flamborough Head. During an attack on a strongly defended convoy a large steamer rammed us, doing major damage to the conning tower. Major flooding followed and we had to surface. We tried to escape from the many enemy ships and an enemy destroyer tried to ram us. Her attempt failed and we rammed her on the starboard side just aft of the bow. The destroyer came around and made a second attempt to ram us that succeeded, but caused only light damage. She then opened fire.

The captain decided to scuttle the boat, which was accomplished by opening the vents. While the crew was in the water, the British fired on us with pistols and rifles. The firing stopped and the destroyer picked up some of us, but others were left in the water and drowned. About twenty minutes after we were aboard the destroyer, she too sank and we were again in the water.

Obermaschinistenmaat Hugo Zipfel, UC-75

A steamer rammed us while we were at twelve meters, causing massive flooding. We surfaced and an enemy destroyer took us under fire. The crew assembled on deck and the vents were opened so that the boat sank very quickly. We were in the water for about a half an hour before we were picked up, but only fourteen were saved. The seventeen who were not rescued must have drowned.

Additional Information

According to the British, SS *Blaydonian* unintentionally rammed UC-75, and the sound of the collision was heard aboard HMS *Fairy.* The destroyer challenged the now-surfaced U-boat and rammed it in the stern and then rammed it again. The Germans dove overboard and *Fairy* fished fourteen survivors from the water before it too sank.

Source

Grant, *U-Boats Destroyed,* 123–24.

Records, T-1022, Roll 1610, PG61997, "Bericht des Kommandanten UC-75"; "Abschrift aus Fragebogen, 4.10.1919"; "Abschrift aus Fragebogen Obersteuermannsmaat Hermann Stengel"; and "Abschrift aus Fragebogen, Obermaschinistenmaat Hugo Zipfel."

UC-76

Date Lost:	10 May 1917
Commander:	Oberleutnant zur See Barten
Location:	Helgoland
Position:	54°10.5' N, 7°54' E
Disposition:	Accident, Own Mine

On 10 May 1917 UC-76 was in Helgoland being armed for a new mission. Someone forgot to close the lower chute hatch. When the first mine was lowered into the chute, it fell through and exploded below the boat. The boat sank immediately in sixteen meters and everyone in the forward part of the boat was killed, including the captain, both watch officers, and the chief engineer.

Source

Spindler, *Der Handelskrieg mit U-Booten,* 4:62.

UC-77

Date Lost:	**July 1918**
Commander:	**Oberleutnant zur See Ries**
Location:	**English Channel or Dover Strait**
Position:	**Unknown**
Disposition:	**Verschollen**

UC-77 departed Zeebrugge on 11 July 1918 to lay mines off the Nab Lightship and Portland. It did not return and there were no survivors. There are no clues as to what happened to UC-77, but it is possible that it either hit a mine in the Folkestone–Gris Nez deep mine barrage or that one of its own mines blew up while it was being laid.

Source

Spindler, *Der Handelskrieg mit U-Booten,* 5:103.

UC-78

Date Lost:	May 1918
Commander:	Kapitänleutnant Hans Kukat
Location:	English Channel or Dover Strait
Position:	Unknown
Disposition:	Verschollen

UC-78 departed Ostend on 2 May 1918 to lay mines off Boulogne and Newhaven, after which it was to attack shipping in the English Channel. The U-boat did not return and there were no survivors. There are no clues as to what happened to UC-78, but it is possible that it either hit a mine in the Folkestone–Gris Nez deep mine barrage or that one of its own mines blew up while it was being laid.

Additional Information

A British account says that patrols forced UC-78 to dive into the Folkestone–Gris Nez deep mine barrage at 0810 on 2 May. A postwar German study discounted that claim on the basis that UC-78 laid its mines off Boulogne and Newhaven as ordered, thus it was still active after 2 May. The French confirmed that the mines had been laid off Boulogne.

Source

Spindler, *Der Handelskrieg mit U-Booten,* 5:88–89.

UC-79

Date Lost:	March 1918
Commander:	Oberleutnant zur See Krameyer
Location:	English Channel or Dover Strait
Position:	Unknown
Disposition:	Verschollen

UC-79 departed Zeebrugge on 20 March 1918 to lay mines off Brest and to attack shipping in the English Channel. It did not return and there were no survivors. There are no clues as to what happened to UC-79, but it is possible that it either hit a mine in the Folkestone–Gris Nez deep mine barrage or that one of its own mines blew up while it was being laid.

Source

Spindler, *Der Handelskrieg mit U-Booten,* 5:90.

UC-91

Date Lost:	5 September 1918
Commander:	Kapitänleutnant Bernard Gerke
Location:	Kiel Harbor
Position:	54°21' N, 10°10' E
Disposition:	Accident, Ramming

UC-91 was commissioned on 31 July 1918 and was conducting diving tests on 5 September in Kiel harbor when the German SS *Alexandria Moermann* rammed and sank it. Seventeen crewmen were killed. The salvage vessel *Vulkan* raised UC-91 on 10 September, but the U-boat was not returned to service. UC-91 was surrendered to the British; on 10 February 1919 it sank while under tow in the North Sea in position 54°15' N, 3°56' E.

Source

Spindler, *Der Handelskrieg mit U-Booten,* 5:103.

The main arena, the British home waters. The Germans operated two independent commands in this area. The oceangoing U-boats were assigned to the High Sea Fleet and the coastal-class UB- and UC-boats operated from Bruges, Ostend, and Zeebrugge in Belgium.

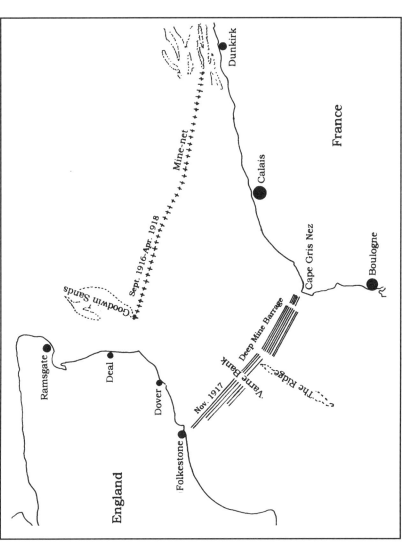

The Dover Strait, showing the two barriers the British constructed in an attempt to close the strait to U-boats. The original net and mine barrier was totally ineffective; U-boat captains used it as a navigational reference. The Folkestone to Gris Nez deep mine barrage was very effective.

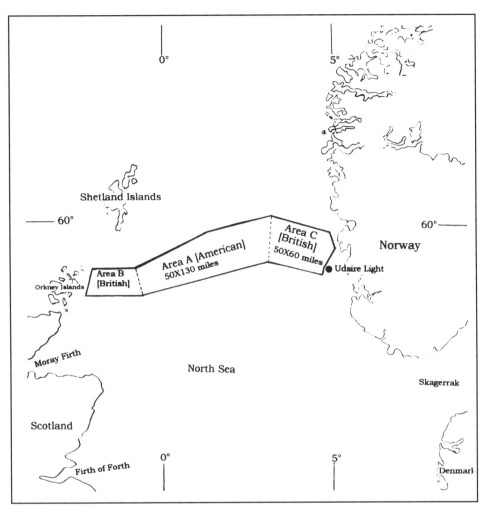

The Northern Mine Barrage probably took five U-boats during its short operational period in 1918. If the war had lasted another year, the Northern Mine Barrage would probably have closed the northern route and effectively confined U-boats to the North Sea.

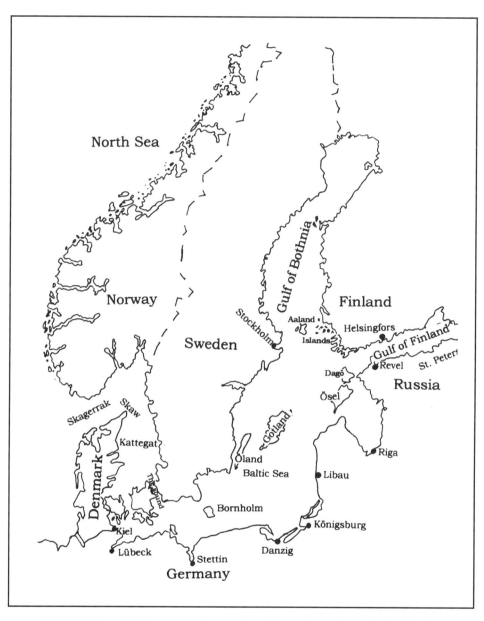

The Baltic was a separate command under Prinz Heinrich. It was the smallest of the five independent U-boat commands and accomplished the least because there were so few targets for U-boats to attack.

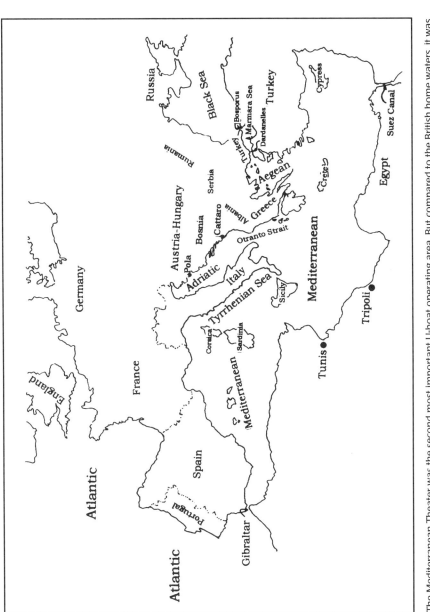

The Mediterranean Theater was the second most important U-boat operating area. But compared to the British home waters, it was very much a secondary theater. The main Mediterranean command was at Pola with a satellite command at Constantinople (present-day Istanbul).

Appendix A

Types of U-Boats

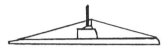

UBI type boat, overall length 93 feet

There were three types of UB-boats, each larger and more powerful than the previous type. This figure illustrates the growth in size as each new class appeared. The type III UB-boats were actually oceangoing warships although the Germans still classed them as coastal types.

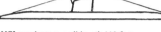

UCI type boat, overall length 112 feet

There were three types of UC-boats; all were minelayers. Like UB-boats, UC-boats grew larger and more powerful with each new type. Type III boats were capable of long ocean voyages and were designed to conduct torpedo and gun attacks as well as lay mines. UC-boats were the most dangerous boats in which to serve.

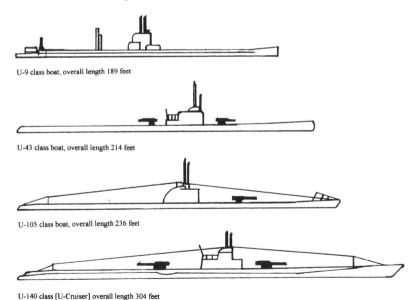

U-9 class boat, overall length 189 feet

U-43 class boat, overall length 214 feet

U-105 class boat, overall length 236 feet

U-140 class [U-Cruiser] overall length 304 feet

The four representative U-boat types are shown. U-9–class boats were primitive warships with limited seakeeping ability. By 1918 the Germans were building U-boats that were capable of transatlantic passages and were as large as a World War II U.S. Navy fleet–class boats.

Appendix B

Rank Equivalents during World War I

Comparative Officers Rank

German Navy	U.S. Navy	Royal Navy
Grossadmiral	—[1]	—
Generaladmiral	—	—
Admiral	Admiral	Admiral
Vizeadmiral	Vice Admiral	Vice Admiral
Konteradmiral	Rear Admiral	Rear Admiral
Kommodore	Commodore	Commodore
Kapitän zur See	Captain	Captain
Fregattenkapitän	Commander	Commander
Korvettenkapitän	Lieutenant Commander	Lieutenant Commander
Kapitänleutnant	Lieutenant	Lieutenant
Oberleutnant zur See	Lieutenant (jg)	—
Leutnant zur See	Ensign	Sub-Lieutenant

[1] No equivalent rank.

Sources: The Bluejacket's Manual, Annapolis: Naval Institute Press, 1918; Department of Languages, U.S. Naval Academy, Naval Phraseology, Annapolis: Naval Institute Press, 1934; Ewegweiser zu den Laufbahnen in der Kaiserlichen Marine, Stuttgart: Bibliothek für Zeitgeschichte, 1917; Jane's Fighting Ships of World War I, New York: Military Press,1990; Tim Mulligan, Guides to the Microfilm Records of the German Navy, 1850–1945, Washington, D.C.: National Archives, 1984; U.S. Navy Office of Information, www.chinfo.navy.mil, accessed November 1999.

Comparative Enlisted Rank

German Navy	U.S. Navy	Royal Navy
Obermaschinist, Obersteurer-mann, Oberheizer (prefix "Ober"; suffix "ist" or "mann")	Chief Petty Officer (E7)	Chief Petty Officer
Maschinist, Steuermann, Heizer (suffix "ist" or "mann")	Petty Officer 1st Class (E6)	Petty Officer 1st Class
Obermaschinisten-maat, Obersteuermanns-maat, Oberheizersmaat (prefix "Ober"; suffix "maat")	Petty Officer 2nd Class (E5)	Petty Officer 2nd Class
Maschinistenmaat, Steuermannsmaat, Heizersmaat (suffix "maat")	Petty Officer 3rd Class (E4)	Petty Officer 3rd Class
Obermatrose (prefix "Ober")	Seaman 1st Class (E3)	Leading Seaman
Matrose	Seaman 2nd Class (E2)	Able Seaman
—	Seaman 3rd Class (E1)	—[1]

[1]No equivalent rank.

Sources: The Bluejacket's Manual, Annapolis: Naval Institute Press, 1918; Department of Languages, U.S. Naval Academy, *Naval Phraseology,* Annapolis: Naval Institute Press, 1934; *Ewegweiser zu den Lauf-bahnen in der Kaiserlichen Marine,* Stuttgart: Bibliothek für Zeitgeschichte, 1917; *Jane's Fighting Ships of World War I,* New York: Military Press, 1990; Tim Mulligan, *Guides to the Microfilm Records of the German Navy, 1850–1945,* Washington, D.C.: National Archives, 1984; U.S. Navy Office of Information, www.chinfo.navy.mil, accessed November 1999.

Bibliography

Primary Sources

Official U.S. Records

Records of the German Navy, 1850–1945, Record Group 242, Microfilm Publication T-1022, National Archives, Washington, D.C.

Memoirs and Personal Recollections

Bauer, Hermann. *Als Führer der U-Boote im Weltkrieg.* Leipzig: Koehler and Amelang, n.d.

Cornford, L. Cope. *The Paravane Adventure.* London: Hodder and Stoughton, 1919.

Crompton, Oberleutnant zur See. *Crompton U-41: Der zweite Baralong-Fall.* Berlin: August Scherl, 1917.

Hashagen, Ernst. *U-Boote Westwärts!: Meine Fahrten um England, 1914–1918.* Berlin: E. S. Mittler und Sohn, 1931.

Sims, Rear Admiral William Sowden, USN. *The Victory at Sea.* New York: Doubleday, Page and Co., 1920.

Technical Monographs and Official Histories

Admiralty Technical History Section. *Technical History and Index: A Serial History of Technical Problems Dealt With by Admiralty Departments,* Part 7 (TH7), "The Anti-Submarine Division of the Naval Staff, December 1916–November 1918," July 1919. Imperial War Museum, London, U.K.

Cowie, Captain J. S., RN. *Mines, Minelayers and Minelaying.* London: Oxford University Press, 1949.

Firle, Rudolf. *Der Krieg in der Ostsee,* vol. 1. Berlin: Mittler und Sohn, 1922.

Gladisch, Walter. *Der Krieg zur See, 1914–1818: Der Krieg in der Nordsee,* vols. 6 and 7. Berlin: E. S. Mittler und Sohn, 1937–65.

Gröner, Erich. *Die deutschen Kriegsschiffe, 1815–1945,* 2 vols. München: J. F. Lehmanns Verlag, 1966.

Groos, Otto. *Der Krieg zur See, 1914–1818: Der Krieg in der Nordsee,* vols. 1–5. Berlin: E. S. Mittler und Sohn, 1922–25.

Herzog, Bodo. *Deutsche U-Boote, 1906–1966.* Herrsching, Germany: Pawlak, 1990.

Lorey, Hermann. *Der Krieg in den türkischen Gewässern,* vol. 1. Berlin: E. S. Mittler und Sohn, 1928.

Rollmann, Heinrich. *Der Krieg in der Ostsee,* vol. 2. Berlin: E. S. Mittler und Sohn, 1929.

Rössler, Eberhard. *The U-Boat: The Evolution and Technical History of German Submarines,* translated by Harold Erenberg. Annapolis: Naval Institute Press, 1981.

Spindler, Konteradmiral Arno. *Der Krieg zur See, 1914–1918: Der Handelskrieg mit U-Booten,* 5 vols. Berlin: E. S. Mittler und Sohn, 1932–66.

Vickers Ltd. *The Submarine Sweep as Fitted on Trawlers.* London: Vickers Ltd., 1917.

Von Gagern, Ernst. *Der Krieg in der Ostsee,* vol. 3. Berlin: E. S. Mittler und Sohn, 1964.

Secondary Sources

Chatterton, E. Keeble. *Beating the U-Boats.* London: Hurst and Blackett, Ltd., 1943.

———. *Danger Zone: The Story of the Queenstown Command.* Boston: Little, Brown and Co., 1934.

———. *Fighting the U-Boats.* London: Hurst and Blackett, Ltd., 1942.

———. *Q-Ships and Their Story.* New York: Arno Press, 1980.

Edwards, Lieutenant Commander Kenneth, RN. *We Dive at Dawn.* Chicago: Reilly and Lee Co., 1941.

Gibson, R.H., and Maurice Prendergast. *The German Submarine War, 1914–1918.* London: Constable and Co., Ltd., 1931.

Grant, Robert M. *U-Boat Intelligence, 1914–1918.* Hamden, Conn.: Archon, 1969.

———. *U-Boats Destroyed: The Effect of Anti-Submarine Warfare, 1914–1918.* London: Putnam, 1964.

Halpern, Paul G. *A Naval History of World War I.* Annapolis: Naval Institute Press, 1994.

Messimer, Dwight R. *Find and Destroy: Antisubmarine Warfare in World War I.* Annapolis: Naval Institute Press, 2001.

———. *The Merchant U-Boat: The Adventures of the Deutschland, 1916–1918.* Annapolis: Naval Institute Press, 1988.

Thomas, Lowell. *Raiders of the Deep.* Garden City, N.Y.: Star Books, 1932.

Wilson, Michael, and Paul Kemp. *Mediterranean Submarines.* Wilmslo, U.K.: Crécy, 1997.

Index

Aberdeen, 27
Acksel, Maschinistenmaat (UC-26), 262
Adam, Kapitänleutnant (*Deutsche Halbflo-
tilla Pola*), 11
Admiralty Ramming Order, 2
Adriatic Sea, 89, 192
Aegean Sea, 127
airships: R-29, 226; SS-Z1, 214
Albrecht, Kurt (U-32), 53
Albrecht, Werner (UC-10), 247
Aldborough Nappes (buoy), 239
Alexandria, 53,189
Algiers, 194
Alia (Norwegian cutter), 93, 95
Amberger, Gustav (U-58), 78–79
Amberger, Wilhelm (UB-108), 219
antishipping campaign, 1–2, 54
antisubmarine warfare (ASW), 2, 25
Arnold, Alfred (UC-33), 267
Arthur, Graf von (U-13), 30
Azores, 12, 220

Babbel, Oberheizer (U-45), 67
Bachmann, Günther (UB-38), 160
Baden, Maschinistenmaat (U-58), 79
Baltic Sea, 11, 45, 216
Bantry Bay, 101
Baralong Affair: first, 46–47; second,
61–64
Barents Sea, 48, 77
Barten, Oberleutnant zur See (UC-76), 313
Bartenbach, Karl (FdU Flandern), 10
Bäthge, Steuermann (UB-81), 202
Bauck, Kapitänleutnant (U-89), 107
Baue, Oberleutnant (84th Uhlans), 272
Bauer, Cäsar (UB-46), 167

Bauer, Hermann (FdU), 9, 10, 87, 109–10
Bay Of Biscay, 103, 109, 157, 161, 297,
303, 310
Beachy Head, 58, 304
Becker, Gustav (UB-82), 207
Befehlshaber der U-Boote (BdU), 9
Beirut, 189
Beitzen, Kurt (U-102), 114
Beizen, Bootsmann (U-40), 60
Bender, Kapitänleutnant (U-76), 93–96
Berckheim, Freiherr von (U-26), 45
Bergen, Norway, 4
Berger, Kapitänleutnant (U-50), 72
Berlin, 191
Berlin, Oberleutnant zur See (UB-114),
225
Bernis, Kapitänleutnant (U-104), 117
Bescwarzowski, Leutnant zur See (UC-16),
254
Bethmann-Hollweg, Theobald von, 227
Beyer, Oberleutnant zur See (U-6), 18
Bieber, Oberleutnant zur See (UB-104),
215
Black Sea, 131, 166, 167, 250, 253
Blavands Point, 42
Bleek, Max (UB-56), 177
Bligh Bank, 244
Blunk, Karl (UB-81), 202, 203–6
Boenicke, Leutnant zur See (U-83), 101
Bohm, Oberleutnant zur See (U-72), 89
Bories, Matrose (UB-81), 202, 206
Borkum Roads, 185, 198
Bosporus Strait, 250
Boston, 124
Böttcher, Oberheizer (U-51), 76
Boulogne, 254, 255, 256, 299, 315

331

Index

Index

Index

Index

About the Author

Dwight R. Messimer served eight years in the Army before becoming a police officer in 1966. After retiring from the San Jose Police Department in 1988, he served as a lecturer in military, aviation, and American history at San Jose State University until 2002, when he retired completely.

Mr. Messimer now writes full time on such historical subjects as World War I naval history, especially German U-boats, and American military aviation 1909 to 1918. He has written six other Naval Institute Press books, including *The Merchant U-Boat, Escape,* and *Find and Destroy: The History of Antisubmarine Warfare in World War I.* He lives with his wife in Mountain View, California.